THE LAST CHARGE
OF THE ROUGH RIDER

The Last Charge of the Rough Rider

of the Rough Rider

Theodore Roosevelt's Final Days

William Elliott Hazelgrove

Essex, Connecticut

An imprint of Globe Pequot, the trade division of
The Rowman & Littlefield Publishing Group, Inc.
4501 Forbes Blvd., Ste. 200
Lanham, MD 20706
www.rowman.com

Distributed by NATIONAL BOOK NETWORK

British Library Cataloguing in Publication Information available

Library of Congress Cataloging-in-Publication Data

Names: Hazelgrove, William Elliott, 1959– author.
Title: The last charge of the Rough Rider : Theodore Roosevelt's final days /
   William Elliott Hazelgrove.
Other titles: Theodore Roosevelt's final days
Description: Essex, Connecticut : Lyons Press, [2023] | Includes bibliographical references
   and index.
Identifiers: LCCN 2022046120 (print) | LCCN 2022046121 (ebook) | ISBN 9781493070909
   (cloth) | ISBN 9781493070916 (epub)
Subjects: LCSH: Roosevelt, Theodore, 1858–1919—Last years. | World War, 1914–1918—
   United States. | United States—Politics and government—1913–1921. | Roosevelt, Theodore,
   1858–1919—Family. | Ex-presidents—United States—Biography. | Roosevelt, Theodore,
   1858–1919—Death and burial. | Oyster Bay (N.Y.)—Biography.
Classification: LCC E757 .H386 2023 (print) | LCC E757 (ebook) | DDC 973.91/1092—
   dc23/eng/20220923
LC record available at https://lccn.loc.gov/2022046120
LC ebook record available at https://lccn.loc.gov/2022046121

For
Kitty, Clay, Callie, and Careen

Contents

A Note to the Reader

In this book I use Teddy, TR, and Theodore interchangeably. It is true Teddy was not a name Roosevelt really liked, but people still called him that. I try to make the name fit the mood, the story, and sometimes I just call him by his last name.

So all things pass away . . . but they were beautiful days.

TEDDY ROOSEVELT

FOREWORD

WHEN WE THINK OF THEODORE ROOSEVELT, WE THINK OF A MAN WITH a pinned-up cavalry hat on a white horse galloping up San Juan Hill with a regiment of Rough Riders close behind him, with his sword high in the air, his glasses dusted, his mustache bristling as he shouts out for his men to charge. What is amazing is this image is true on the whole. And what is more amazing is that charge won a war and propelled that man on a trajectory that led to the presidency in 1900. The Rough Rider is etched into our national consciousness of a time when a single man could make a difference and be a catalyst to end a war. The Rough Riders really belong to the great cavalry charges of the Civil War and the plains wars of the late 1800s with the American Indians. Theodore Roosevelt squeaked in one last charge in 1898 before warfare changed forever.

So it is no wonder TR would return to his supreme moment of action in the declining years of his life. It was a way to celebrate his life and a way to end it. The heroic life must have a heroic ending. "I would literally and gladly give my life to command a brigade of regulars under Pershing," he later wrote. "It would have mattered very little whether or not I personally cracked from pneumonia in the trenches or shell fire, or exhaustion or anything else. . . . If I should die tomorrow, I would be more than content to have as my epitaph and my only epitaph, 'Roosevelt to France.'"[1]

The last five years of Roosevelt's life were a quest to regain power at a time when his own health was in steady decline, and what better way to do that than going back to the well of action. TR always followed failure with action. It was his balm, his salve to soothe melancholia, or "overthought" or "black care," famously writing to his sister Bamie from South Dakota that "black care rarely sits behind a rider who is fast enough."[2]

So it was in his last years after the debacle of 1912 where he split the Republican Party and handed the election to Woodrow Wilson, making him persona non grata among most Republicans and a pariah in American politics, that his course to soothe this catastrophe was to go down the Amazon and nearly kill himself. But when he returned, shaken, forty pounds lighter, his health never to be the same, he began to think of a return to power, and what better way to do that than to replay his most glorious moment when he surmounted incredible odds and charged up San Juan Hill with his Rough Riders.

TR had never quite shaken the idea of another Rough Rider charge. When war almost broke out with Mexico, he had let President Wilson know he could be ready at moment's notice with a division of Rough Riders to go fight the Mexicans. War did not break out, but this let Woodrow Wilson know that his nemesis of the 1912 election, who had hurled invectives his way during the campaign and had kept up a steady barrage after the campaign, was not going away any time soon. Wilson would have abnormal power over Roosevelt's final years when war broke out with Germany and TR played his final hand of action with a proposed division of Rough Riders to go take on the Germans.

Most historians scoff at Teddy Roosevelt's plan to lead a division of Rough Riders to fight the Germans in World War I as the foolish dreams of an old man at the end of his life. This final plan has been put into the category of the wild fantasies of a man who wanted to go on a suicide mission and literally go out with a bang. After all, this was mechanized warfare and Roosevelt and his Rough Riders would be cut down in seconds by .50 caliber machine guns or gassed or obliterated with high-explosive shells. This may all be true, but in 1917 Teddy Roosevelt's plan to lead a brigade against the Germans was taken very seriously and many saw it as a game changer in the stalemate that had become the death by inches trench warfare of the last four years.

The New York Times front-page article on Tuesday, May 8, 1917, declared that a "New Rush Sets in to Join Roosevelt. . . . Predicted that 250,000 Will be enrolled for division by end of week."[3] Theodore Roosevelt was revered as a great president, but more than that he was revered as a great military leader by most of the populace—a man who had literally won the war with Spain. The military establishment did not see Roosevelt the same way. To them he was a relic of a bygone era of warfare where cavalry charges could win the day. More than that, he was regarded as a man who did not play by the rules, and they remembered the man who stole the show in the last war. "They recollected what a pain Roosevelt had been in 1898 with his entourage of reporters and his constant carping about the deficiencies of the regular regiments compared to his volunteers." Still, Roosevelt was beloved, and the press could not get enough of the Rough Riders resurrected.

A *New York Tribune* magazine front-page article was titled "GETTING INTO THE WAR WITH THE COLONEL."[4] The article went into depth, defining the type of man Roosevelt sought and why Roosevelt and his Rough Riders would prevail. "As in the Rough Riders every man on the Roosevelt roll is an outdoor man by choice or calling, trained to take hard knocks and give them."[5]

The writers of the day conveniently ignored the mega carnage of World War I as they calmly explained how real American men knew how to shoot and had lived hard, strenuous lives and they could prevail over the puny Germans hacking it out in the trenches in France. It was to be an egalitarian force of fighting men presented to President Woodrow Wilson as the best America had to offer. "Literally what the Colonel has offered the President is a cross section of American life, the most representative fighting force ever assembled in America. In the 20,000 all walks of life all of life are represented."[6]

This then would be American exceptionalism taken to its logical conclusion. Teddy Roosevelt was an exceptional man who would lead exceptional men who would destroy the less-than-exceptional Huns. All President Wilson had to do was unleash TR and his Rough Riders and they would set sail immediately for France and turn the tide of war for the Allies.

And why not? America had never participated in a world war before. America had never faced the modern carnage of mechanized warfare with millions of dead into the grinding maw of machine guns, tanks, chlorine gas, and shells the size of small cars. No, in America's last war, the war with Spain, Teddy Roosevelt and his Rough Riders *had won the war.* Men on horseback—and most were not even on horseback—had literally charged up San Juan Hill and turned the tide of the battle against Spain and ultimately forced a defeat on the army occupying Cuba. A contingent of cowboys, New York socialites, roughnecks, lawyers, doctors, coal miners, a virtual smorgasbord of men largely without military training except that which Roosevelt and Lieutenant Colonel Wood had been able to give them hurriedly in Texas, sailed over to Cuba and with American courage, fortitude, grit, insanity (the Spanish soldiers claimed the Americans were crazy and just kept coming even though they were shooting them down from entrenched positions) had forced the Spanish into an untenable position and won America's first foreign war. So why should this war be any different?

A naïve assumption, but in the twenty years that had passed since Roosevelt led his men to glory and death against the Spanish, the view of warfare had not changed in America; one American, a real outdoors, dead eye, shooting American, a rough-and-tumble cowboy, a frontiersman, could easily defeat ten men from any other country. Besides, had not our American Revolution been fought by rabble from local militias that banded together under George Washington to defeat the mightiest army known to man? Why, yes, they had. And if we dig a little deeper answering the critics of the day who pointed out TR's experience in warfare was less than extensive, confined to his foray in Cuba, then we could also point out that George Washington had been minding his wife's plantation for fifteen years when he was called to take over the Continental Army outside of Boston and didn't know what he was doing in the beginning either.

So there you go. Yes, Roosevelt was older than Washington had been by about fifteen years, but he was a vigorous man who had led a vigorous life and doctors pointed out that his health was that of a man half his age. This was not true, but it didn't matter; American exceptionalism would take care of the rest. The reality is that the newspapers, the pundits, even the men of the Senate, all saw Teddy Roosevelt's plan to take ordinary citizens across the ocean in a homespun brigade modeled on his Rough Rider motif used so well in Spain as logical and maybe even strategic if not brilliant. The Europeans themselves were begging for American troops and the French premier was fairly salivating at the prospect of a Rooseveltian division led by none other than the TR himself as a way to counter the dark gloom that had descended on the Allies as the Germans launched another offensive. Even if Roosevelt and his division were obliterated, then so much the better. The Americans would then be in it, following up with a blood lust to avenge their dead president.

And they may have been right. The PR bonanza of Theodore Roosevelt on a white stallion leading the first American division against the Germans would have been titanic. The Germans, too, would have known that the Americans had joined the fight and the sense of dread that a million-plus men were on the way would be palpable. People all over the world would take heart that a great man like Teddy Roosevelt had put Americans on the line and if he were killed, which surely he would be, well then what a lightning rod that would be for the mega bolt of pent-up American might that would fry the Germans in their trenches. There really was an upside to what many regarded as another crazy scheme by the kamikaze that was Teddy Roosevelt.

TR really just had to get beyond the Princeton president turned American president, whom he had spent the last five years turning on a spit over the Roosevelt coals of indignance and vituperation on Wilson's lack of action against the Germans. Now that the war had begun, TR began his campaign to woo the coldly reticent academician and convince Wilson it was in both their interests that he go to France for a final glorious charge that would help the Allies and give Roosevelt the fitting epitaph the man of action required. For he was not a well man and TR, who had always said he would work up until he was sixty, was now fifty-eight, and he knew full well this would be the Final Charge of the Rough Riders for him.

From 1917 to 1919 the race was on against his rheumatism, gout, septic infection, high blood pressure, obesity, a rheumatic heart, pleurisy, a ticking embolism, pathogens in his blood, a bad leg from an accident, a bullet in his chest from an assassination attempt. This would all be behind him once he saddled up and faced the oblivion of the German machine guns on his white steed. A shadow of himself, he was still the beloved man of his country, headed for another run for president in 1920. He was still giving speeches, writing for several magazines, positioning his sons to get into the fight before it was all over, holding court at Sagamore Hill, keeping a wary eye on Woodrow Wilson, all the while plotting a political comeback after his devastating loss of 1912. Win, lose, or draw, the Final Charge of the Rough Riders would solve all his problems. If he lived, he would surely be president in 1920; if he died, well, then he would go out in the blaze of blinding energy that had burned a comet's trail against the black coal of the universe his whole life. Inaction was the only real enemy and Woodrow Wilson was the keeper of that poisoned arrow. Teddy Roosevelt just had to take it from him.

PROLOGUE

Destiny

APRIL 25, 1865

IN 1957, HISTORIAN STEPHAN LORANT STARED AT THE PHOTOGRAPH of Lincoln's funeral heading past Broadway on Thirteenth Street. It was one of those sepia-toned prints that seemed to be in danger of fading away. The mansion on the left belonged to Cornelius van Shack Roosevelt. This he knew. Lincoln's procession was a black-draped affair of horses, soldiers, and caissons. Lorant had stared at the photograph many times and considered using it in his book. But now he was staring at two little apparitions in the window of Roosevelt's home. How had he missed this? These two little faces in the silver nitrate of the developer, peering out at the world. The revelation was a thunderclap. The two boys appeared to be leaning on the windowsill watching the procession. Could it be? Lorant peered closer and took out his magnifying glass. He did some research that proved his hunch might be right, but then of course the only person who could really confirm it was the now-widow of one of the grown boys. Both were now dead. One had committed suicide after being committed to an insane asylum by his brother for flagrant alcoholism and adultery. The other had died peacefully in his sleep after changing the world. Historian Lorant traveled to Long Island and showed the photograph to the surviving widow. She held it in her lap in the large home, still drafty from the wood-burning fireplaces. She nodded and looked up at Lorant. She smiled faintly.

"Yes, I think that is my husband and next to him is his brother,"[1] said Edith Carow Roosevelt, wife of Theodore Roosevelt.

CHAPTER ONE

The First Charge

1898

THEODORE ROOSEVELT STOOD IN THE TROPICAL DARKNESS STARING AT the honey-speckled sky of pinwheel stars. He was on his way to the Great Adventure aboard the *Yucatan* with his Rough Riders bedded down below deck and on the deck to stay cool and out of the stifling reek of men and mules and the offal they produced. Captain Buckey O'Neill, a one-time Arizona sheriff turned Rough Rider who had shot down his fair share of bad men and Indians in the past but could recite Balzac and identify the signs of Apache, stood next to TR, staring up at the star-filled sky. Die or win, Roosevelt was headed for what he would later refer to as his "crowded moment" and standing in the close warmth with the whoosh of the great ship the only sound; heading down toward Cuba he looked for answers in the heavens.

"Who would not risk his life for a star,"[1] Buckey O'Neill murmured and Teddy turned to the grizzled officer and nodded. It was just the answer he was looking for. The next day they came to a halt off the coast of Cuba and awaited orders. Roosevelt and his Rough Riders gazed at the island nation they had come to liberate from the tyrannical rule of Spain. "Every feature of the landscape," wrote Richard Harding Davis, "was painted in highlights; there was no shading, it was all brilliant, gorgeous, and glaring. The sea was an indigo blue, like the blue in a washtub, the green of the mountains was the green of corroded copper, the scarlet trees were the red of a Tommy's jacket, and the sun was like a limelight in its fierceness."[2] TR and his men had a lot of time to gaze at the tropical paradise as battle orders didn't arrive until the following evening for the thirty-one transport ships.

Roosevelt out west in the Badlands had patented a war dance when he shot his first buffalo, and he repeated it for the troops when he got the news they would be going in. He put his hand on one hip and then waving his hat in the air, he danced like a Russian cowboy, singing, "Shout hurrah for Erin-go-Bragh ... And All the Yankee Nation!" His men were much amused, and his officers drank a toast that night, raising their cups "to the officers, may they get killed, wounded or promoted!"[3] The night was long as men contemplated their fate. Some knew they would never sleep again. Others, like Roosevelt, saw only glory ahead.

After a naval bombardment, the Rough Riders disembarked onto a slimy wooden pier with their ships riding up and down in the surf like elevators. Horses were simply pushed into the sea with the hope they would swim to shore; many drowned until a bugler sounded his horn and the horses headed for shore. For Roosevelt, the cosmic moment of the night before had given way for the very terrestrial work of getting men and horses ashore off a ship that was moving up and down. His two horses were not to be pushed into the water but off-loaded per his instructions.

TR swore, snorted, gesticulated in the hot Cuban sun as he watched his horse Rain in the Face lowered to the water in a harness. A sudden breaker caught the horse and before she could be released the horse drowned. Roosevelt was outraged and "snorting like a bull, split the air with one blasphemy after another,"[4] wrote Albert Smith, the vitagraph cameraman. Not to be caught again in the crosshairs of the red-faced Roosevelt, the men were so tenuous in handling his second horse, Texas, that she hung in the air with legs dangling above the water like a trapeze artist looking for land until Roosevelt roared out, "*Stop that Goddamned animal torture!*"[5]

Texas was then unceremoniously dropped into the water, where she swam to shore. Roosevelt, who had landed with not much more than his toothbrush and extra glasses sewn into the brim of his hat, turned to look at the leafy steaming green effulgence that was Cuba. The forty-three-year-old former assistant secretary of the navy could only marvel at the events that had brought him so close to having "his crowded hour."[6] Ever since his own father had hired a substitute for himself in the Civil War, young Teddy had fantasized about the highest baptism for a man: that of being blooded in battle. Not that he blamed his father for hiring the substitute (he would never blame Great Heart for anything—the only man he ever admitted to being afraid of), but still there was that one blemish on the great edifice that he could never quite reconcile and so for his own life it had become an obsession to find his own moment, his own "crowded hour" where he could put himself to the ultimate test and to do this he had created his own war.

When Secretary of the Navy McKinley had gone on summer vacation, his young assistant secretary of the navy set about firing up the battle fleet by filling the ships' bunkers with coal, positioning the ships to be ready to go at a moment's notice, and basically putting the US Navy on a war footing. When the *Maine* obligingly blew up in Havana harbor, TR tendered his resignation, told his wife Edith and four young children goodbye, and set about rounding up cowboys from his ranching days, socialites, Harvard men, and politicians from his own patrician class and then headed off to Texas to march and gallop in the dust after being outfitted in an immaculate grey and gold-fringed cavalry uniform from Brooks Brothers.

Reporters had flocked to San Antonio, Texas, to watch Roosevelt and his Rough Riders charge across the dusty prairies, writing in romantic terms about the men who would go first to Cuba to fight the Spanish. *Remember the* Maine. *Remember the* Maine. Banners flew from ships, from trains, as the Rough Riders journeyed to their disembarkation point. Women and children gave them flowers. Letters promised love and marriage for any Rough Rider who made it through the war. Teddy Roosevelt and his Rough Riders boosted circulation for newspapers across the country. Beyond the cowboys, it didn't hurt that a few senators' sons had joined as well. Craig Wadsworth, a nephew of Congressman James W. Wadsworth, had joined and was front-page news. The papers quickly built the Rough Riders into a new brand of supermen. "Judging from the reports of the surgeons who have examined the men who enlisted here, there never was such a body of men in the world enlisted in the regiment.

3

They are the flower of American manhood and of the regiment fully nine tenths are men who have college diplomas. They are nearly all able to bear their own expenses. Many of them are millionaires and every man of the 1200 has joined the regiment out of pure patriotism and for the one purpose of fighting."[7]

Most of the men were not millionaires, but no matter. The Rough Rider was part cowboy, frontiersmen, ivy leaguer, millionaire, scout, soldier, an omnibus of American character bundled into one man on a horse who would show American strength to the world. *The Kansas City Star* led with a star-studded headline: "New York Heavy Swells Bound for the Front"[8] and went on to stress that though the Rough Riders had their fair share of "Leaders in the Cotillons Given by the Four Hundred,"[9] the egalitarian nature of the Rough Riders was preeminent. "New York's men of fashion will ride flank to flank with the untamed cowboys of the wild and wooly west. And there will be no good lines drawn. One man will be as good as another in this organization, physical strength and endurance being the only qualification."[10]

Even the trip down to Florida to disembark was a publicity junket with every train stop met with cries of "Where's Teddy!" Eventually, Roosevelt obligingly came out to wave or speak to the crowds. America was going to fight the Spanish to free the Cuban people and this great foreign adventure was the first war since the Civil War that bound the nation together in common cause against oppression and barbarity and the man with the brimmed hat, spectacles, riding boots, and the grey and yellow tunic was going to lead the way.

His former boss, Secretary of the Navy John D. Long, wrote that Roosevelt might well be crazy after he turned in his resignation to go fight in Cuba. "He has lost his head," he wrote in his diary. "He means well but it is one of those cases of aberration—desertion—vain-glory; of which he is entirely unaware."[11]

It was a zero-sum game for the ambitious Roosevelt. He would either be killed in Cuba or come back a national hero, and he was fine with either. He really didn't have time to think about any of that; it had been a herculean task just to get to Cuba. When he found out that the Rough Riders could not take their horses because there was not enough room on the *Yucatan*, his force then became the Rough Walkers, but Roosevelt and some of the officers kept their mounts and of course now he was down to one horse, Texas.

Six thousand troops were on the sands of Cuba by sundown and the campfires of the Rough Riders soon speckled the beach. In the morning they began a seven-mile march to Siboney on a hard coral road through jungle. The green jungle, so brilliant in the noon sunshine, now became a hellish damp hot clinging labyrinth of winding roads running up and down. The heat was well over 100°F with humidity so high the men's clothes looked like they had passed through a rainstorm. The heat became the first foe to face the Rough Riders along with the other six thousand soldiers who walked in single file into the unforgiving foliage that was Cuba. Men began to shed equipment and clothes with the insects hovering over rotting fruit and harassing the sweat-soaked men who swatted futilely at the mosquitoes that would introduce many of the men to Cuba's greatest export, malaria. "I shall never forget that terrible march to Siboney,"[12] wrote Edward Marshall of the *New York Herald*. Roosevelt, who could have ridden his horse, walked along with the men, refusing suggestions he ride. This went on for two days.

Theodore Roosevelt had passed up commanding the Rough Riders for a man of experience, General Wood. On the first night General Wood met with an ex-Confederate general Fighting Joe Wheeler to strategize. Wheeler, who kept mixing up wars, wanted to make contact with the enemy as soon as possible to encounter "the Yankees—damnit—I mean the Spanish."[13] While the generals strategized, Roosevelt ate hardtack and pork and drank fire-boiled coffee in his yellow slicker, as it had begun to rain. On the morning of the second day, the men came upon a dead guerrilla on the trail. Reports of Spanish soldiers just ahead had the men marching quietly with guns at the ready. Roosevelt spied some barbed wire to the left of the trail and said to the soldier next to him, "My God, this wire has been cut today."[14] The next sound would be remembered by Roosevelt and every Rough Rider for the rest of their lives. "*Zzzzzzzz-eu!*" It was the dreaded sound of a high-speed Mauser bullet, a vicious stinging wasp of a bullet that while small, killed men efficiently, leaving many times a hole smaller than a dime drilled between the eyes.

The bullets started cutting through the leaves, leaving a sickening thud in their wake as they found flesh. Sergeant Hamilton Fish was the first to die in the Spanish-American War; then Captain Capron was shot through the heart along with six other Rough Riders. Roosevelt was literally surrounded by whizzing bullets as a bullet glanced off a tree by his face and blew splinters of bark into his eyes. Roosevelt took three men, headed for the right side of the trail, and stepped across the barbed wire that had let him know the Spanish soldiers had been close. Private Marshall wrote later that when Roosevelt crossed the barbed wire a different man emerged.

"He stepped across the wire himself and from that instant, became the most magnificent soldier I had ever seen. It was as if that barbed wire strand had formed a dividing line in his life and that when he stepped across it he . . . found on the other side of it in that Cuban thicket the coolness, the calm judgement, the towering heroism, which made him, perhaps the most admire and best beloved of all the Americans in Cuba."[15]

Roosevelt couldn't tell where the shots were coming from thanks to the Spanish soldiers using smokeless powder. TR pushed through some trees and saw a clearing that led to a ridge where the Spanish were entrenched with Santiago Road below where General Young's men were pinned down. "There they are Colonel," cried a newspaper man, Richard Harding Davis. "Look over there, I can see their hats near that glade."[16] Roosevelt peered through his binoculars, ordering the Rough Riders to pour fire upon the Spanish in the trenches. Another nine Rough Riders went down but the Spanish soldiers ran for the jungle behind them. TR turned and ordered his men back to the trail where the Mausers cut down several more men, but Roosevelt now had the "wolf rising in his heart";[17] he took his men on the left and broke into the open where the Americans were charging. Nine hundred men charged and TR led the left side as the Spanish retreated from their rock forts along the ridge and ran in the direction of Santiago. *We've got the damn Yankees on the run,*[18] roared Fighting Joe Wheeler, the former Confederate general. The Rough Riders had their first victory. The Battle of Las Guasimas had lasted less than two hours.

Roosevelt picked up some Mauser cartridges from the ground as he ran with his troops to the ridge. The first battle of the Spanish-American War was over and Roosevelt had survived. He stared into the distance at the city of Santiago and closer in a hill, San Juan. He would later joke about the difficulty of running with his sword flapping between his legs and his fogged-up glasses that left him "firing at any target that was not a tree."[19] For Roosevelt his baptism of fire had left him with a sense of his own worth as a leader of men. "As throughout the morning I had preserved a specious aspect of wisdom and had commanded first one wing and then the other wing, the fight really was a capitol thing for me, for practically all the men had served under my actual command, and thenceforth felt enthusiastic belief that I would lead them aright."[20]

The fighting was over the for the day but tomorrow the Americans would attempt to take Santiago with the last defenses on San Juan Hill between them and the city. Roosevelt assumed he had his moment in battle, but his crowded hour was yet to come.

CHAPTER TWO

The Great Big Boy

1914

THEODORE ROOSEVELT FACED THE MOST POWERFUL MAN IN AMERICA over two sweating glasses of lemonade. President Woodrow Wilson was well aware of Roosevelt's exploratory descent down the River of Doubt, the Amazon, and he was also well aware it had mirrored his descent in American politics. Both expeditions had started out well and full of hope. The 1912 election should have been a shoo-in for TR's appointed man, William Howard Taft. Taft was facing off with an unknown to American politics, Woodrow Wilson, a Princeton president turned New Jersey governor. Vice President Taft was the proclaimed victor, trailing in the wake of the most beloved president of modern times, Theodore Roosevelt.

But Roosevelt's return from an African safari left him restless and he decided he did want to be president after all; when the party didn't give him the nomination, he split the party in Chicago and proclaimed himself a Bull Moose and formed the progressive Bull Moose Party. The disaster to follow was predictable with any split party and Theodore Roosevelt was universally blamed for handing the election to Woodrow Wilson.

The expedition into the Amazon should have been a capstone and the needed balm Roosevelt needed after the 1912 election disaster. The president would regain national prestige and through action redeem himself once again with a trip down the uncharted River of Doubt in the deep jungles of the Amazon. Things immediately began to go wrong. The men quickly began to run out of food and one of the Brazilian paddlers murdered another man. Roosevelt's son Kermit came down with severe malaria and then TR cut his ankle on a rock. The infection raced through his body, his temperature soared, and sepsis set in. Roosevelt told his son and the commander of the expedition to leave him in the jungle where he would take a lethal dose of morphine he always carried on such trips. Kermit for the first time refused his father and Roosevelt realized he must make it out of the jungle alive or his son would die also.

A month later TR emerged from the Amazon after rumors of his death had circulated, fifty-five pounds lighter, haggard, unable to walk, a shadow of the man who had gone into the jungle three months before. The Amazon had done what trips out west, a war, safaris, numerous hunting trips, assassination attempts, trolley accidents had not done—it had broken the bulldog strength of the president. But he was back and now he was waiting for President Woodrow Wilson in the Red Room of the White House after an invitation to lunch had been extended when Wilson heard Roosevelt was speaking to the National Geographic Society. They quickly moved out to the South Portico to escape the heat. Ostensibly, TR had come to Washington to address the National Geographic Society on May 26 about his hellish trip into the Amazon, but he also had an eye on seeing Wilson, who had serendipitously invited him to lunch. Roosevelt now had malaria and other Amazonian pathogens circulating in his blood and he was feverish. The day was hot, and he couldn't decide if he was warm from the malaria that never went away but came on like the flu with soaring temperature, night sweats, trembling, chills, fatigue. When President Wilson suggested they have lemonade on the South Portico because of the heat, he had already soaked his shirt from perspiration.

They had just sat down when Wilson was called inside; Roosevelt leaned back in his chair and felt a cooling breeze cross the White House lawn. He had been here just ten years before and allowed himself to drift back into the past. Small American flags fluttered along the White House fence and a lilt of music reached his ears. It was the summer of the early century, and he remembered his son Quentin running down the hallways playing cowboys and Indians and his eyes lifted to the bars on the upstairs windows he had installed so his children would not fall out.

When Ike Hoover, the president's valet, had brought out the two glasses of lemonade, TR exchanged pleasantries with his former valet. He knew Wilson's wife Ellen was gravely ill with Brights disease, a kidney disease that had killed Roosevelt's first wife, Alice Lee, who died on the same day as his mother and sent him into the Badlands of South Dakota on a three-year hijra to renew himself. Roosevelt didn't allow himself to think about Alice Lee usually but coming close to death in the Amazon and sitting in the early summer heat, he allowed himself to drift back.

On October 18, 1878, he wrote, "I shall never forget how sweetly she looked and how prettily she greeted me."[1] The Harvard man with the lacquered dog cart was instantly smitten with the girl who looked like she had walked off the pages of a Victorian novel. Her family was wealthy. She was blond with blue eyes, petite, the daughter of a great family with more money than the Roosevelts. Teddy would take his dogsled over to the family home to see her in snowstorms that would leave him frostbitten. One time he had been dragged out of his sled when the horses bolted and plowed along one hundred yards in the snow.

Roosevelt entered in his diary a vow that he would marry Alice Lee, but she was a hot catch for the mutton-chopped, squeaky-voiced suitor who would ramble on in explosive fits that labeled him eccentric if not strange. Besides, she had many suitors. Alice Lee did like the attention of the young man with the high voice (a trait Roosevelt put down to his asthma) and his unceasing energy for adventure. Chestnut Hill, the Lee mansion, was twelve miles from Harvard and Teddy had his horse Lightfoot shipped to school to pay court to his sweetheart. He studied early in the morning, cramming six hours of study in, and then headed over to Chestnut Hill. On May 13, he headed over for dinner and then left late at 10:15. Going down a hill in the darkness at full gallop, the horse stumbled, pitching Teddy off.

"I rode like Jehu, both coming and going and as it was pitch dark when I returned we fell while galloping downhill—a misadventure which I thoroughly deserve for being a fool."[2] The horse took a long time to recover and Theodore had to walk the twelve-mile journey back to school.

In his senior year Teddy pressed the issue. Still, Alice Lee had not made up her mind and when he asked her to marry him, she turned him down. Teddy was beside himself. "Oh the changeableness of the female mind,"[3] he wrote home. After an offensive where TR entertained the entire Lee family in New York, he still had not managed to get Alice to consent to be his. To make matters worse, Boston's eligible bachelors began to court the prettiest girl of the season. Theodore in a deep gloom pointed across the room at a Harvard Hasty Pudding function toward Alice. "See that girl," he proclaimed. "I am going to marry her. She won't have me but I am going to have her!"[4]

But Alice Lee had other plans and the lovelorn suitor could no longer sleep; he began wandering the woods near Cambridge, reciting Swinburn and not returning until morning. When he refused to go back to his room, a classmate let the Roosevelts know what was going on and his uncle James West Roosevelt went to see Teddy and soothed his distressed nerves. But TR ordered dueling pistols to take on any rival suitor and after a long ride on his horse he shot a dog who barked at him. He was stressed, but after Alice Lee tantalized him for months, talking of others who might steal her heart away, she consented to marry the young man who dressed like a dandy.

On January 25, TR wrote in his diary, "At last everything is settled; but it seems impossible to realize it. I am so happy that I dare not trust in my own happiness. I drove over to the Lees determined to make an end of things at last; it was nearly eight months since I had first proposed to her and I had been nearly crazy during the last year and after much pleading my own sweet, pretty darling consented to be my wife."[5]

The engagement was kept secret until her family approved, and Teddy went back to his work at Harvard. He had decided on law and then politics, taking on a controversial topic for his senior thesis, "Practicability of Giving Men and Women Equal Rights."[6] Roosevelt went against most of his classmates' views with his egalitarian declaration that "a cripple or consumptive in the eye of the law is equal to the strongest athlete or deepest thinker and the same justice should be shown to a woman whether she is or is not the equal of the man.... As regards the laws relating to marriage there should be the most absolute equality preserved between the two sexes. I do not think the woman should assume the man's name.... I would have the word obey used not more by the wife than the husband."[7]

It is hard to know how much his relationship with Alice Lee had on his views of the sexes, but she had already veered him away from a career as a naturalist, disapproving of the smelly carcasses that would be his life's work. TR graduated and noted "only four months before we get married ... my cup of happiness is almost too full."[8] But a visit to Dr. Dudley A. Sargent, the college physician, cast a small dark cloud across the halcyon sunshine. After a complete physical he told TR he had gained twelve pounds but there was a problem. "Theodore's heart, strained by years of asthmatic heavings and over exercise was in trouble. Far from climbing mountains in Maine, he must in future refrain from even running upstairs. He must live quietly, and choose a sedentary occupation, otherwise, sergeant warned, he would not live long."[9]

"Doctor," came the reply, "I'm going to do all the things you tell me not to do. If I've got to live the sort of life you have described, I don't care how short it is."[10] And that was that.

After a honeymoon in Europe, the couple settled down in New York and went on the social whirl open to those of the patrician class. TR was smitten and moved about as in a dream. Their favorite pastime was to take a sled and go around Central Park with Alice Lee bundled up under furs and Teddy whipping the horse to go faster. When he became an alderman in Albany, all the stars seemed to be lining up for the young couple with a baby on the way. Teddy would often spend the week in Albany and come home on the weekends to their cozy brownstone on the Upper East Side. They were rich, in love, and the world was opening like the roses TR showered upon his young bride. But to the representatives in Abany, the man with the short-waisted coat and silk shirt was The Dude. That was how the older assemblymen saw Roosevelt with his dandyish dress and his full muttonchop whiskers. He ran into the wall that was Tammany Hall and immediately took the role of reformer. Tammany Hall delegates tried to intimidate Roosevelt. Big John MacManus proposed to "toss that damned dude" in a blanket and whatever this meant, it got to Roosevelt. Marching straight up to MacManus, who towered over him, he hissed, "I hear you are going to toss me in a blanket. By God! If you try anything like that I'll kick you, I'll bite you, I'll kick you in the balls, I'll do anything to you—you'd better leave me alone." And McManus did. But other

Tammany Hall bullies lay in wait for the young alderman who had just installed Alice Lee in a hotel nearby the Capitol.

Sporting a cane, doeskin gloves, and the style of a short pea jacket popularly known in England as a "bum freezer," he went walking along Washington Avenue. Along with two other young aldermen, he stopped into a saloon, where Roosevelt was confronted by a large man named J. J. Costello, another Tammany enforcer. There was an insult hurled at TR to do with his coat: "Won't mama's boy catch cold?" Hunt, the alderman with him later recalled, "Teddy knocked him down. And he got up and he hit him again and when he got up he hit him again and he said, 'Now you go over there and wash yourself up. When you are in the presence of a gentleman, conduct yourself like a gentleman.'"[11]

And all seemed well when he received the telegram in Albany telling him that Alice Lee had gone into labor but not to worry. It was the second letter from his brother Elliott that got him on the train. Alice Lee was deathly ill with Brights disease and his mother was dying from typhoid fever. The train was slow, and Teddy jumped off into a strange fog that had shrouded Manhattan, bolting up the stairs to his parents' manse where his young wife lay dying after having a daughter, Alice Lee. And incredibly, upstairs his mother lay dying as well from typhoid fever. Alice Lee died before daylight and his mother died the next afternoon. Roosevelt scrawled in his diary a large X and wrote "the light had gone out of his life forever."

Theodore Roosevelt knew what grief could do to a man and as he watched Woodrow Wilson return to the portico, he wasn't surprised to find him looking haggard, with dark circles of ill health under his eyes. The two men exchanged pleasantries. Even the breeze from the Potomac did little to stir the heat rising from the White House lawn. Woodrow Wilson thought his guest looked like a much smaller man. He had lost fifty pounds, they said, in the Amazon, and he faintly swam in his collar and loose suit. There was something haggard about him. Well, they were both haggard men now. Ellen, his wife, was dying. There was no doubt about that. Brights disease. What an awful thing. This kidney disease that seemed to carry off women like so many falling buds from a rose. He had gone back to hold her hand in the unholy darkness with the nurse placing cool washcloths on her brow. That was the way of it now. He could not stand to be away from her, certainly not to spend time with the blowhard who had insulted him on the 1912 campaign trail like a man with a Gatling gun.

No, he had invited "the Colonel" to the White House as a courtesy when he heard he was in town to address the National Geographic Society. It was a courtesy he now regretted. He only had so much strength these days and listening to this man who at times seemed like a loud-mouthed boor was not something he wished to expend energy on. Intellectually, they were very different men. Roosevelt was reading Booth Tarkington's *Penrod*, essentially a boys' novel and something Woodrow Wilson would not deign to even look at. Nor would Wilson touch *Histories of African Game Animals*, Roosevelt's latest two-volume effort. Nor were their biggest literary outpourings any way similar. Roosevelt's four-volume *The Winning of the West* and Wilson's five-volume *A History of the American People* had little in common in style or content except a desire to create history more than to write about it.

Beyond that, Wilson was a dry academician in style and lacked the purple prose TR so readily indulged in when describing the West of his youth: "In the soft springtime, the stars were glorious in our eyes each night before we fell asleep; and in winter we rode through the blinding blizzards, when the driven snow dust burnt our faces."[12] Roosevelt was not only a big game hunter who marched through Africa with a retinue that would befit a king, he was also half naturalist, taking delight in animal carcasses, flora and fauna, and bugs. Wilson did not recognize the natural world except when it impeded on his travel or when it allowed him to take pleasure in a sunny, warm clime. The very heroics that Teddy Roosevelt exulted in were foreign to the man who wrote *Division and Reunion*, a discussion of the polemics of the Civil War. He could no more have read, appreciated, and certainly not written *The Rough Riders*, which showcased Roosevelt's shining moment that propelled him to high fame and the White House that Wilson now occupied.

Woodrow Wilson had never hunted, camped, roped cattle, fished, swum in the icy Potomac nude as Roosevelt was wont to do when he was president. He had not charged up San Juan Hill leading a division of

Rough Riders to victory and essentially become the hero of America's war with Spain. But Wilson had been on the receiving line of Roosevelt's ire where names came tumbling down from on high and he was called everything from a mollycoddle to a coward to an egghead. Woodrow Wilson had the dry flint of an academician that he used to hide a fiery soul that loved the passionate side of life, especially the passionate side of women. He had an affair with socialite Mary Peck that almost derailed his 1912 election and gave TR the opportunity to expose him when the press came his way. Roosevelt declined, stating he did not want the public to think Wilson was a passionate man. He preferred they see him as the piece of dry toast that radiated from his cold demeanor. The scandal passed with his own wife Ellen later writing that the only sadness Wilson had caused her was over the Mary Peck affair. TR may have regretted not going public with Wilson's affair after his defeat, but he never mentioned it again.

Roosevelt saw the world as a naturalist, the physicality of the world giving meaning to life. Wilson preferred the opaque glass of a garret, viewing the world at arm's length and keeping his own interior world a secret that would find flower in less than a year with a widow named Edith Bolling Galt. Still, the sunburned man who had survived the Amazon and the wary president nursing a dying wife drank lemonade together and stared out at the swelting heat.

Their conversation centered on books and Roosevelt's trip down the Amazon. Wilson found his vigor, his voice, his arm-swinging histrionics not unlike a play where he was allowed to sit back and watch the drama unfold. Roosevelt inquired after his wife and Wilson listened to the tale of his near-death escape from the Amazon. Roosevelt had dominated the papers since his return and had regaled editors all over the country with his exploits. He was a force to be reckoned with and Wilson believed in keeping his friends close but his enemies even closer. So why not have the Rough Rider Amazonian explorer ex-president to the White House to take his temperature. There was an election coming up in 1916 and there were already rumblings of Roosevelt getting into it.

So they chatted, but mostly Roosevelt pontificated, explained, pronounced, laughed. And finally, after an awkward, cold beginning, Wilson thawed and laughed too. The man was radioactive. Something a young boy, Lincoln Lang, had said of him years before when he met out in the Dakotas. Radioactive. And while the Amazon had taken some of the punch out of the Rough Rider (he did not have his cane anymore and he had gained back most of the weight he had lost in the Amazon), you just couldn't help liking the man. He saw Roosevelt as one step away from a demigod and he shuddered to think what kind of country they would be in if he were to occupy the White House again.

Roosevelt thought Wilson was pleasant, but he seemed to be observing him like a man going to a zoo and content to lean back and watch the animals. Roosevelt was sweating profusely and now he was sure the malaria was kicking up again. Also his right leg ached where surgeons had scraped all the way down to the bone to dig out the infection that had set in on his trip down the Amazon. So he held court, getting a few chuckles out of Wilson, and trying to listen as Wilson described his own readings and told a few stories of his own but he was no raconteur and quickly turned the floor back over to Teddy.

And then it was time to go. The two men finished their lemonade and Wilson walked Roosevelt to the north door of the White House, watching him hobble out into the hot sunshine. He noticed people had gathered around Teddy and a young man belted out "Hurrah for Teddy! Hurrah for our next President!"[13] Woodrow Wilson watched Roosevelt swing off his Panama hat and tap the boy's head. Secretary Joseph Tumulty walked up and stood by the president and asked what he thought of Roosevelt.

"He is a great big boy," Wilson answered. "There is a sweetness about him that is very compelling. You can't resist the man. I can understand why his followers are so fond of him."[14]

Tumulty nodded and walked back into the shade of the hall while Wilson continued to watch the man who would be king. It was then Roosevelt started to limp and Wilson realized he had put on a show and the aging president had much to hide. In that way, they were the same. Physically both men were fighting their own private battles. Wilson had been plagued by high blood pressure and arteriosclerosis, something that had given him several mini-strokes already, most undiagnosed with strange paralysis in his hands afflicting him, sending him off to Bermuda for various rest cures. The excruciating headaches of hypertension sent him into darkened rooms where he slept with cold washcloths on his head to bring down the thump of cardiac pressure.

The press gave the Roosevelt-Wilson tête-à-tête front-page space, stressing it was only the second time TR had been back to the White House and how cordial the visit was. There was a definite Roosevelt slant that surely would have irritated the sitting president.

"Today 300 or more persons who waited to see Mr. Roosevelt's departure from the White House applauded vigorously as the well known figure appeared in the doorway followed by President Wilson. Mr. Wilson shook hands with Mr. Roosevelt as the latter took his departure and the President smiled as the crowd paid its compliment to the former President by handclapping and the raising of hats. 'I had a perfectly charming visit with President Wilson,' said Mr. Roosevelt. 'By the way, did you know that the President invited me to lunch.' Mr. Roosevelt answered the question himself. 'Yes the President invited me to lunch but I was unable to accept as I did not reach the city in time.'"[15]

It was a little boy's wistful desire to be liked at that moment. The president invited him to lunch but he could not make it. Teddy wanted the world to know that. The paper then covered his departure. "As the machine which bore Mr. Roosevelt started from the White House cochere port, the ex-president waved his hand in an adieu to Mr. Wilson. The President bowed, smiled and paused for a moment as the Roosevelt motor passed from the White House ground into the street."[16]

Woodrow Wilson turned and walked back into the White House with the frozen smile still on his face. By the time he reached Ellen the dark sorrow had returned and he resented the energy and time he had lost with the Roosevelt visit. Wilson sat down by the bed in the darkened room and took his wife's hand. The drowsy heat of the day lulled the president. There was little sound. America was settling in for another lazy summer of the new century. Not much was happening. Two years before, *Titanic* had sunk on April 15, 1912. That was big news. No one suspected that in less than a month, Archduke Ferdinand of Austria would be assassinated and the world would be engulfed in flames.

Chapter Three

The Fuse

1915

It was a smudge. A charcoal smudge against a palate of light blue in Commander Schweiger's binoculars. A German U-boat 20 commander, Schweiger had despaired of finding any ships to train his torpedoes on. In fact he was heading home, coming out of a fog into a brilliantly clear day after trailing a British destroyer that he could never catch up with and resigning himself to the fact that between evasive maneuvers, Marconi wireless, and the sheer luck of British ships avoiding U-boats on the open seas, his mission was doomed to failure.

Hours of boredom had not been broken for days by the high excitement of finding a defenseless ship that could be rent asunder by the 350-pound TNT-topped brass torpedoes matched with a high-explosive Hexanite that would create a furnace of heat at nine thousand degrees and a pressure that would collapse hulls, bulkheads, and send ships to the bottom of the Atlantic. But then he saw the smudge that transformed itself into "a forest of masts and stacks."[1] He would later tell Max Valentiner that "at first I thought they must belong to several ships . . . then I saw it was a great big steamer coming over the horizon. It was coming our way. I dived at once, hoping to get a shot at it."[2]

He dived to periscope depth and recorded in his log at 1:20 p.m., "Ahead and to starboard four funnels and two masts of a steamer with course triangular to us comes into sight . . . ship is made out to be a large passenger steamer."[3] The ship, growing ever larger in his periscope, was moving at twenty-two knots. The best the U-20 could do was fifteen

19

knots on the surface and nine knots submerged. Many ships simply ran away from the German U-boats. To be sunk, a ship had to stumble across a U-boat, and even then it could stoke up its boilers and make a getaway. The torpedoes had no homing capabilities at all. They were lumbering bullets going forty miles an hour that had to be lined up with rudimentary calculations on speed and distance, and then like a geometry equation, the perpendicular line of their trajectory had to transect the hull of a passing ship. Most of the time the torpedoes missed, didn't go off, or sunk; sometimes they blew up in the tube, taking the U-boat down.

U-boat commander Schweiger tempered his excitement even as the four masts grew larger with the thick black coal smoke trailing. The ship suddenly veered away, moving too fast for the U-20 to catch her. "I had no hope now, even if we hurried at our best speed, of getting near enough to attack her."[4]

The problem was, it was a brilliantly clear day. The white splash of his periscope could be easily spotted. It had happened before. Once when he was trailing a British royal steamer she suddenly turned and tried to ram the U-20. Still Schweiger trailed the behemoth in the hope she might change her course, slow down, or even stop. Realistically, he knew none of these possibilities were going to happen. Usually the ship just became smaller and smaller in the periscope and Schweiger gave up the chase. This was why he was shocked to see the ship slow and change course, coming straight for the U-20. Schweiger calculated the ship's speed at twenty-two knots and the distance from the U-boat at seven hundred meters. "She could not have steered a more perfect course if she had deliberately tried to give us a dead shot."[5] Schweiger was going for a clean shot that should transect the hull at a 90-degree angle. A clean bow shot would put the torpedo in range at a speed of forty-four miles an hour and would reach the ship within thirty-five seconds. Schweiger thought it was odd a ship of this size would have no escorts but that was why he must act quickly. A destroyer appearing on the horizon would change everything.

Even so, with the clear weather and his shot perfectly lined up, the torpedo's wake, created by the compressed air turning gynocentric propellors, would be plainly visible and the captain could reverse engines, turn hard to starboard, or even just slow down and the torpedo would miss her. Worse, the lookouts above the big steamer could spot his periscope and call in destroyers. There was no time to lose. Schweiger ordered the torpedoes to run ten feet below the surface as his firing crew armed the torpedo and flooded the tube. Sinking this ship would be more than enough to satisfy the tonnage requirements of his patrol. At 2:10 p.m., Schweiger gave the order to fire and the torpedo's gyroscope took over and began to guide the death missile to the iron hull of the *Lusitania*.

Passengers on board looked up from shuffleboard games or their books and saw a long white streak growing toward the ship like an underwater chalk line. The torpedo was running only ten feet below the surface and when it came closer, the long silvery fish-like torpedo was visible and the word was passed in stupefaction that this was the dreaded murdering torpedo the voyagers had been obsessed with and was the topic of discussion over many dinners and lunches. The Germans had made it clear that passengers traveled at their own risk and here was this risk in the long dying trail running up to the ship like a phantom from the deep.

The torpedo disappeared from view, smashing into the iron hull, which set off a contact explosion that set off the TNT and Hexanite, creating a nine-thousand degree fireball of gas that punched through bulkheads, coal bunkers, and boiler rooms, creating a hole the size of a small house that gulped in water at a rate of one hundred tons per second. The empty coal bunkers filled with water and became an anchor pulling the stern up and the ship to starboard. A second explosion sealed her fate as the *Lusitania* began to sink and took 120 Americans to their watery grave. The fuse to America's entry into World War I had been lit.

CHAPTER FOUR

Teddy Unleashed

1915

THEODORE ROOSEVELT WAS A DRUNK. OR HE WAS INSANE. THESE TWO rumors followed him on the campaign trial of 1912 and beyond. In 1912, Dr. Allan Lane of Cornell (professor of mental diseases) wrote an article, "The Perils of a Progressive Administration." Lane went right for the throat and warned people away from "the very great danger of electing Presidential candidates about whose sanity there was any doubt." He went on to finger TR as "the querulent lunatic who may quarrel or find fault with everything and everybody."[1]

The grandson of Alexander Hamilton summed up, saying Roosevelt "is really a psychopathic individual and should be looked upon with pity or properly protected."[2] The second, more insidious rumor that adhered like gum on Roosevelt's shoe was that he was a pitiless drunk. George Newett, the publisher of *Iron Ore*, jumped on the bandwagon and proclaimed in his Michigan newspaper that "Roosevelt lies and curses in a most disgusting way, he gets drunk too and that not infrequently and all his intimates know about it."[3] The truth was Teddy Roosevelt was close to a teetotaler and as Henry Adams observed, the man "was drunk with himself and not with rum."[4] Still, Roosevelt had enough and sued Newett for $10,000. Newett's one witness, newspaperman J. Martin Miller, fled during the trial after passing a bad check. Newett's defense collapsed and he apologized, TR let the $10,000 go and asked for minimum damages. Six cents.

But now he was back in court on the other side of the witness stand, defending himself against the charge of slander. TR had been on the witness stand all day in Syracuse fighting off a $50,000 lawsuit by William F. "Billy" Barnes for besmirching his reputation when Roosevelt blasted the New York State Republican chairman. "The State government is rotten throughout in almost all of its departments directly due to the dominance in politics of Mr. Murphy and his sub bosses, aided and abetted when necessary by Mr. Barnes."[5]

Boom. Roosevelt was pulled into a trial on April 19 and had spent many days in the witness chair regaling the jury with stories, anecdotes, memories. The trial dragged on with Barnes's attorneys scoring point after point against the former president. TR for his part was reading newspapers during the trial and between testimony. He read the notice posted by the imperial German embassy on April 22:

NOTICE Travelers to embark on the Atlantic voyage are reminded that a state of war exists between Germany and her allies and Great Britain and her allies that the zone of war includes waters adjacent to the British isles that in accordance with formal notice given by the Imperial German Government, vessels flying the flag of Great Britain or any of her allies, are liable to destruction in those waters and that travelers sailing in the war zone on the ships of Great Britain or her allies do so at their own risk.[6]

He had been following the progress of the war very closely. He read how London's fleet had blockaded Germany and begun to systematically starve her for food and supplies. He followed Germany's retaliation with her sinking of three British cruisers in one hour, killing 1,459 sailors. Then the SM UB-65 sunk the *Harpalyke* with a white flag and a large banner, Commission for Belgian Relief. The Germans didn't care. The British were starving them and they would sink as many ships as possible. The US oil tanker *Gulflight* went down with three lives lost.

The court had adjourned for the day and Teddy Roosevelt emerged in the dim twilight outside the Syracuse courthouse and went right to the newspaper boy shouting the news. The headline floated against the crepuscular light, a clarion call to war as far as Roosevelt was concerned: "LUSITANIA TORPEDOED."[7] The *Lusitania* was the bloody flag waved at the Bull Roosevelt. He read the paper outside the courtroom. The trial now mattered not at all; 1,198 lives had been lost with 121 Americans among the dead. The worst were the babies. One Canadian newspaper led with the headline, "One Hundred and Fifty Innocent Babies Die When Lusitania Sinks."[8] But then the real impact of the sinking was brought home: "The babies were the talk of the ship, and everybody tried to look after them when the time came. There are numerous cases recorded when both passengers and the crew stripped themselves of their own lifebelts to put around the little ones, but it was useless, and about 150 of the infants, it is calculated, died from exposure. They were afterwards seen floating in the water with lifebelts tied around their little bodies, but they were past saving."[9]

Undoubtedly TR read this; it was carried in all major newspapers. The sputtering colonel had received the telegram in the courtroom telling him *Lusitania* had sunk but now to read about the carnage shocked and enraged him. The trial had at times been comical and frustrating. Many of the exchanges set up by the prosecution backfired. It was a tricky proposition getting a popular ex-president to testify. Ivins, the attorney for Barnes, walked in front of TR.

> Ivins: Has your occupation in life, apart from your public service, been that of an author?
>
> TR: An author a ranchman and an explorer.
>
> Ivins: Then you had three professions?
>
> TR: I have followed all three vocations or avocations.
>
> Ivins: And more or less simultaneously?
>
> TR: More or less simultaneously (laughter).[10]

The jury sat spellbound each time Roosevelt spoke, leaning forward to hear better. Ivins continued to badger his witness when he asked if he included Barnes in his autobiography as a man of high character. When Roosevelt begged off and said it was not a yes or no question, Ivins snapped, "If you cannot answer it, I do not care for your feelings. I want to know whether you can answer yes or no."

TR: Now—

Ivins: No, one moment—I ask for a categorical answer. Yes or no?

TR: Then I must answer you, no . . . that I did not include him.

Ivins: Then I will ask you this. If you did not regard him as a man of high character, why did you invite him in the Capitol? Why did you associate with him? Why did you advise with him?

TR: Because I thought he was above the average of ordinary political leaders. . . . I believed that he had it in him . . . to become a most useful servant of the state and I believed that there was a good chance of him so becoming.[11]

Ivins felt he had scored well on that interchange, but he did not know that TR was already far away after learning that the *Lusitania* had sunk. Teddy returned that night to the mansion of Horace S. Wilkinson, where he was staying for the five weeks of the trial. He knew many of the first-class passengers. Alfred G. Vanderbilt and Miss Theodate Pope were among the dead. One newspaper led with the story, "Vanderbilt Places His Life Belt on Girl as *Lusitania* Sinks." The article went on to say that Vanderbilt was standing with his life vest on when he saw a woman without one. He took off his vest and put it on the woman. "There was nothing in the way of heroics. The self sacrifice was made as a matter of course," said an English passenger. Vanderbilt was not seen again until he was found in the morgue with the other drowned passengers. A Mr. Bernard remarked, "When I saw his body in the morgue his face was among the most peaceful of all I saw there. There was no trace of agony and unlike others his features were not disfigured in any way."[12]

Roosevelt undoubtedly heard this and other stories over time. In the days that followed, the bold headlines spoke directly to him: "OH FOR A DAY OF ROOSEVELT."[13] But now all he was reading was the carnage of the sinking. He paced the floor in front of Wilkinson that night, agonizing about what to say, tempered by the fact that the jury had three men with German-sounding names. The phone rang with an Associated

Press reporter on the line asking for a statement after he told him that only 520 of the 1,918 souls aboard had been rescued.

"That's murder. . . . Will I make a statement? Yes. I'll make it now. Just take this." The statement TR dictated on the phone spread across the country, carried as a front-page story:

> *I can only repeat what I said a week ago when in similar fashion the American vessel the* Gulflight *was destroyed off the English coast and its captain drowned. . . . This represents not merely piracy but piracy on a vaster scale of murder than any old time pirate ever practiced. This is the warfare which destroyed Louvain and Dinant and hundreds of men, women and children in Belgium . . . it seems inconceivable that we can refrain from taking action in this matter, for we owe it not only to humanity but to our national self respect.*[14]

TR then went to bed, returning to the courthouse the next morning and apologizing to his defense team: "Gentlemen I am afraid that I have made the winning of this case impossible . . . we have two German American jurors whose sympathies I have likely alienated . . . but I cannot help if we lost the case. There is principle . . . far more vital to the American people than my personal welfare."[15] In other words, TR was willing to take a $50,000 hit ($500,000 in today's money) to speak his mind, and he was not a rich man anymore. He was notoriously bad with money and had to keep up a steady flow of books and articles to supplement his income. He was no Vanderbilt, that was for sure.

Roosevelt then went from shooting himself in the foot to the head with German Americans when editor Henry J. Whigham of the *Metropolitan Magazine* asked for his thoughts on the *Lusitania*. "Murder on the High seas" was a diatribe against Germany and the inaction of one Woodrow Wilson, who had not seized German ships or asked for a declaration of war and so far had said little about the sinking. Teddy went for the jugular of his lemonade-drinking partner:

> *In Queenstown there lay by the score the bodies of women and children, some of the dead women still clasping the bodies of the little children*

they held in their arms when death overwhelmed them. The action of the German submarines in the cases cited can be justified only by a plea that would likewise justify the wholesale poisoning of the wells in the path of the hostile army . . . we earn as a nation measureless scorn and contempt if we follow the lead of those who exalt peace above righteousness if we heed the voice of those feeble folk who bleat to high heaven for peace when there is no peace. For many months our Government has preserved between right and wrong a neutrality which would have excited the emulous admiration of Pontius Pilate . . . unless we act with immediate decision and vigor we shall have in the duty demanded by humanity at large and demanded even more clarity by the self respect of the American public.[16]

Woodrow Wilson had responded with little so far. A New York headline blared, "ONE HUNDRED AND FIFTY INNOCENT BABIES DIE WHEN LUSITANIA SINKS!"[17] TR went back to the courtroom resigned to taking a $50,000 bath now that he had fully alienated all German Americans. On Monday, President Wilson gave a speech in Philadelphia in a convention of naturalized immigrants. Many expected a declaration of war or a call for revenge. But Wilson, who had been hard at work wooing his new girlfriend Edith Bolling Galt, could not escape the love light and didn't even mention the *Lusitania*, winding up with, "The example of America must be the example of not merely of peace because it will not fight, but of peace because peace is the healing and elevating influence of the world and strife is not. There is such a thing as a man being too proud to fight."[18]

Henry Cabot Lodge, majority leader of the Republicans in the Senate and the biggest supporter and friend of Teddy Roosevelt, would later say that Wilson's proclamation of being too proud to fight was "the most unfortunate thing he ever said."[19] Lodge detested Woodrow Wilson as much as Roosevelt did, but for different reasons. He believed Wilson's progressivism was a cancer and his smug belief that he was the smartest man in any room grated on Lodge. He had gleaned what the tight-lipped smile meant when Wilson would often finish someone's sentence or jump to a conclusion before a thesis was offered. He detected the thin skin behind the supercilious gleam that made others call him cold. Wilson was a Calvinist who believed he was doing God's will and this more than anything else drove Lodge to the wall. Such arrogance.

Lodge would have been shocked to know that Wilson would have liked people to call him Woody the way people called Roosevelt Teddy. But no one ever did. Like many retiring academics, he had a secret desire to the be the extrovert people wanted to be around. And in private he was "a lover of dinner table repartee, limericks, and the songs of Gilbert and Sullivan which he would sing in a pleasant tenor voice."[20] But all this was locked away from view. If anyone was doing God's will, it was Lodge. Besides, the Brahmin from Boston knew he was the smartest man and it galled him that this southerner from nowhere should assume his mantle.

After that it was just chemistry and the fact he had defeated his best friend, Teddy Roosevelt, in the 1912 election. Roosevelt, for his part, could have strangled Wilson with his own words, "too proud to fight," but the world breathed a sigh of relief. Stocks surged, William Howard Taft, who never forgave TR for turning on him, expressed his support and William Randolph Hearst pointed out that Germany had every right to sink a ship carrying munitions. It was later certified that the *Lusitania* was carrying "260,000 pounds of brass, 60,000 pounds of copper, 180 cases of military goods, 1271 cases of ammunition and 4200 cases of cartridges."[21] In a letter to his son Archie, Roosevelt vented and declared war on Woodrow Wilson:

> *Every soft creature, every coward, and weakling, every man whose god is money, or pleasure, or ease, . . . is enthusiastically in favor of Wilson and at present the good citizen as a whole are puzzled . . . the murder of the thousand men, women and children in the* Lusitania *is due solely, to Wilson's cowardice and weakness in failing to take energetic action when the* Gulflight *was sunk . . . he and Bryan are morally responsible for the loss of the lives of those American women and children . . . they are both of them abject creatures and they won't go to war unless they are kicked into it.*[22]

Roosevelt then signed up his sons, Ted, Archie, and Quentin, for a military preparedness camp in Plattsburgh, New York. The camp's function was to train civilians for military duty; it lasted for one month in August. If Woodrow Wilson was not going to go to war, then so be it. This did not stop Roosevelt from going to war and getting his sons ready to accompany him. He promised to visit the camp and to advertise it with articles and in speeches. The jury in Syracuse deliberated for three days and even though everyone agreed Billy Barnes had proved his case that Roosevelt had slandered him, he lost. One could not compete against the force of personality that still burned brightly in America. TR emerged from the courthouse to reporters proclaiming his victory and rising from the politically dead candidate of 1912 as the crusading man of action, the man of war. He was once again, Teddy, the beloved president.

The *Lusitania* had pushed TR's stock up, but not so with Woodrow Wilson, having received much damning criticism for his statement of "a man being too proud to fight." He later confided to Edith Bolling Galt on one of their many drives that "I do not know just what I said in Philadelphia . . . my heart was in such a whirl."[23]

Indeed it was.

CHAPTER FIVE

Romeo and Juliette

1915

"WHO IS THAT BEAUTIFUL WOMAN?"[1]

The question lingered in the air passing over the Pierce-Arrow. Cary Grayson, Woodrow Wilson's personal physician, craned his neck and recognized the woman, Edith Bolling Galt, from an introduction by his niece, Helen Bones. He turned back around and looked at the president. He had been very worried lately. Ever since Ellen Wilson had died, his patient had been in a deep depression, talking about resigning, mooning around the White House in a dark torpor, some days not even getting out of bed. He complained of having no direction in life anymore and had stopped eating. He was not a well man, with high blood pressure, arterial sclerosis, a tendency toward brooding and melancholia, and now there was the death of his wife. Grayson was afraid it might have pushed him over the edge.

Wilson had taken to walks without his Secret Service agents. In November 1914 he went for a walk in Manhattan with his campaign manager and trusted advisor, Colonel House. In the evening, the two men strode down Fifty-Third Street to Broadway and stopped to listen to a man speaking on the sidewalk when people began to recognize the president of the United States. A crowd trailed the two men into the Waldorf Astoria, where they disappeared into an elevator, crossed over on a top floor, and went down the elevator and back out again. They took a bus back to House's home after walking down Fifth Avenue. Wilson later told House he wished someone had killed him while he was unprotected. Such was the grief of the sitting president.

But here was this ray of hope: Grayson quickly arranged a meeting at the White House between the fifty-nine-year-old president and the forty-three-year-old widow, owner of her late husband's jewelry store. Edith Galt beguiled Wilson with her wit, her blue eyes, her southern background where they compared notes on the end of the Civil War, and her Junoesque figure that radiated sexuality. Wilson recited poetry and Edith vamped with one-liners that Wilson enjoyed. Another dinner was quickly arranged and then drives in the country with Agent Starling and the chauffer in the front seat with Wilson and Edith in the back, separated by a curtain.

Wilson relished these drives into the Virginia countryside, but he relished the young woman beside him more. Woodrow Wilson had simply come back to the living when Edith Galt entered his life. He was a sensual man and lost no time, bombarding Edith with love letters, dinners, and more. "For God's sake try to find out if you really love me or not," Edith chastised him after one of their rides in the country. "I need strength and certainty for the daily task and I cannot walk upon quicksand," he countered.[2] Wilson sent her books: *Round my House: Notes of Rural Life in France in Peace and War.* A note followed the book. "I hope it will give a you a little pleasure. . . . I covet nothing more than to give you pleasure—you have given me so much." Wilson's letters continued to rain down. "If it rains this evening, would it be any fun for you to come around and have a little reading—and if it does not rain are you game for another ride?"[3]

Wilson's letters were elegantly written, the penmanship of an erudite Virginia gentlemen evident in the cursive script. Edith's letters were studies in curlicues, block letters, circles, and dots, betraying her three years of formal schooling and homeschooling at the hands of a dyed-in-black matriarchal aunt with a sharp tongue. She forgot the tradition and inherited the sharp tongue.

Woodrow Wilson had simply been reborn when he started courting Edith and found a bulwark, a safe haven to a world barreling toward war. "It's a great privilege to be permitted to share any part of your thought and confidence. It puts me in spirits again and makes me feel as if my private life had been recreated. But better than that it makes me hope that I may be of some use to you, to lighten the days with whole hearted sympathy and complete understanding. That will be happiness indeed."[4]

The evening rides in the Pierce-Arrow or on horseback or the golf games played even in winter with the Secret Service painting their balls red began to become unofficial meetings where Wilson let down his guard and ruminated on world events. Edith listened attentively and later wrote, "From the first, he knew he could rely on my prudence and what he said went no further."[5] Neither of them understood that this was the beginning of Edith Wilson's education for a position neither could have ever predicted.

The White House staff saw their boss come alive and Ike Hoover, the White House usher, commented, "He's no mean man in love-making when once the germ has found its resting place."[6] Arthur Brooks, his valet, summed up Wilson's smitten state in one sentence, "He's a goner."[7] Indeed he was, and one night at a dinner for two in the White House he asked Edith to marry him. She stared at the president sitting close to her. "Oh you can't love me, for you don't really know me and it is less than a year since your wife died."[8]

"Yes," Wilson responded, "I know you feel that but little girl in this place time is not measured in weeks or months or years but by deep human experience and since her death I have lived a lifetime of loneliness and heartache. . . . I would be less than a gentleman if I continued to make opportunities to see you without telling you what I have told my daughters and Helen; that I want you to be my wife."[9]

Still, Edith stuck to her guns and after an hour of talking the president escorted her home. That night Edith could not sleep and sat by a window thinking how Wilson had "made her whole being vibrant!"[10] She then wrote Wilson a letter saying, "I am a woman."[11] And she was trying to get used to the "thought that you have need of me."[12] She turned him down, but it was complicated. Edith astutely thought many would think she had trapped the president with her sexual wiles. "There was the fear that some might think I loved him for that, then the terrible thought of the publicity inevitably entailed and the feeling that I had in training for the responsibilities such a life held."[13]

Wilson was not to be undone and began a full-court press to woo the young widow; the truth was, Edith had not shut the door. A torrent of epistolary testimonials to his love fluttered down on the head of Edith Bolling Galt. The love letters were Wilson's forte, having sent many to his wife Ellen, his mistress Mary Peck, and now his latest conquest, the young woman with a jewelry company, an electric car, a sassy repartee, and a very consuming figure. The drives in the country, the golf, the horseback riding, and above all the letters continued.

Wilson was hard at work on a five-page letter on May 6, the night before Schweiger sent the *Lusitania* to the bottom of the ocean. "If you cannot give me all that I want—what my heart finds it's hard now to breathe without—it is because I am not worthy. I know instinctively you could give it if I were—and if you understood—understood the boy's heart that is in me and the simplicity of my need, which you could fill so that all my days would be radiant."[14]

Wilson had the letter posted the next morning May 7 and waited for a reply. He finished lunch and was going golfing when news came that the *Lusitania* had been sunk by a German U-boat. Woodrow Wilson, who had resisted the previous sinking of the American ship *Gulflight*, which many had thought might push America into war, now had a stick of dynamite thrown into his lap.

He canceled his golf game and met the news with a retreat from the White House by slipping away from his Secret Service agents and walking the rainy streets of Washington with his hat pulled low and his hands plunged in his overcoat pockets as newsboys shouted the fate of the *Lusitania* with massive loss of American life. President Wilson stared at the newspaper the boy held up. The liner had sunk in eighteen minutes; 1,198 people had died and 128 had been Americans. Wilson returned to the White House, then went to church, then went for a long drive in the country—with Edith of course.

The county was quaking with revenge. Henry Cabot Lodge summed up the feeling: "The country was horrified, and at that moment the popular feeling was such that if the President after demanding immediate

reparation and apology to be promptly given, had boldly declared that . . .
it was our duty to go to war, he would have behind him the support of the
whole American people."[15] Wilson's own secretary of state, William Jennings Bryan, was a pacifist and pointed out that the Germans had posted
advertisements in fifty American papers telling people that a state of war
existed between Germany and Great Britain and "that travelers sailing in
the war zone on British or Allied ships did so at their own risk."[16] Bryan
also pointed out the fact that the *Lusitania* might have been carrying
munitions. She was, of course, and even the early evidence revealed "4200
cases of rifle cartridges, and 1250 cases of shrapnel, along with cases of
fuses, shell castings and high explosives."[17]

In Bryan's view, both parties, the Germans and the British, were at
fault. But this was not the prevailing view. Colonel House, Wilson's unofficial advisor who had managed his campaign, wired that an "immediate
demand should be made upon Germany for assurance this shall never
happen again."[18] He also said Wilson should consider the possibility of
going to war and that the country "must determine whether she stands
for civilized or uncivilized warfare."[19] The general populace sent telegrams
and letters to the White House. One telegram asked Wilson "in the
name of God and humanity, declare war on Germany."[20] But Woodrow
Wilson had other things on his mind, namely how to get one young jewelry store owner to become his wife. His literary output was three letters
a day and he agonized over them as only a professor could, completing
multiple drafts. Edith was showing cracks in her resistance.

"You ask why you have been chosen to help me! Ah dear love," he
wrote on May 9, "there is a mystery about it . . . but there is no mistake
and there is no doubt!"[21] The next day Edith and Woodrow saw each
other; the dam broke and love was declared on both sides. "The most
delightful thing in the world . . . is that I am permitted to love you,"[22] he
told her and then he got a train to Philadelphia, where he spoke to fifteen
thousand people in a convention hall waiting to hear if Woodrow Wilson
would take the nation to war over the *Lusitania*. What they heard was a
man in the clouds, smitten, floating in the ether of new love. His speech
was not a polemic of war but a dissertation on peace.

"The example of America must be a special example . . . not merely of peace because it will not fight, but of peace because peace is the healing and elevating influence of the world and strife is not." He must have paused then and felt the warm glow that his new world of a life with Edith had given him. If love is a chemical reaction, then Woodrow Wilson was on a mighty drug as he let loose with the lines that would haunt him. "There is such a thing as a man being too proud to fight. There is such a thing as a nation being so right that it does not need to convince others by force that is right."[23]

Even Wilson knew he had gaffed the next day. "It was not the moment for fine words or false idealism,"[24] Lodge later remarked. At the bottom of the Irish Sea lay 128 Americans, and Wilson's tone-deaf words hung out for anyone like Teddy Roosevelt to hit with a bat over and over. Wilson later wrote Edith that his mind was blotted with images of her. "If I said what was worth saying to that great audience last night . . . it must have been because love had complete possession of me."[25]

Woodrow Wilson may have been lovesick during his speech but he also knew the effects of total war, having seen Jefferson Davis paraded through the streets of Virginia in handcuffs at the end of the Civil War. "I could go to Congress tomorrow and advocate war with Germany," he told Secretary Tumulty, "and I feel certain that Congress would support me, but what would the country say when war . . . finally came and we were witnessing all of its horrors and bloody aftermath."[26]

Wilson then sat down to his typewriter and tapped out a note to the German foreign minister, holding the Germans responsible for the sinking of the *Lusitania*. Then he turned to the real work at hand and wrote another love letter to Edith Galt.

Chapter Six

Standing Fat in Pink Tights

1915

On the evening of June 10, a mail boat approached the Roosevelt yacht anchored off Battledore Island, Louisiana, with the pilot shouting the news from the AP that William Jennings Bryan had resigned as secretary of state. Edith Galt recorded in her diary that same day, "Hurray the old pacifist Bryan is out!"[1] Indeed he was. The Great Commoner had proved too common for the president by trying to equate the sinking of the *Lusitania* with the iron blockade Britain had around Germany. "Why be shocked at the drowning of a few people if there is no objection to starving a nation?"[2] Bryan pointed out.

The pacifist did not believe Wilson should side with Britain and should condemn allied violations even though Woodrow had told Joe Tumulty, "England is fighting our fight."[3] Bryan believed the United States should be friends to both sides and it came to a head in a cabinet meeting where Colonel House's latest cable questioning American neutrality after the *Lusitania* sinking was discussed. Bryan, feeling outnumbered, accused Wilson's cabinet of favoring Britain over Germany. Wilson stared at him coldly. "Mr. Bryan, you are not warranted in making such an assertion. We all doubtless have our opinions in this matter, but there are none of us who can justly be accused of being unfair."[4] But the damage was done and when Wilson and family members, including Edith, went on a cruise on the *Mayflower* that weekend, it was Edith who sealed Bryan's fate.

37

"The night was clear and the Potomac River like silver,"[5] Edith later wrote. After dinner she and Woodrow walked on deck alone until Wilson stopped and leaned against the railing. "I am very much distressed over a letter I had late today from the Secretary of State, saying he cannot go on in the Department as he is a pacifist and cannot follow me in wishing to warn our country and Germany that we may be forced to take up arms, therefore he feels it's his duty to resign." Edith was no student of realpolitik, but she had good instincts and said, "Good," without a moment of hesitation, "for I hope you can replace him with someone who . . . would in himself command respect for the office at home and abroad."[6]

Robert Lansing quickly replaced Bryan, a pro-Britain, rigidly correct bureaucrat who had penned the phrase "strict accountability" in Wilson's response to the Germans over the *Lusitania*. Meanwhile on the yacht, Teddy Roosevelt squinted, not sure had heard right, but he had. This meant only one thing: war. And he didn't have a moment to lose. After the trial, Roosevelt had fled to the Barrier Islands of Louisiana to fish, examine the flora and fauna, and become the naturalist he had once thought of becoming when he was a boy embalming rats, mice, and bats in his parents' house. The naturalist was always there in his safaris into Africa, his trip into the Amazon, or his forays in the American West. In the waters of the gulf, shrimp, mullets, and sardines darted just beneath the surface. The life-and-death struggles of his own life were always mirrored to Roosevelt in nature. "Nature is ruthless and where her sway is uncontested there is no peace save the peace of death and the fecund stream of life, especially of life on the lower levels."[7]

To Roosevelt, the news in the hot sun of the Gulf of Mexico meant only one thing there was going to be a war and he wanted go back immediately to sign up for military service. But Roosevelt's people on the yacht did not share his enthusiasm that the sacking of Bryan meant war and so they stayed on another night with Roosevelt settling for a statement to the AP. With a kerosene lantern swinging above in the dark wainscoting of the yacht and the halyards whistling in the wind, he scribbled out his view.

"Of course I heartily applaud the decision of the President and in common with all other Americans who how are loyal to the traditions handed down by the men who served under Washington and by the others who followed Grant and Lee in the days of Lincoln, I pledge him my heartiest support in all the steps he takes to uphold the honor and the interests of this great Republic."[8] His total political reversal on Wilson was front-page news across the nation: "ROOSEVELT SUPPORTS WILSON." The papers quoted Roosevelt directly, still in the wilds of Louisiana as late as June 11, that he was glad Bryan was gone. "I pledge my heartiest support in all the steps he has taken to uphold the honor and the interests of this great republic."[9] Another article, "ROOSEVELT WARMLY SUPPORTS WILSON IN CABINET RUPTURE,"[10] had Roosevelt discovering Bryan had resigned from the newspapers brought by the mail boat. It was the first papers he had seen in several days, and he asked the people in the boat, "Has war broke out? Had I better return immediately?"[11] The paper reported TR and Edith would be back in New York by Monday.

The Rough Rider was throwing in his lot with Woodrow Wilson against the Germans. Roosevelt returned and was immediately talked about as a potential candidate for the 1916 Republican ticket. More than that, military men began to line up to serve under Roosevelt, who now very much wanted to lead a "super force" of Rough Riders into battle and assumed the war department would not stand in his way. TR assumed his rank would be major general, and he wrote down his plan in a letter to General Frank Ross McCoy on July 10.

"My hope is we are drawn into this European war to get Congress to authorize me to raise a cavalry division, which would consist of four cavalry brigades each of two regiments and a brigade of Horse Artillery of two regiments, with a pioneer battalion or better still, two pioneer battalions, and a field battalion of signal troops in addition to a supply train and a sanitary train." He then clarified to the general that he meant motor trains, "and I would like a regiment or battalion of machine guns."[12]

Roosevelt was looking to duplicate his charge up San Juan Hill with the same kind of charge against the entrenched Germans who had been engaged in the deadly slaughter of trench warfare for the past two years. Military glory followed a cavalry charge and even if it proved to be suicide by charging into a Maxim gun, then so be it. Better to go out in a blaze of glory than this death by inches that seemed to be assaulting him every day. Forget the fact he was so heavy he could barely lift himself onto a horse, but once he was on the horse, he could certainly point it in the direction of the German trenches and, if need be, raise a saber to lead the charge.

This was his vision for the new Rough Riders of World War I. They would be the same tough breed of men who had followed him in 1898. True, they were almost twenty years older, but no matter. Roosevelt did not understand or did not care that the heroic age of the cavalry charge had been snuffed out by mechanized warfare that churned up hundreds of thousands of men with machine guns, gas, flamethrowers, and high-explosive shells. The real casualty of total war was anonymity. No one stood out under such slaughter, and no one could rally anyone to overcome impossible odds. The mechanization that allowed Henry Ford to churn out cars on an assembly line by lining up workers and relegating them to one simple mundane task of putting on a tire or a bolt or a windshield had also been applied to war. Men were now cogs in a giant war machine and the cogs had no names, merely numbers. And many did not have that after a high-explosive shell literally obliterated human beings.

TR had yet to understand the technology that highly industrialized nations were bringing to mass slaughter. Romance and chivalry were as dead as the English poets of the trenches; Kipling and others had realized the real carnage of the First World War was a way of being, of viewing life. Teddy still believed in the individual effort that could change world events. From a butterfly's wing came massive change. A brave man on horeseback, followed by other brave, outstanding men, could surmount any enemy, banish any foe, right any wrong. This was Theodore Roosevelt's credo.

But in the cold-blooded truth of the twentieth century, fear would be the only thing that could save a man from going over the top and being mowed down by crisscrossing .50 caliber machine guns. Without this fear, man was committing suicide. But Roosevelt saw the world one way and even if he were cut down, which he surely would be, it would be on the altar of sacrifice for his country and would be the capstone of a life well lived. In this at least, Teddy Roosevelt had it right. He had lived his life in his mind, but of course he expected his four sons to follow him as well. "I should expect all four to go in if there was a serious war and would of course go in myself,"[13] he told a reporter. The only problem was his sons were young and had yet to live their lives. In this case, tragedy was the inverse of glory.

But the country had begun to catch war fever and Teddy's stock rose accordingly. He went to the Panama Pacific Exposition World's Fair in San Francisco in July to speak on "War and Peace." His topics would include "bleaters," the name TR gave to ultrapacifists and "mollycoddles." The colonel told the gathered press when he arrived, "I am heartily sick and tired of this bleating . . . inane cry about having peace at any price," he declared. "This thing of standing fat in pink tights like an angel of peace praying that no one will do or say anything to offend us may be all very lofty and ideal but what happens when men with real guns come to offend us. . . . I shall talk on war and peace at the exposition tomorrow but I might just as well have entitled my address, 'damn the mollycoddles.'"[14]

Nobody bothered to mention that William Jennings Bryan had spoken to a crowd of 23,000 people at the exposition the month before. But the mood had changed since the sinking of the *Lusitania* and ten thousand people lined up on Market Street as Roosevelt was escorted to the Hotel St. Francis in an open car. The crowd pushed in, and Roosevelt's car came to a halt when a veteran of the Rough Riders leaped upon the step of TR's automobile. The ex-president of the United States and the rancher shook hands as the car rolled along. Then with a parting clasp and a wave of his hat the Rough Rider jumped off the step and vanished into the crowd.

Roosevelt continued on to the hotel, but surely he felt the old warm glow of the Rough Rider who had jumped up on the running board of his car. In that moment he was the young lieutenant colonel, and this cowboy represented the men who would follow him to the gates of hell if necessary. Surely it was a sign that it was time to resurrect that heroic group of men who had charged into the annals of history and left their mark forever. It was time for the Rough Riders to charge again.

CHAPTER SEVEN

Rough Rider Camp

1915

IN THE PICTURE, TEDDY ROOSEVELT IS STANDING IN CAVALRY BOOTS IN what looks like a Boy Scouts tunic with a wide-brimmed hat. His boots strain against his large calves. He is talking to man also in cavalry boots and jodhpurs with his hands clasped behind his back in military fashion. Both men look like they could be at summer camp for Boy Scouts for the over fifty-five set. Roosevelt is clearly having a great time talking with the man who was his old commander of the Rough Riders, General Leonard Wood. Wood, whose tunic is bursting at the seams, appears to be having less of a great time, but that is probably because he has a camp to run.

Some people want to go to war. Some want peace. Teddy Roosevelt wanted war and if Woodrow Wilson wasn't going to give it to him then he would do what he did in the hot months of 1898 when he stoked up the battleships with coal and then quit his job as assistant secretary of the navy and hurried down to Texas to start whipping his cowhands, cowboys, socialites, and adventurers into shape. It was where wild men from the West could train and play soldier and where a forty-three-year-old family man who had been working in Washington could also play soldier with the real possibility of getting killed in Cuba. The Rough Riders were born in the dust of Texas by men who still believed the life of adventure was the only one worth living.

Yet the Rough Riders were not atypical. There was a long tradition of volunteer militias in America, going back to Bunker Hill and Concord. These were not soldiers but farmers, merchants, lawyers, professors, shopkeepers who met the British in the opening battles of the Revolution. George Washington would command a ragtag army of volunteer militias from the colonies when he took over the Continental Army and tried to pry the British out of Boston. It was a bookseller with no military experience who would drag 120,000 pounds of cannons three hundred miles to George Washington outside of Boston that would force the British out of Boston. The Civil War on the Confederate side was closer to the Rough Riders. On the Union side the army of the Potomac would have more in common with the drafted armies of World War I.

But that didn't mean America didn't believe in the men who made it up as they went along. Some would later say the fine spirit of improvisation that still exists in the US Army was responsible for America winning the war in Europe against the Nazis. Theodore Roosevelt had not had time to set up any sort of Rough Rider camp, but he did have the Plattsburgh preparedness camps set up by Major General Wood in Plattsburgh, New York, and Fort Oglethorpe, Georgia. Wood, who had been with Roosevelt in Santiago, was now commander of the US Army's eastern department and was a passionate believer in preparedness. Wood believed even more than Roosevelt that America was woefully underprepared for the war that was coming in Europe and that all young men of eighteen and over should have universal compulsory training for two months a year for four years. This was not Woodrow Wilson's belief, but if a bunch of bluebloods and businessmen from New York wanted to play soldier, he had no problem with that. At least they would lose weight.

TR viewed these summer camps for training college-educated men who had never been in the military as feeders for Rough Rider camps to come. His old commander of the Rough Riders, General Wood, put out a bulletin picked up by the press:

> *The training given at these camps is very intensive, covering in a period of four weeks as much as possible of the fundamental education of an officer. This calls for a well trained mind. In the second place, past experience has shown that this class of young men is the first to join the colors in time of war and many of them regardless of their skill in military matters, receive commissions. This has been the procedure in times past. It is right and necessary that these young men should be*

fully informed as to the tremendous responsibility which will come to them with the command of men and the irreparable loss which may be caused by unskilled leadership.[1]

The upstate camp was "sixteen rows of tents stretched for half a mile on the grounds of an army base that beautifully overlooked Lake Champlain."[2] Ted, Archie, and Quentin Roosevelt had joined the camp and were not atypical in being from the Ivy League pipe-and-cane set. It was distinctly a gentlemen's camp and lacked the rude dust and sweat of the Rough Riders in Texas. Ted later noted that half of the 1,400 nascent soldiers had graduated from Harvard. "I suppose some Yale men would fight if there was a war, but it is more clear than ever that Yale is the great middle class college and the middle classes are naturally gallant."[3]

There was a bit of snobbery in the Plattsburgh training camp, but Lieutenant Colonel Wood meant to beat the starch out of the Covington collars that appeared before him in the line of new recruits. "The training program as laid out by Wood was intense, compressing four years of regular army education into four weeks of dawn to dusk discipline. Men of all ages were learning how to drill, shoot, and run with forty pound bags on their shoulders until the oldest and plumpest were half dead from fatigue. Among them were John P Mitchell [*sic*] playing hooky from his peacetime job as mayor of New York. He was flanked by his police commissioner and a platoon of the city's finest."[4]

Roosevelt arrived at the camp in August of 1915 and felt like the boy unleashed again, much as he had when he arrived in Texas two decades before. This was a time when men could still play at being soldier as the US Army had yet to deal with a major European war where uniformity, machination, and a massive draft would generate millions of men to turn the tide of battles. In Plattsburgh there was still the shadow of the nineteenth century, where gentlemen could drill and play at war in Brooks Brothers uniforms.

When TR arrived, he stared across Lake Champlain to the Green Mountains of Vermont. The war fever was stirring in his blood as he went to meet his old commander. Roosevelt had pushed for Wood to command the Rough Riders in 1898 but Teddy emerged as the lieutenant colonel hero of the war while Wood's name was mostly lost to history.

When Roosevelt became president it was clear who had really profited by the charge up San Juan Hill, but Wood remained the ramrod-straight career soldier now in a reversal of fortune. TR was coming to see the man who held the reins of power while Roosevelt had been cast into political exile after the election of 1912.

In another sense, the Plattsburgh camp was a sort of early Outward Bound trip for the well-to-do of Manhattan and had the bonus of being a fat camp as well. Most of the men came back pounds lighter with the belief that if the Germans docked in the harbor or sailed up the Hudson, they would be ready for them. TR toured the camp on August 25 and was impressed by Wood's training regimen that compressed years of army discipline into a month of dawn-to-dusk hell. The men learned to march with forty-pound bags on their backs, run, shoot, charge, and run some more, until the middle-aged among them collapsed in the heat. The upper echelons of New York City were among the sweating recruits. Mayor John P. Mitchel ran with the rest of the recruits diving to the ground, learning the art of the bayonet, breaking down a rifle in the field, sleeping in a hot, steamy tent with other men. He was not alone; a few tents down, the police commissioner collapsed into his tent each night along with Corporal Robert Bacon, the former ambassador to France and Private Frank Crowninshield, editor of *Vanity Fair*. The rest of the two battalions divided into eight companies were a hodgepodge of "bankers, lawyers, retailers, and former college jocks."[5]

Cartoonists around the country had already lampooned the attendees as TBMs: tired businessmen playing at being soldiers. Wood himself was a Harvard graduate, Rough Rider, former chief of staff, and medal of honor winner. If there was to be any legitimacy to the Plattsburgh training camp, it came from Major General Wood, who was deadly serious about the mission of the camp to form a highly professional military reserve. And now a former president, a very popular former president who was already rumored to be recruiting for his own Rough Rider battalion, had come to the training facility. And now we are back to that picture of Wood and Roosevelt talking at Plattsburgh, both men in cavalry boots and straining tunics. Wood is ramrod straight with his hands clasped behind his back, while Roosevelt is leaning toward him; both men could easily be at a reunion of the Rough Riders, reliving their glory days.

But TR was energized by the camp; he ate with the regiment in the evening and gave a speech afterward abusing those who would shirk from joining the fight with stinging words of "poltroon, college sissies and hyphenated Americans"[6] The only thing he didn't do was attack Woodrow Wilson, who was now dealing with another German sinking of an American ship, the *Arabic.* Teddy behaved himself right up to the train ride home, when he let loose with a salvo to rival the bombardments the Germans were unleashing with guns lobbing shells the weight and size of small cars.

TR turned in the train station, his cheeks sunburned from spending days in the field and with dust still on his high cavalry boots.[7] He declared that "any peace loving prose stylist living in a house once inhabited by Abraham Lincoln should emigrate to China."[8] The only thing he didn't do was name Wilson, but it didn't matter. The man busily writing love letters to Edith Bolling Galt would later read in the papers a direct quote from the boy soldier of Plattsburgh. "Let him get out of the country as quickly as possible. To treat elocution as a substitute for action, to rely upon high sounding words unbacked by deeds, is proof of a mind that dwells only in the realm of shadow and of shame."[9]

Undoubtedly, Wilson read Roosevelt's words in the newspapers. Annoying yes, but a small speck of shadow in the brilliant sunshine that had become his life. The rides in the Virginia countryside had become steamier. Helen Bones, Woodrow's cousin and the woman who introduced Edith to the president, sat up front in the Pierce-Arrow with the driver. The curtain was drawn and what happened next was revealed in Edith's letter to Woodrow. "For God's sakes try and find out whether you really love me or not."[10] The sensual president was a frustrated lover and returned with a letter. "You owe it to yourself and you owe it to the great love I have given you. . . . Remember that I need strength and certainty for the daily task and I cannot walk upon quicksand."[11] Edith was not ready for the sexual tiger that was Wilson and told him she did love him but did he have to move so fast. "But you," she concluded, "must conquer."[12]

Wilson did have to conquer. He doubled down on love letters, filling Edith's apartment with roses and then a ring. "There is no one else in the world for me now,"[13] he wrote her on June 1. Edith assured him that though she removed her other rings every night this one would stay on her finger. Romeo needed no more than that and increased the dinners at the White House and the letters now spoke of "gentle caresses" and "precious kisses."[14] Cupid's arrow was a vacation in Cornish, New Hampshire, where Wilson secretly met Edith and managed to even shake the Secret Service. "He was like a boy home from school,"[15] Edith recalled. After breakfast every day, they went through the official mail together and then took walks along the Connecticut River. Then came Edith's favorite time, when they made a fire and sat together and read to each other.

Wilson's daily epistolary output increased to 250 letters over the next two months. Edith on her part began to research American history and read up on foreign affairs. She had only three years of formal schooling, but she had a quick mind and a photographic memory. During a drive, Wilson put all his cards on the table. "And so little girl . . . I have no right to ask you to help me by sharing this load that is almost breaking my back, for I know your nature and you might do it out of sheer pity."[16] Edith turned to Wilson and in front of Agent Starling, the chauffeur, and Helen Bones, she put her arms around his neck. "Well if you won't ask me I will volunteer."[17] They would marry in December.

The Germans and Theodore Roosevelt could not stop the man who now had joy in his step. Agent Starling would later see the president in the presidential rail car on the day of his wedding, "a figure in top coat, tailcoat, and gray morning trousers, standing with his back to me, hands in his pockets, happily dancing a jig." And then to Starling's amazement, the president of the United States clicked his heels in the air and sang, "Oh you beautiful doll! You great big beautiful doll!"[18]

Woodrow Wilson looked forward to a life filled with romantic bliss while TR rode the train taking him back to New York from Plattsburgh and stared out the window at the receding twilight. The empty fields of his youth passed outside the window, and he remembered a very different train ride taking him away from the world as a grief-stricken young man, going west with no return date. He had been in love as Woodrow Wilson, but his young bride had died; he felt he had little to live for and so he had gone west. The Wild West was really where the Rough Riders began.

CHAPTER EIGHT

Genesis of the Rough Rider

1883

THE TRAIN CARRYING THE YOUNG MAN INTO THE DAKOTA TERRITORY plunged deeper into the west, rolling past fantastic rock formations and blue lignite fires burning like pyres in the darkness. Theodore Roosevelt was leaving the world after his wife, Alice Lee, and his mother, "Mittie," had died on the same day. He was headed into the Badlands where Geronimo still roamed and Billy the Kid had been gunned down a few years before. The asthmatic from New York with the glasses, the buckskin coat, and the engraved pistols slept with his head against the window while one world passed for another.

And then he was standing in the dew, watching the Northern Pacific fade down the track, leaving only the burned coal smoke and the caboose lights winking into darkness. He had come to Little Missouri, "the toughest town on the line."[1] He had been there once before to hunt before he married and had spent days out in the red mud of a rainstorm trying in vain to find an elusive buffalo. He didn't know then that most of the buffalo had been killed off by the Indians who wanted the bounty the government paid for each buffalo head, knowing that the West cleared of buffalo would soon be cleared of Indians. The rest were finished off by Americans who liked to shoot the buffalo from train platforms.

Then young Teddy Roosevelt was looking for a buffalo head to put over the fireplace of the manse he and his new bride would live in. After days of tracking, he had found one and headed back with the thirty-five-pound head wrapped in burlap. That was an adventure that led to him buying a ranch with cattle and returning to the East to boast of his Wild West adventures. Now he was leaving to get away from the unsustainable grief of losing his wife. He had given his daughter, Alice Lee, to his sister Bamie to care for and headed into the unknown.

And now, now would begin TR's greatest education. He had to start over. Roosevelt had left his old self behind and adopted the mantra of "black care rarely sits behind a rider whose pace is fast enough."[2] He would adopt the code of action as balm for his loss and in the West there was plenty of action. The man who suffered from acute asthma and Crohn's disease was now in the Badlands. General Alfred Sully called it "hell with the fires out."[3] It was a land of extremes, 120 degrees in the summers and forty degrees below in the winter. The Indians were still there, and Roosevelt now had disappeared into the fabled West that would be declared closed by 1890.

When Teddy Roosevelt looked out over the Badlands, he saw a geologic extension of his own existential hell. Here is where he would die or live. He immediately rode off for four days into the Badlands by himself, into the fantastic buttes and cliffs that resembled a mini Grand Canyon. In a letter to his sister Bamie, he marveled at the desolation.

> *I grow very fond of this place and it certainly has a desolate grim beauty of its own, that has a curious fascination for me. The grassy, scantily wooded bottoms, through which the winding river flows are bounded by bare jagged buttes, their fantastic shapes and sharp steep edges throw the most curious shadows, under the cloudless, glaring sky and at evening I love to sit out in front of the hut and see their hard gray outlines gradually growing soft and purple as the flaming sunset by degrees softens and dies away; while my days I spend generally alone, riding through the lonely rolling prairie and broken lands.*[4]

Roosevelt saw the beauty of his own ragged soul in the lignite fires that dotted the landscape, burning from the volcanic pressures below in the night along with the pearled landscape from a low moon. Few men could see beauty in a landscape that swallowed men, never to be seen again. It was the country of outlaws and renegade Indians; few could venture into the hostile environment in pursuit of a wanted badman and come out alive. The sickly asthmatic from New York with a waist so small one cowboy said he could span it with his hands suddenly began to find a rude animal health. Action was his tonic, and he roamed over thousands of miles on foot and in the saddle and camped "with winds powerful enough to over turn the wagon and huge hailstones thudding into the earth with the velocity of bullets."[5] He camped at altitudes well over eight thousand feet in the Big Horn and hunted elk and bear with a ferocity that would have left other men exhausted. "We had been running briskly after elk uphill through the soft heavy loam in which our feet made no noise but slipped and sank deeply; as a consequence, I was all out of breath and my hand so unsteady that I missed my first shot . . . we raced after them at full speed opening fire, I wounded all three . . . they trotted on and we panted afterward, slipping on the wet earth, pitching headlong over charred stumps, leaping on dead logs that broke beneath our weight. . . . I sobbed for breath as I toiled at a shambling trot after them, as nearly done out as well could be."[6]

Long, hard days in the saddle transformed the dude from New York who now sported the latest in cowboy apparel. "You would be amazed to see me," he wrote Henry Cabot Lodge, "in my broad sombrero hat, fringed and beaded buckskin shirt, horse hide chaparajos or riding trousers, and cowhide boots, with braided bridle and silver spurs."[7] And if Roosevelt had a bucket list of experiences he wanted out of the Wild West, he would begin with facing down the proverbial gunslinger in a saloon.

He had been out looking for lost horses one evening when he headed for Mingusville, Montana, a drifting sleepy town, to bed down. There in the Nolan Hotel legend would be created in the old West where grit, courage, and a man's word were the highest measure. Roosevelt, who would later write many books on his time out West, tells the story best in his own words.

It was late in the evening when I reached the place. I heard one or two shots in the bar room as I came up, and I disliked going in. But there was nowhere else to go, and it was a cold night. Inside the room were several men who, including the bartender, were wearing the kind of smile worn by men who are making believe to like what they don't like. A shabby individual in a broad hat with a cocked gun in each hand was walking up and down the floor talking with strident profanity. He had evidently been shooting at the clock, which had three holes in its face.[8]

As soon as he saw me he hailed me as "Four Eyes," in reference to my spectacles and said, "Four Eyes is going to treat." I joined in the laugh and got behind the stove and sat down, thinking to escape notice. He followed me, however, and though I tried to pass it off as a jest this merely made him more offensive, and he stood leaning over me, a gun in each hand, using very foul language. . . . In response to his reiterated command that I should set up the drinks, I said, "Well if I've got to, I've got to, "and rose, looking past him.[9]

As I rose, I struck quick and hard with my right just to the one side of the point of his jaw, hitting with my left as I straightened out, and then again with my right. He fired the guns, but I do not know whether this was a convulsive action of his hands, or whether he was trying to shoot at me. When he went down he struck the corner of the bar with his head . . . if he had moved I was about to drop on my knees, but he was senseless. I took away his guns and the other people in the room, who were now loud in their denunciation of him, hustled him out and put him in the shed.[10]

Roosevelt's stock rose higher in the West as he joined other cowboys on the spring roundup where the cattle were driven in, sorted, branded, then driven to market. He spent days and days in the saddle with men who lived by their wits and who accepted the man from the East who alternated between grief and despair and exhilaration at the new life he had found in the West. These men's values of hard work, honesty, plain truth, grit, and courage would become values that Roosevelt himself would put above all else and form the ethos of the future Rough Riders. Many of the men he rode with in the roundups would follow him years later to Cuba and accompany him in his charge up San Juan Hill.

After writing a memorial for his dead wife, "Fair, pure and joyous as a maiden; loving, tender, and happy as a young wife; when she had just become a mother, when her life seemed to be but just begun . . . then by a strange and terrible fate, death came to her. And when my heart's dearest died, the light went from my life forever,"[11] he rode across the Badlands and told a hired hand, Bill Sewall, that he had nothing to live for and his daughter, "she would be just as well off without me." The tough Maine lumberjack who had come West upon Roosevelt's urging told him, "You won't always feel as you do now and you won't always be willing to stay here and drive cattle."[12]

His training as a Rough Rider continued. After donning moccasins to track a grizzly that had left a trail after snacking on a carcass, TR advanced when the twelve-hundred-pound grizzly reared up not ten feet in front of him. "Doubtless my face was pretty white, but the blue barrel was as steady as a rock as I glanced along it until I could see the top of the head fairly between two sinister looking eyes: as I pulled the trigger I jumped aside out of the smoke, to be ready if he charged; but it was needless, for the great brute was struggling in the death agony . . . the bullet hole in his skull was as exactly between his eyes as if I had measured the distance with a carpenter's rule."[13]

And then the ultimate experience of the cowboy, facing down hostile Indians, came to Roosevelt when he was once again out riding on a lonely plateau. There had been atrocities on both sides with Indians shot down by settlers and men found buried up to their neck with their own penis stuffed in their mouth. Roosevelt knew of these encounters, and he knew he was far out and had ventured into debatable territory when he saw five Indians gallop over a rise. "The instant they saw me they whipped out their guns and raced full speed at me, yelling and flogging their horses. I was on a favorite horse, Manitou, who was a wise old fellow, with nerves not to be shaken at anything. I at once leaped off him and stood with my rifle ready."[14]

Roosevelt was in real danger as the Indians approached. At the least, the Indians would take his horse and rifle and leave him alone in the Badlands, which was a sentence of death. But more than that they would probably just shoot him. So there he was with his Winchester over the pommel of his saddle. "I waited until they were a hundred yards off and then drew a bead on the first . . . in a twinkling every man was lying over the side of his horse and all five had turned and were galloping backwards . . . after this one of them made the peace sign with his blanket first and then, as he rode toward me, with his open hand. I halted him at a fair distance and asked him what he wanted. 'How, me good injun, me good injun,' and tried to show me a dirty piece of paper on which his agency pass was written."[15]

Roosevelt kept his rifle pinned to the Indian when another one tried to flank him. "I once more aimed with my rifle, whereupon both Indians slipped to the side of their horses and galloped off."[16] TR managed then to turn around and gallop away with the Indians shadowing him, but this encounter made the rounds and Roosevelt had his moment of truth where he demonstrated his creed once again. "I found that by doing what I was afraid of I was no longer afraid anymore."[17]

In the spring roundup he fractured his arm when a horse threw him. But when a stampede erupted during a storm he was up and on his horse, racing through the darkness across a landscape flashing with lightening and rain, gullies and cliffs. "I kept on one side and the cowboy on the other and never in my life did I ride so hard. In the darkness I could but dimly see the shadowy outlines of the herd as with whip and spurs I ran the pony along its edge . . . the ground was cut up by numerous little gullies, and each of us got several falls, horses and riders turning complete somersaults. We were dripping with sweat and our ponies quivering and trembling like quaking aspens."[18]

Roosevelt would then play sheriff and apprehend three men who stole a boat from him on the Little Missouri River. He took off in pursuit down the river in a buffalo robe while they closed the gap to apprehend the three outlaws. Going down the Little Missouri in pursuit of the men, he read Tolstoy's *Anna Karenina* as they made their way through ice floes. Roosevelt saw smoke and reached shore, rushing the outlaws in camp where only one man sat by a fire. They waited for the other two to return in the bushes, one of whom was Finnegan, a known gunman. "We heard them a way off and made ready, watching them for some minutes as they walked toward us, their rifles on their shoulders and the sunlight glittering on their steel barrels. When they were within twenty yards or so we straightened up from behind the bank, covering them with our cocked rifles, while I shouted them to hold up their hands."[19] Finnegan didn't drop his gun, evaluating the man with glasses in the buffalo robe. "I walked up within a few paces, covering the center of his chest so as to avoid overshooting and repeating the command, he saw that he had no show and with an oath, let his rifle drop and held his hands up beside his head."[20]

He then travelled forty miles to Dickinson with the three men, collecting fifty dollars as a deputy sheriff for bringing them in. After giving up his prisoners he ran into a Dr. Victor Stickney, who afterward attended Roosevelt, whose feet were badly blistered from walking and standing guard over the men for two days. The doctor later wrote,

> *The stranger struck me as the queerest specimen of strangeness that had descended on Dickinson in the three years I had lived there. . . . He was all teeth and eyes. His clothes were in rags from forcing his way though river bottoms. He was scratched and bruised and hungry but gritty and determined as a bulldog. . . . I remember he gave me the impression of being heavy and rather large. As I approached him he stopped me with a gesture, asking whether I could direct him to the doctor's office. I was struck by the way he bit off his words and showed his teeth. . . . I told him I was the only practicing physician. . . . "By George," he said emphatically, "then you're exactly the man I want to see . . . my feet are blistered so badly that I can hardly walk." . . . when I went home to lunch an hour later, I told my wife that I had met the most peculiar and at the same time the most wonderful man I ever came to know.*[21]

But it was the nights around the campfire with the other cowboys that Roosevelt cherished above all else. Here, after a day of hard riding, he came to know the men who made their living in the saddle and would probably die in the saddle, leaving their bones strewn across the West. It was the egalitarian quality of the West that was branded into Roosevelt's soul and these men and the landscape had produced a man many would not recognize. The respect for Roosevelt by the men who worked for him or came to know him on the roundups increased when they saw he was no "dude" from the East come for his piece of the West. He could stay in the saddle for forty hours on a roundup and rope calves with his hands burned from the friction and break ponies with his gun, spectacles, and hat flying in all directions. After being out on the roundup for thirty-two days and riding nearly a thousand miles, he wrote his sister, Bamie. "It certainly is a most healthy life," he exulted. "How a man does sleep and he enjoys the coarse fare!" After one particularly wild horse fell back on him and broke his shoulder, he just kept working "as best I could until the injury healed of itself. As one old cowboy said in wonder, "that four eyed maverick has sand in his craw aplenty."[22]

When he returned to the East few recognized him. One press report had him as "rugged, bronzed and in the prime of health."[23] Even his accent had changed to the flat drawl of the west. Another reporter who encountered Roosevelt commented on his "sturdy walk and firm bearing."[24] Gone was the asthmatic with cholera morbus and in his place was a hardened cowboy. When William Roscoe Thayer saw TR, he couldn't believe the transformation. Here was this man "with the neck of a Titan and with broad shoulders and stalwart chest."[25] Another person who could not believe the skinny, squeaky-voiced youth who had once courted her had been transformed into a rugged man of the West was an old childhood sweetheart, Edith Carow. "He was a mahogany-brown stranger, slim of leg and forearm, inclining to burliness about the head and shoulders. Most changed of all was the bull-like neck, heavy with muscle and bulging out of his city collar as if about to pop its studs. His hair was sun-bleached and cropped shorter than she had ever seen it . . . the reddish-brown mustache had been allowed to sprout freely and droop at the corners in approved cowboy fashion."[26]

Edith and TR became secretly engaged and when he returned West he knew his adventure was almost over. A once in a lifetime winter in 1887, called the Winter of the Blue Snow, wiped out his herd and Roosevelt lost his investment, close to half a million dollars today. When he shut the door on his cabin he knew he would not return, but he was taking with him the genesis of the man who would lead others in war in a scant eleven years. The very concept of the Rough Rider was born out West under hardship and adventure. It is here the boilerplate for the type of man Roosevelt would look for years later to follow him was established. He would later write unknowingly of the men who would follow him in battle in Spain and the quite possibly in France:

> *They had narrow, bitter prejudices and dislikes, the hard and dangerous lives they had led had run their character into a stern and almost forbidding mold . . . they felt an intense although perhaps ignorant pride in and love for their country, and looked upon the lands hemming in the United States as territory which they or their children should one day inherit; for they were a race of masterful spirit . . . they prized highly such qualities as courage, loyalty, truth and patriotism, but they were as a whole poor . . . stern, rude, and hard, like the lives they led, but it was the character of those who were every inch men, and were Americans through to the very heart's core.*[27]

Theodore Roosevelt had unknowingly just described the ethos of the American Rough Rider.

The Man against the Sky

1916

It was still cold in Milwaukee with snow by George McNally's mailbox. In Wisconsin, spring didn't really come until May, if it came at all. McNally opened his mailbox and saw a hand-addressed envelope with a return address of Oyster Bay, New York. He opened the envelope right there and began to read, feeling his skin crawl with excitement. He immediately took the letter and let the local paper know that Teddy Roosevelt might not have to wait for Woodrow Wilson to declare war on Germany to have his Rough Riders.

The article picked up by the *Montana Standard* in Butte declared that "the famous Roosevelt 'Rough Riders' are reorganizing." The article went on to say that "should a war be declared with Mexico, a cavalry regiment which will include in its roster many of the fighters in the Spanish-American War will assemble at Butte Mont and from there will go straight through Mexico." It would seem a George McNally, whose brother was killed in the charge on San Juan Hill, had received a letter from Oyster Bay asking him if he was ready to join the Fourteenth Montana Rough Riders. There was also a request to "obtain the promise from all other former Rough Riders or their sons that I knew," said McNally, "that would join a brigade of cavalry along the lines of the old troop and possibly headed by Colonel Roosevelt."[1]

McNally got about the business of contacting other sons and brothers of former Rough Riders while Teddy Roosevelt fairly licked his chops. He owed it all to Pancho Villa, whom Woodrow Wilson had initially supported to become president of Mexico, and then Villa became furious that Wilson had thrown his support to another candidate and wanted to make the president pay. Early in the morning of March 9, his force of 484 men attacked the town Columbus, New Mexico, three miles from the border. His army burned buildings, shot down townspeople, and were only driven off by the Thirteenth Cavalry after killing ten soldiers and eight civilians. Villa lost 90 to 170 dead and stirred the ire of the lovelorn Wilson, who had just returned from his honeymoon and who was also dealing with the sinking of the cross-channel ferry *Sussex* by the Germans with four Americans onboard.

America was furious and demanded action. On January 11, Villa had taken eighteen Americans off a train and executed them. The attack on Columbus was the last straw. The sixty-three dead Villa soldiers were dragged south of the stockyards, soaked with kerosene, and burned. The six captive soldiers were hanged. But America wanted revenge. President Wilson sent General John Pershing after Villa with a force of 6,600 men along with four regiments of cavalry to track down the elusive Villa, but after six months he remained at large. When General Carranza, the de facto ruler of Mexico, complained about Pershing's incursion into his country, Wilson ignored him. Carranza then attacked, killing fourteen American soldiers and taking twenty-three prisoner. Pershing needed help and it would come from Sagamore Hill, where Roosevelt had just returned from a trip to the Caribbean while fighting off the nomination of his party for the 1916 election. He was done with being a progressive splinter candidate and he had just come back to Sagamore Hill to find a book of poetry waiting for him. The name of the book was *The Man Against the Sky*.

Roosevelt had taken on Edwin Arlington Robinson at the request of his son Kermit, who asked the president to find something for the poet, who was busy drinking himself to death while writing poetry few would publish. His one book, *Children of the Night*, had fallen out of print and Roosevelt had persuaded Scribner's to bring it out again. Robinson had written Kermit, "I don't know where I would be without your astonishing father. He fished me out of hell by the hair of the head and so enabled me to get my last book together and in all probability to get it published."[2]

Robinson had visited Sagamore Hill in 1913, "A mousy deaf little man," but Roosevelt had since lost track of the poet. Now the accompanying note explained he had completed the book after a depressive slump. "Your letter deeply touches me," TR responded. "There is not one among us in whom a devil does not dwell, at some time, on some point, that devil masters each of us . . . it is not having been in the dark house that counts . . . but having left it that counts."[3] The central metaphor of title poem, "The Man Against the Sky," was that of "a giant figure reaching the top of a black hill, gazing with inscrutable emotion at a world on fire beyond, then descending by slow stages out of sight."[4]

Roosevelt felt this hit more than a little close as he pondered the years before him. But Pershing's trouble in Mexico energized him and even though Robinson believed there was more to Roosevelt than "biceps and sunshine," action was still his best tonic for the blues. President Wilson, dealing with multiple crisis while golfing, going to ball games, riding horseback, reciting poetry, and more than all that enjoying the sexual fruit of a younger woman in his marriage to Edith Galt, wrote stern letters to Germany, addressed Congress, and answered the question of whom he would rather face in the November election, Teddy Roosevelt or Charles Evans Hughes: "It matters very little, Roosevelt deals in personalities and does not argue upon facts and conditions. One does not need to meet him at all. Hughes is of a different type. If he is nominated, he will have to be met."[5]

The truth was Edith Wilson had proved to be more than just a wife and was deciphering top secret codes, accompanying Wilson to the Oval Office, blotting his signature on official documents, and acting as a sounding board for what to do about Germany. The papers described the new First Lady as "an unusual beauty gifted with natural charm. Mrs. Galt is not quite as tall as Mr. Wilson, has dark hair and dark eyes, and always is in stylish attire."[6]

When the cross-channel ferry *Sussex* went down, Wilson addressed Congress, declaring that "tragedy had followed tragedy. . . . Great Liners like the *Lusitania* and *Arabic* and mere ferryboats like the *Sussex* have been attacked without a moment's warning."[7] Wilson then issued an ultimatum to Germany in the form of a note threating to break off diplomatic relations. Three days later the Germans came back with the *Sussex* pledge, promising to respect the rights of noncombatants. For now, Wilson could still play the peacemaker and return to ball games, dinners, and drives in the countryside with his young bride.

But there was still Pancho Villa, whom Pershing could not track down. If Roosevelt had known Wilson's view of him, he might have thought twice about casting about for recruits. A division of reconstituted Rough Riders would be perfect to track down the elusive Pancho Villa. "I don't believe this administration can be kicked into war, for Wilson seems about as much as a milksop as Bryan," he wrote Seth Bullock, contemplating war with Mexico. "But there is, of course, the chance that he may be forced to fight. If so, are you too old to raise a squadron of cavalry in South Dakota?"[8]

His boys had already signed up for another training camp under General Wood, all except Kermit, who was working in New York, but he would join the camp in July. War footing was about, Roosevelt could feel it. Even Woodrow Wilson admitted to his secretary of war, Newton D. Baker, "The break seems to have come."[9] But then Carranza released the American prisoners and offered to let Pershing continue to operate in Mexico in pursuit of Villa. One war was postponed but another raged on with the Battle of the Somme, where twenty-one thousand men died in a single day under unrelenting machine guns, flamethrowers, gas, and shells. Roosevelt was so fixated on Mexico, he didn't take notice that mechanized warfare had just taken another gruesome step forward, nor did he slow down in his drive to raise a division.

Roosevelt's true view of Wilson as any type of war commander and his view of his marriage to Edith Wilson was recorded in a letter of Charles C. Bull, superintendent of Yosemite National Park:

I am very glad to get your letter. I do not think that anything would wake Wilson up. He is exactly in the attitude of Artemis Ward hero, who would be willing to see all his wife's relatives sacrificed on the altar of his country. Thank Heaven that for a year and half I have been hammering him and his policies at a time when I was pretty lonely in doing so. In marital affairs, by the way, the worthy gentle-

men's motto seems to be, "My wife is dead! Long live my wife!" His conduct in Mexico, his conduct in the face of Germany, and his conduct in the face of the hyphenated Americans at home, stamps him as being, the most wretched creature we have had in the Presidential chair, and we have had some pretty weak sitters there.[10]

Fortunately for Roosevelt, this letter would not see the light of day for many years because he needed all the goodwill of the Wilson administration now. A tidal wave of applications to join the division of Rough Riders under Roosevelt had come flooding in. Roosevelt felt it was time to request formal permission from the administration, moreover from Woodrow Wilson, to organize a division of Rough Riders. He wrote to Secretary of War Newton D. Baker on July 6, 1916, and laid out his case:

In the event of war with Mexico and of volunteers being called for, I have the honor to apply for permission to raise and command a division. My purpose would be to have the division raised by men who as brigade, regiment, squadron or battalion, troop or company, platoon or squad, commanders, would be chosen carefully with their efficiency in warfare, and who would, in at least a large number, probably a large majority of the cases, raise the men under them. I would with your permission submit the division to you with its organization practically complete, so far as the personnel is concerned. I would raise a cavalry division if you so desire, but in view of the possibility that that there may be difficulty in obtaining horses and of the possibility of the attack being made against the City of Mexico by way of Veracruz, I should like your permission to raise the division on the following lines.[11]

TR then laid out his first plan for the reconstituted Rough Riders. Up to now the Rough Riders "resurrection" had been bandied about in letters and in speeches and conversations. It wasn't the first time. Roosevelt himself had brought up a resurrected Rough Riders with President Taft in 1911 to go fight in Mexico. "I would wish immediately to apply for permission to raise a division of cavalry such as the regiment I commanded in Cuba." So this idea of the Rough Riders had always been the trigger Roosevelt kept his finger on in case of war. "The division would consist of three brigades of three regiments each. If given a free hand, I could render it, I am certain, as formidable a body of horse rifleman, that is, of soldiers such as those of Sheridan, Forest and Stuart as has ever been seen."[12] What is interesting is TR is looking back to the Civil War as a model of a cavalry-based regiment. Even in 1911 he tips his hand that his idea of the Rough Riders remained fundamentally unchanged from 1898.

It had been speculated in the press and for Roosevelt it was a dream that had yet to take form. But now he was laying down the actual form and function of his reconstituted volunteer force for the secretary of war, Newton, taking the idea of another Rough Rider force out of the realm of speculation and putting it square in the lap of the Wilson administration.

I would make it an infantry division, with a brigade of divisional cavalry instead of a regiment of divisional cavalry; I would raise one and perhaps two of the brigades as mounted infantry. For service in Mexico I do not believe that it would be necessary to have a brigade of artillery and instead I should ask permission to raise one regiment of artillery and one motorcycle regiment with machine guns. In addition I should of course raise an engineering regiment, an aviation squadron, a division of the signal corps, together with surgical, supply and other services. I would respectfully ask permission that I be permitted to request the detailing of regular army officers in the proportion of about one to every thousand men. In the event of war being declared and of my being permitted to raise the division I shall immediately submit to you the names of the regular officers I would like to have as divisional chief of staff brigade commanders, lieutenant colonels and majors. I should like to be permitted to assemble the division at Fort Sill, Oklahoma. . . . Of course I understand that nothing can be done at the present moment; but I desire to have my application before you for action if the emergency arises. I have the honor to be, sir, with great respect, Very truly yours.[13]

TR must have known he was paddling upstream. After lambasting the Wilson administration for years and turning up the heat over the sinking of American ships by German U-boats in the past few months, his grand request had a good chance it might be unceremoniously dropped in the waste can. But like a little boy who has been bad, he believed all was in the past with a few kind words. But it was read by Secretary of War Baker sitting in his hot office in Washington. One can imagine Baker reading this incredible letter from an ex-president of the United States proposing to essentially create another branch of the army that would answer to Theodore Roosevelt. A motorcycle regiment with machine guns, aviation regiment, surgical, cavalry, signal corps, two brigades of mounted infantry—and he wanted to assemble his division at a US fort. This was not the Rough Riders going down to San Antonio and kicking up dust for a month before shipping out for Cuba. This was a real army with machine guns and planes and all the complexities that would constitute an unofficial force under a man outside of government. The Rough Riders TR envisioned were no longer the charging brigade on horseback with him at the front, though this undoubtedly still was the way it would play out in his mind, but Roosevelt had now put himself at the head of a full-fledged army. A sort of General Patton of the Rough Riders. Unfortunately, his letter had the tang of an old man no longer connected with the modern world . . . still it was Teddy Roosevelt and Secretary Baker had to respond.

So he did the next best thing. He kicked up Roosevelt's letter to the adjutant general of the army who must have had a similar headache when he read the four-page proposal. The adjutant general replied as Taft had when Roosevelt had brought the issue of another Rough Riders army years before. His proposal would be considered "in the event of war." This was a convenient dodge for the moment and defused the prospect of turning down Teddy Roosevelt's proposal. TR had no choice but to wait for events to take their course. It was just as well. He was fighting off an attack of dry pleurisy that would make it difficult to lead an army anywhere. He could blame that on the bullet he carried from an assassination attempt in 1912.

CHAPTER TEN

The Assassin and the Bull Moose

1912

THE DRY RATTLING WIND OF OCTOBER CUT DOWN THIRD STREET OUT-side the Kilpatrick hotel in Milwaukee. Teddy Roosevelt sat in the seven-seat automobile and waved to the gathered crowd. He had napped in the hotel and was tired from the grueling campaign stops but now he was feeling better. The electricity of the crowds always energized him and he sat in his large army coat and waved. He noticed the fall air of the Mid-west and felt ready for his speech at the Milwaukee Convention Center. He stared into the crowd, his eyes passing over a short man with receding hair and absurdly large shoes. He waited in the open car, feeling the bulge of his folded speech and his glasses case inside his coat pocket. He looked at the crowd again, a perfect target for an assassin.

President Taft had been sidelined when Roosevelt split the party and went rogue with the Bull Moose Progressive wing in Chicago. He believed the people loved him enough still to return him to the White House and to that end he had been going nonstop. His train car, the *Mayflower*, had arrived at six and TR stopped at the Kilpatrick hotel for dinner. His eight-page speech was folded in his pocket along with his glasses case. Outside the hotel was a New York bartender, John Shrank, who believed the dead President McKinley had spoken to him and said no one should run for a third term. A letter later found in his coat dated September 15, 1912, stated, "In a dream I saw President McKinley sit up in a monks attire in whom I recognized Theodore Roosevelt. The dead president said, 'This is my murder avenge my death.'"[1]

After a quick nap, Roosevelt emerged into the dimly lit street with several bodyguards and walked along the sidewalk to a waiting seven-seater car with an open roof. A rope stanchion kept onlookers at bay as he took his seat and waited for the car to start toward the convention center. The crowd pressed forward, and TR then stood up and doffed his hat; that's when Elbert Martin, his stenographer, a powerfully built man, saw the flash of a pistol no more than seven feet away. Martin later told the press his version of events:

> I walked down the stairs with the colonel and out to the car and had taken my seat before anything happened. As Colonel Roosevelt was standing in the car, waving his hat to the crowd, the flash of metal caught my eye. I did not stop to think what I was doing and before I really knew it, jumped over the side of the car and had my arm around the neck of a man I had hardly seen. Everything seemed to happen at once. There was a flash, a sound of a shot and I was on the ground with the man. I threw one arm about his neck and held him fast. At the same time I caught his gun hand with my free hand and wrenched the revolver from him.[2]

Martin had Shrank in a half nelson while bodyguards Alfred Girard and Cecil Lyon jumped on Shrank with Lyon pulling out his Texas-sized revolver and warning the crowd to stay back. Philip Roosevelt, who was also in the car, saw TR fall back from the impact of the shot and thought "he'll never get up again."[3] In a letter to Edward Gray, Roosevelt later described the events: "The bullet passed through the manuscript of my speech and my iron spectacle case, and only went three or four inches into my chest, breaking a rib and lodging against it. I never saw my assailant, as it was dark and he was mixed with the dense crowd beside the automobile, and as I was standing unsteadily I half fell back for a second. As I stood up I coughed and at once put my hands to my lips to see if there was any blood."[4]

Martin and Roosevelt's bodyguards had their hands full with the crowd that was already crying out, "Lynch him! Lynch him!" and moving to take Shrank away. "I picked up the man and held him where Colonel

Roosevelt could see him," Martin later recalled. "Don't hurt him, bring him here," Roosevelt shouted, "I want to see him."[5] Martin dragged him to the side of the car where TR took his head in both hands and stared into his eyes. "What he saw was the dully eyed unmistakable expressionless of insanity, along with the clothes that looked as though they had been slept in for weeks, and an enormous pair of shoes."[6]

"Why did you do it?"

Shrank stared dully back at TR and shook his head.

"What's the use . . . turn him over to the police."[7]

It was then Roosevelt discovered he was bleeding and Dr. Terrell demanded the car to go directly to the hospital. Roosevelt shook his head. "You get me to that speech."[8] And so the car with the bleeding president went to the auditorium where Roosevelt spoke for ninety minutes while bleeding under his coat. He stood at the podium unsteadily and faced the crowd. "Friends, I shall have to ask you to be as quiet as possible. I do not know whether you fully understand that I have just been shot, but it takes more than that to kill a bull moose." Roosevelt then held up the manuscript perforated by the bullet. "So you see I was going to make a long speech. And friends the hole is in it that the bullet went though and it probably saved it from going into my heart. The bullet is in me now so that I cannot make a very long speech, but I will try my best." At one point Roosevelt opened his coat for the audience. "I don't know who the man was who shot me tonight. He was seized by one of my stenographers, Mr. Martin, and I suppose he is in the hands of the police now. He shot to kill me. I am just going to show you."[9] Roosevelt then showed the gasping audience his blood-stained white shirt.

He managed to ramble through, feeling hot, weak, a pain in his ribs each time he breathed. He almost tottered over several times as he half read and half improvised the speech. After three quarters of an hour, he said he would speak for fifteen more minutes and then spoke for another half hour. At the end he turned from the thundering applause and, ashen, he walked unsteadily toward Dr. Terrell on the side of the stage and said, "Now I am ready to go with you and do what you want."[10]

Roosevelt was rushed to Milwaukee Emergency Hospital, where he was examined and x-rayed, and then the wound dressed. By midnight

TR was back on his private car, the *Mayflower*, and undressed by himself, shaved, and fell asleep before the train left for Chicago Mercy Hospital, where surgeons decided to leave the bullet where it had embedded itself in his fourth right rib. The trajectory through the folded pages of his speech, his steel glasses case, his army coat, his shirt, suspenders, and flannel undershirt had slowed the bullet down enough to only crack his rib. But it was too risky to remove and for the rest of his life he would carry it with him.

In a letter to Edward Gray, Roosevelt ruminated on why he insisted on giving his speech even after being shot. "There was then a perfectly obvious duty, which was to go on and make my speech. In the very unlikely event the wound being mortal I wished to die with my boots on, so to speak. It has always seemed to me the best way to die would be in doing something that ought to be done, whether leading a regiment or doing anything else." Roosevelt invoked the old ethos of the Rough Riders then. "I believe half the men in my regiment at the least would have acted just as I acted . . . why, even in our little San Juan fight there were thirteen men of my regiment who after being shot continued in the fight.[11]

The ethos of the Rough Rider not only was something his men and the country could latch onto, but also was a benchmark TR referred back to the rest of his life. The bravery of his own men stood as a bar he held himself to and expected in any future Rough Rider. "I expect to be judged by their standards and not by the standards of that particular kind of money maker whose soul has grown hard while his body has grown soft, that is, who is morally ruthless to others and physically timid about himself."[12]

Woodrow Wilson sent a sympathy telegram and suspended his campaign until Roosevelt was well again. "My thought is constantly of that gallant gentleman lying in the hospital at Chicago."[13] Crowned heads and dignitaries around the world sent their get-well wishes. A ten-dollar campaign donation came from Vincent Curtis Baldwin of Chicago. He told Roosevelt he had made the ten dollars from selling flowers, "For I want you to be our President. If I was a man I'd help you and work hard for you, and tell people how good you are, but I am only ten years old."[14]

The dry cough that would come on all his life was a reminder of John Shrank's attempt to end his life and while TR recovered at Sagamore Hill in 1916, he could only watch as Woodrow Wilson was now back in the ascendency as the great peacemaker. Pancho Villa had released the prisoners in Mexico and Secretary of War Baker could now file away TR's letter outlining his super Rough Riders. Charles Evans Hughes had just clinched the Republican nomination and the phone had stopped ringing at Sagamore Hill after Roosevelt declined to represent the progressive wing of the party.

All TR could do now was wait for events to unfold. War with Mexico had not come but he was sure war with Germany would become a reality. The inflamed linings of his lungs gave his breathing a rattling quality, the wheeze of a tired engine. The assassin's bullet still in his chest was a reminder on how life could change in the flash of a moment. All TR could do was prepare himself for the war he was sure would resurrect the Rough Riders and grant him his final wish, "To die with his boots on."[15] Roosevelt was sure his four sons felt the same way.

The Sensitive Son

1916

THE SCRIPPS-BOOTH TORPEDO ROADSTER WAS RED WITH CHROME wheels and a chrome radiator shell. Low slung, it was built for speed, beauty, grace, and the one percent. Flora Whitney, the daughter of Gertrude Vanderbilt Whitney, zoomed on winding roads past estates in Long Island with slick-haired boys who smoked and drank only the best gin or champagne or whiskey. Flora smoked straw tipped Benson and Hedges, which she pulled out from a red beaded case that was more arty than chic. She mixed jewelry with clothes in an unconventional style that smacked of the bohemian; her mother, after all, was a famous sculptor and if she sculpted her daughter she would have a creamy complexion with aquiline eyes and a designer's posture.

Flora came out on August 4, and her father, the owner of *Metropolitan Magazine*, threw his nineteen-year-old a party in Newport. She was the first of the debutante season, a single rose among many to come, and the five hundred guests foxtrotted the night away in the Whitney ballroom, tastefully garnished in blue and gold as Flora, in a white dress, spun in the arms of her escort for the night, Quentin Roosevelt.

Flora could have had her pick of potential suitors as she was the first clipped bud of the magnificent bouquet of debutantes to follow, but she picked the somewhat sad, slight, large-toothed youth who had just returned sunburned from a military training camp in Plattsburgh. He was on a pass from the camp under the stern rigidity of Major General

Wood and by proxy his father, who had visited, but was glad to get away and in fact would be glad not to return at all.

Blasphemous to say it, but Quentin Roosevelt was not a warrior. He was a poet with an engineer's bent. He had just graduated from Harvard and did not feel the great call to have his "crowded hour" that his father spoke of. In fact, he found camp life a bore and thought that drilling was ridiculous. His worldview was more in common with his wild stepsister Alice Lee, who had harassed his father for years in the White House while Quentin ran up and down the halls playing cowboys and Indians and being so rambunctious his father put bars on the upstairs windows to prevent him from falling out. He was the youngest and as the youngest he had his father's favor; parents realize too late that raising children has an end date. He was frail and had inherited the Rooseveltian ethos of putting one's body to the test but a bad back that caused him excruciating pain and parade ground drill seemed to aggravate the condition.

The son of the former president had been driving up to Westbury for the last year and had discovered the hazel eyes and winged brow of the girl who liked to have fun more than anything else. They were the same age, and he found a lightness more in tune with his view of the world that more resembled his mother than his father. None of the stuffed heads of lions and bears in the brooding Rooseveltian library, Flora, her parents, and their friends had the light touch of artists and pursued life as a pleasure rather than an obligation. Of all her children, Edith Roosevelt felt Quentin was closest to her own personality "of gallic tastes and temperament. The others spoke French, but Quentin did so with instinctive rapidity, gesturing as he talked. He identified with the *gaité*, the elegance and subtle snobbery of French culture, as opposed to the Nordic, Slavic, and Mongol militarism his father admired. Archie and Ted were warriors, cut from a coarser cloth."[1]

No wonder Quentin hated the faux soldiers in training at Plattsburgh who dreamed of charging the Germans in France or defending the homeland from the Huns sailing down the Hudson. He was much more interested in the girl with the sun in her hair with an appreciation for poetry and fast cars. So far their relationship had been platonic; he was the younger brother of Archie Roosevelt, who had originally dated the incorrigible Flora but she had seen something in the younger, slightly tragic brother and so he was her escort at the ball. Flora's parents, while appreciative of the president's son, were not crazy about the "name-but-no-money college boy they wanted to protect her from."[2]

Now that she had come out, the young men of "the Four Hundred" would be knocking on the Whitney mansion door. Still, Quentin did carry the cachet of his father's name, his charm, and a sense of inheriting life's finest moments that came from growing up in the White House. He felt little need to impress anyone and was used to deference when he walked into a room. In a sense, Quentin's furrowed brow and Roos-eveltian teeth could not compete with the slicked-back smooth-talking scions who had escorted her from one sleepy-eyed party to another. But Flora was not conventional and the Swinburnian young man who talked of flying airplanes if the war should come had already captured her heart.

And that war, if Quentin's father had his way, would be at his door-step tomorrow. TR had given a speech on August 31 where he compared Woodrow Wilson to Pontius Pilot; then he went to brood about his inaction since the sinking of the *Lusitania*. The speech was picked up by the newspapers, but many felt it was too pugnacious to print. Naturalist John Burroughs, who had accompanied Roosevelt in a tour of the Grand Canyon and the Redwoods of California, wrote in his journal, "Roosevelt would be a really great man, if he could be shorn of that lock of his hair in which that strong dash of the bully resides."[3]

Meanwhile, President Woodrow Wilson appeared nonchalantly on the porch of Shadow Lawn, his summer cottage in Long Branch, New Jersey, and thanked the Democratic Party for nominating him again to run for president in 1916. He was the man with the wind behind his back in white pants and a dark blazer with the radiance of a man who had found love again in his new wife. He could have danced a jig on the porch, and it would not have been out of character to the breezy, youthful air radiating from the presidential retreat. Though he was almost sixty he seemed much younger than Roosevelt, who resembled to many reporters a more squat battleship that was taking on ballast with the prodigious meals he had at breakfast, lunch, and dinner.

And why shouldn't Wilson be the young man? He had settled the railroad strike and come down on the side of the working man, negotiating a six-hour workday from ten. The United States was enjoying prosperity and more than all that he had kept America out of the war so far. Fall was nipping already with cool nights and shortening days but so far the coast was clear and Americans turned inward once again. Charlie Chaplin's movie *The Count* opened in New York while department stores stocked up on black velvet caps and new zebra boas while yachts were moored for the winter and summer houses were closed. The truth was Woodrow Wilson had more in common with Teddy Roosevelt's son than he did with the former president. Quentin Roosevelt returned to college to finish up with images of Flora in her orange bathing suit from an amazing summer and realized quite suddenly he was in love, while Woodrow Wilson sat on the porch of Shadow Lawn in deep twilight, holding the hand of his young bride, smitten as a schoolboy.

CHAPTER TWELVE

U-53

1916

NOT FAR FROM WHERE FLORA DANCED WITH QUENTIN ROOSEVELT, A long, sleek 212-foot iron shark slid into the inner harbor of Newport, Rhode Island, and docked like many of the yachts the young debutante's slippers had graced. Residents stared in stupefaction as the bearded, smartly dressed captain, sporting an iron cross, popped out the conning tower and waved. A small German flag on the bow flapped in the wind. He did not speak English but Miss Margaret Fahnestock, another debutante who was friends with Flora, spoke German and translated for the captain. The bearded man standing in front of the small crowd that had now gathered identified himself as Lieutenant Hans Rose and he held out a letter for the German ambassador in Washington, Count Bernstorff. An AP reporter volunteered to mail it for him as the surreal moment veered again when someone asked the lieutenant if he needed supplies.

"We require nothing, thank you," Rose replied and added that he and his crew of thirty-three men had been at sea for seventeen days but had more than enough fuel and food to return to Wilhelmshaven. He then smiled and shrugged. "Maybe soon, maybe never!"[1] Lieutenant Rose then offered a tour of the U-boat to anyone who would like to see the interior of a working submarine. To the people of Newport, this was the equivalent of seeing a flying saucer; men, women, and children took turns climbing down the stairwell and touring the German U-boat. The six torpedoes that could mean death to the very people who stared at them were impressed by the efficiency, cleanliness, and hospitality of the German sailors. "A constant comment of those permitted on board,"[2] the AP man noted, "was on the thorough preparedness which the vessel seemed to exhibit despite her many days at sea. A Newport resident presented one of the officers with an Irish Republican flag and the officer responded, grinning, 'the first British ship we sink, we will hoist this flag in honor of Ireland.'"[3]

After a day of Newport residents streaming through the U-53, at 5:17 p.m. the Germans waved and the U-boat snorted a dark cloud of diesel exhaust and backed away from the dock. The German sailors waved with the Irish flag already affixed to the bow. The carnival-like atmosphere continued as a flotilla of Newportian pleasure boats trailed the German submarine that remained on the surface until it cleared the harbor. U-53 then settled low in the water and began to accelerate, pulling away from the boats in a sea of foamy wash. The pleasure crafts stopped, and passengers watched the submarine settling lower, its running lights still visible, and then as it crossed a slash of moonlight the serpent sank into the water and disappeared.

On Sunday morning, distress calls flooded into Naval Station Newport. The SOS signals were from eastbound merchant ships that had been sunk by the U-53, including a British ocean liner with a large contingent of Americans. Lifeboats had been allowed to be lowered, but there were eighteen children among the rescued. Residents of Newport had a hard time connecting the courteous Germans with their immaculate machine with the hideous death and destruction on the high seas. But Rear Admiral Albert Greaves, the commander of the US Atlantic fleet, had no problem making the connection and sent every warship he had in the vicinity to hunt for the U-boat. He had not taken a tour of the U-53 or met the dapper Lieutenant Rose. The Royal Navy sent out wireless messages to the naval shore station as the destroyers looked for the U-boat as well. But the U-53 had slipped into the depths and simply disappeared. Two hundred survivors from the ships were brought to Newport and many stayed in the luxurious mansions of the Beckmans and Vanderbilts.

No other event illustrated the unreality of the war for Americans. The U-boat was a curiosity, its commander and sailors straight out of a Hollywood movie. The danger was offshore, somewhere out in the Atlantic, but in Newport the WASPish world of debutantes, mansions, and old-world money carried on as if it were all part of a fine melodrama put on for the one percent and now the Germans had returned to their roles as predators of the seas, faceless monsters beneath the deep, but they were actually very nice fellows, quite polite in fact.

President Wilson was golfing with Edith, taking walks along the beach, having coffee on the porch of Shadow Lawn, and like the people of Newport found the news of the U-boat docking in Newport more curious than anything else. Besides, Wilson had no "official" knowledge of the sinkings, but all the same he dictated a statement from his cottage, "The country may rest assured that the German government will be held to the complete fulfillment of its promises to the government of the United States."[4] He finished dictating the statement, then took Edith for a ride in the Pierce-Arrow where their courtship began. It was still the president's favorite escape where he simply pulled the curtain separating him and his bride from the rest of the world.

TR was furious that the Germans were so brazen to pull up to an American dock like a car pulling into a gas station. In fact, if the Germans had needed diesel fuel, then the Newportians would have accommodated. "Now the war has been carried to our very shores,"[5] he sputtered. To Roosevelt, the Germans having the temerity to tie up to an American dock in broad daylight and requesting that a letter be mailed to the German ambassador was a direct result of Wilson's weak-kneed response going all the way back to the *Lusitania*. He fired off the broadside that the American and Royal navies had failed to do. "Now the war has been carried to our very shores. The administration's dismissive attitude to sea-born terrorism, going back to the *Lusitania*, had made it inevitable that something like this would happen. President Wilson's ignoble shirking of responsibility has been clothed in an utterly misleading phrase, the phrase of a coward, he kept us out of war. In reality, war has been creeping nearer and nearer until it stares at us from just beyond our three-mile limit, and we face it without policy, plan, purpose or preparation."[6]

Then Roosevelt went on a high-speed tour for the Republican nominee, Hughes, where he gave one incendiary speech after another attacking Wilson's inaction. He burned down the house at Cooper Union in New York:

> *During the last three years and a half, hundreds of American men, women and children have been murdered on the high seas and in Mexico. Mr. Wilson had dared not stand up for them. . . . He wrote Germany that he would hold her to "strict accountability" if an American lost his life on an American or neutral ship by her submarine warfare. Forthwith the* Arabic *and the* Gulflight *were sunk. But Mr. Wilson dared not take any action. . . . Germany despised him and the* Lusitania *was sunk in consequence. Thirteen hundred and ninety-four people were drowned, one hundred and three of them babies under two years of age.*[7]

Teddy then dramatically threw his script to the floor and continued in the pin-drop silence. "Mr. Wilson now dwells at Shadow Lawn. There should be shadows enough at Shadow Lawn, the shadows of men, women, and children who have risen from the ooze of the ocean bottom and from the graves in foreign lands; the shadows of the helpless whom Mr. Wilson did not dare protect lest he might have to face grave danger; the shadows of babies gasping pitifully as they sank under the waves; the shadows of women outraged and slain by bandits." Now Teddy wound up, throwing everything at Wilson but the kitchen sink. "The shadows of troopers who lay in the Mexican desert, the black blood crusted round their mouths, and their dim eyes looking upward, because President Wilson had sent them to do a task, and then shamefully abandoned them to the mercy of foes who knew no mercy. Those are the shadows proper for Shadow Lawn, the shadows of deeds that were never done; the shadows of lofty words that were followed by no action; the shadows of the tortured dead."[8]

One can imagine Roosevelt was fairly exhausted after his emotional evisceration of Woodrow Wilson. On the drive home he knocked down any idea he would run in 1920, telling a young aide, John Leary, "You are wrong there, this was my year, 1916 was my high twelve. In four years I will be out of it."[9] Of course, this was the man who said he would never run again after turning it over to William Howard Taft. And while TR roasted Woodrow Wilson on a spit over the hot flames of his indignation for candidate Hughes, life in Newport returned to the placidity of the landed gentry after the German submarine departed. Undoubtedly, Flora's fellow debutante Margaret Fahnestock relayed the day's events and her role in translating for the dapper U-boat commander Lieutenant Rose. Such adventures during the season could only add to the conversations around dinner tables and breakfast. And while the lion roared at Sagamore Hill, the consensus among Newportians was that the Germans were actually very nice fellows. Quite top drawer really.

The Snows of the Sierra Nevada

1916

THE WAGONS CREAKED ALONG THE SNOW-MUFFLED ROAD WITH KERO-sene lanterns throwing a halo of yellow light not ten feet ahead. Still the snow came down on the Sierra Nevada mountains, coating the horses' manes and stinging the eyes of the two men huddled together on the buckboard, squinting into the white-rimmed darkness. The roads were all but impassable and they had waited until there had been a lull in the storm but now it had begun again with a vengeance. The snow on the road was level with the forest and to the two men there was no longer a road and the horses were slowing with each step. They would have turned back with their locked boxes of ballots if the entire country weren't waiting to hear who the next president of the United States would be. That answer was in the snow-covered crates behind them.

The New York Times had already given the election to Charles Hughes. A colored light on the top of *The New York Times* building was to denote the winner for all the world to see. White would be Wilson and red would be Hughes. The red light beamed over the cavern of Times Square and Teddy Roosevelt at 10:00 p.m. had issued a statement, "I am doubly thankful as an American for the election of Mr. Hughes. It is a vindication of our national honor."[1] Woodrow Wilson at Shadow Lawn drank a glass of milk at 10:30 and announced to his family he was going to bed. Edith joined him a few minutes later. He had lightly chastised her in the morning when she told him how happy they would be if he lost the election and could lead their own lives. "What a delightful pessimist you are! One must never court defeat. If it comes, accept it like a soldier; but don't anticipate it, for that destroys your fighting spirit."[2]

Edith had gone so far as to look at the house that she and Woodrow were to occupy. Things were not looking good, and Edith hoped that Woodrow would lose in November and that she and the president could lead a quiet life together. She had married him thinking he might lose and that she would only have to endure a year in the White House. And now it was coming down to the night of the election and it wasn't looking good for Woodrow Wilson. Edith had another reason to rejoice in Wilson losing the presidency. He was not a well man.

Woodrow had been suffering from high blood pressure and arteriosclerosis for years and Edith's obsessing over what he ate, getting up early to supervise his breakfast, lunch, and dinner, taking the long drives in the country, golf, poetry; it was all therapy to keep the stress levels low and fight the rising systolic pressure that gave Wilson excruciating headaches that forced him to retreat into darkened rooms with a damp cloth over his forehead. No beta blockers. No real understanding of a salt-free diet to push down the creeping blood pressure that had as much to do with the hardening of arteries that thickened the walls of Wilson's veins and heart.

For the first time in history, a First Lady had inserted herself into the daily routine of the president and her role approached what might even be called a copresident, as Scott Berg outlined in *Wilson*:

The President now took to rising at six o'clock in the morning, at which time he would have a small sandwich and a cup of coffee from a plate and thermos that had been set on a small table outside his bedroom. Then he and Edith would go to a course for at least an hour of golf. They would be home in time for breakfast together at eight o'clock sharp and then go to his study together to check "the drawer" bin in the desk in which all documents demanded immediate attention had been placed. Edith would sort the papers placing those requiring his signature before him and blotting each as she set down the next item. Time permitting, he discussed each document with her. By nine o'clock, stenographer Charles Swem would arrive and Edith would sit close by, listening to Woodrow dictate replies to his mail, marveling at the lucid answers that came apparently with no effort form a mind so well stored.[3]

No, losing the election was just fine with Edith, and the sooner the better. She didn't like Washington, where everyone looked down on her because she was younger, outspoken, came from the "trades," and had ensnared the president into their view with her sexual wiles. She especially couldn't stand Henry Cabot Lodge and his protégé, Teddy Roosevelt, who never lost an opportunity to attack her husband for his He Kept Us Out of War slogan, which TR called "the phrase of a coward,"[4] which sent Woodrow's blood pressure up with the incessant war talk that made it harder to keep America out of the war.

So on the night of November 6 it looked as if Hughes had clinched the election and now *The New York Times* had called it for Hughes and Wilson looked at Edith in their bedroom. "Well, little girl, it looks like you will get your wish and we can move into that house you have been looking at. Frankly I did not, but we can do some of the things we want to do."[5]

Edith nodded, not looking at the newspaper that had Roosevelt's latest attack on Wilson. "Instead of speaking softly and carrying a big stick, President Wilson spoke bombastically and carried a dishrag."[6] The paper also had the latest British steamers the Germans had sunk, the *Marina* and the *Rowanmore*, with eight Americans lost. Wilson had been able to throw off the actions of the U-53, but these attacks showed the *Sussex* pledge was dead where the Germans had pledged not to sink noncombatant ships.

TR had been doing a tour of the West and the Southwest for Charles Evan Hughes and at one stop there was talk of his red face and speculation that he had arteriosclerosis. When asked if he suffered from a hardening of the arteries at Cooperstown, he stared at the reporter.

"Just what is that?"

The reporter explained.

"Well they are right."[7]

Roosevelt left the hall exhausted, hobbling along from an infected left ankle. When he reached the car, he got in the back and tried to position his foot so the throbbing would stop. It had been that way ever since the trolley accident. He shut his eyes against the pain. It was fourteen years ago, 1902. He had been on a tour of New England and piled into an open carriage with Governor Winthrop Murray Crane of Massachusetts and up front his bodyguard, Bill Craig. He had just finished a speech in Pittsfield, Massachusetts, and the open carriage started down the road, grooved in the center with a trolley track. Everyone assumed this part of the trolley line was closed. The horses kept to the right of the track but then the track swung across their path. Roosevelt and others heard a loud rumbling behind as the horses galloped into the grooved center of the track.

The bodyguard, Craig, turned around and cried out, "Oh my God," and then Roosevelt, the governor, and his secretary were thrown in different directions as Craig fell under the eight wheels of the trolley that had struck the open carriage. Roosevelt hit the road with his face and lay there while the trolley car and wrecked carriage crashed to a stop in a cloud of dust. TR searched for his spectacles as Captain Lung ran over: "Are you hurt Mr. President?"[8]

"No, I guess not," he muttered through bleeding lips.[9]

Roosevelt saw the coachman lying on the road with blood oozing out of his ears. The governor seemed unhurt, and Roosevelt went to the wrecked trolley and carriage and looked under the wheels; he saw only blood and bone. His bodyguard had been chopped to pieces by the eight wheels of the trolley car. He saw the engineer standing dazed and staring. TR bunched up his fist and put it in his face. "Did you lose control of the car?" The man stared at him. "If you did," said Roosevelt, voice shaking, "that was one thing, if you didn't it was Goddamned outrage!"[10] Roosevelt had escaped Craig's fate by inches and by luck he was thrown clear. The engineer seemed to wake up.

"You don't suppose I tried to do it, do you?" The president and the man stood face to face; then Roosevelt remembered himself and stepped away as deputies led him off. "Well, I had the right of way anyway," the engineer shouted back. But TR was already kneeling by the twisted body of his bodyguard. "Too bad, too bad," he murmured. "Poor Craig . . . how my children will feel that."[11] Quentin, the little boy in the White House, was bereft that the big man whom he spent time with was gone. The black and blue marks on TR's face faded but the damage done to his ankle was permanent, even after surgeons scraped infection from the bone. His trip down the Amazon had reignited the infection and now as so many things were becoming, it was chronic.

But Charles Evan Hughes had won, and TR believed his division of Rough Riders would now become a reality. Still, there was high snow in the Sierra Nevada and California had not come in because the ballot boxes could not be brought in by horseback on the blocked roads. Woodrow Wilson had gone to bed thinking he had lost the election, but the counting continued, and it was all coming down to the thirteen electoral votes for California and uncounted ballots from the Sierras. California would call the next president of the United States. Margaret Wilson knocked on her father's door in the morning when he was shaving and told him an extra edition of *The New York Times* was printed. The election was still in doubt but was now leaning toward Wilson.

While the counting went on, Roosevelt started packing up his papers at Sagamore Hill for deposit in the Library of Congress. There were already rumblings that Roosevelt's pro-intervention, pro-war stance might have cost Hughes support in the Midwest. The count should have been over by now. There was always the unexpected. Snow in the Sierra. A trolley car that crosses over into the path of speeding carriage. Roosevelt picked up another box, feeling the pain in his left ankle that was infected once again. His old friend Hamlin Garland found him in his spurred boots but moving slowly, favoring one leg.

"I am no use, Garland. I feel my years," he said.[12]

The roads in the Sierra Nevada were finally cleared and the count was finished on the night of November 7. Woodrow Wilson was elected by just 3,773 votes. Charles Evan Hughes was so disbelieving that he didn't concede for two weeks. Edith Wilson also had a hard time believing that snow in the mountains of the Sierra Nevada had held her future and seemly given her the life she wanted and then taken it away. She was now signed on for four more years in the White House. Life was like that—always the unexpected. Charles Evans Hughes knew that feeling very well. And so did Teddy Roosevelt. Once again he was being blamed for the Republicans losing the election and the debacle of the Hughes candidacy for being the pro-war oracle attached to Hughes's shoe. A vote for Hughes became a vote for war and most Americans did not want war. Roosevelt's attacks on Wilson were now the anchor of Republican defeat and it looked once again as if his political career was dead.

"I hope you are ashamed of Mr. Roosevelt," Alice Hooper wrote Frederick Jackson Turner. "If one man was responsible for Mr. Wilson he was the man—thus perhaps Mr. Roosevelt ought to see the Shadows of Shadow Lawn and the dead babies in the ooze of the sea."[13] As Teddy Roosevelt plodded around Sagamore Hill, he could only wonder how he had ended up on the wrong side when he began on the side of the right-eous. The truth was, it had happened many times before.

Chapter Fourteen

Commissioner Roosevelt

1895

TEDDY ROOSEVELT MADE HIS WAY IN THE COLD DARKNESS OF THE Lower East Side of New York, which smelled like death at 2:00 a.m. to the man with the turned-up collar and soft hat pulled low over his brow. He walked with two other men with hands in their pockets eastward along 42nd Street. The smell of beer, sweat, salt from pickle barrels, the open doors of saloons pouring out the rank smell of human debauchery with perfume, body odor, excrement. A night watchman trailed the three men who looked to be up to no good for several blocks, then turned back. They paused outside an all-night restaurant when the owner emerged. "Where in thunder does that copper sleep?"[1] he groused, rapping the ground. The three men continued on, rousing some officers who were conversing outside a liquor store.

They continued through the pale globes of gaslight and entered an oyster saloon and came upon officer William E. Rath drinking beer and inhaling oysters. The man with the slouch hat and glasses stepped in front of the officer.

"Why are you not on your post, officer?"

"What the — is it to you?"

A counterman stepped up to the bar.

"You gotta lot of nerve coming in here and interfering with an officer."

The man stepped up close to the officer now, eyeing him.

"I'm Commissioner Roosevelt."

William Rath snorted.

"Yes, you are. You're Grover Cleveland and Mayor Strong all in a bunch you are. Move on now or—"

The counterman's jaw dropped.

"Shut up Bill, it's His Nibs, sure, don't you spot the glasses?"

"Go to your post at once."[2]

The officer took off running as the new police commissioner frowned. Teddy Roosevelt had come in on a wave of reform, sweeping New York City and promising to clean up the police force. His nocturnal wanderings were just the beginning. He had been elected police commissioner and 300 Mulberry Street, the headquarters of New York's finest, would never be the same. A reporter remembered TR's first day:

> He came on down the street, he yelled, "Hello Jake!" and running up the stairs to the front door of Police Headquarters he waved us reporters to follow. We did. With the police officers standing around watching, the new Board went up to the second story. . . . TR seized Ries, who introduced me and still running he asked questions: "Where are our offices?" TR then called a meeting of the board and made his first public statement. "The public . . . may rest assure that so far as I am concerned, there will be no politics in the department, and I know that I voice the sentiment of my colleagues in that respect."[3]

There would be no more payoffs for positions. There was a new sheriff in town to clean up the department and the press headlines jumped on for the ride.

"ROOSEVELT'S NEW GIRL SECRETARY"

"REIGN OF TERROR AT POLICE HEADQUARTERS"

"RATTLED THE DRY OLD POLICE BONES"

"ROOSEVELT AS JUDGE"[4]

TR understood the role of the press in his campaign to stamp out corruption and invited reporters daily into his large office for chats. He was a young thirty-six, dashing, volcanic, and made great copy. Theodore Roosevelt, the cowboy turned commissioner, quickly became the story.

When he asks a question, Mr. Roosevelt shoots it at the poor trembling policeman as he would shoot a bullet at a coyote . . . he shows a set of teeth calculated to unnerve the bravest of the Finest. His teeth are very white and almost as big as a colt's teeth . . . they seem to say, "Tell the truth to your Commissioner or he'll bite your head off . . . this interesting Commissioner's face is red . . . his hair is thick and short . . . under his right ear he has a long scar. It is the opinion of all the policeman who have talked with him that he got that scar fighting an Indian out West. It is also their opinion that Indian is dead. But Mr. Roosevelt's voice is the policeman's hardest trial. It is an exasperating voice, a sharp voice, a rasping voice. It is a voice that comes from the tips of the teeth and seems to say in tones, "What do you amount to anyway?"[5]

Roosevelt's ritual was to arrive around 8:30 and turn the corner on Mulberry Street with his pace increasing until he bounded up the front stairs and into the lobby of the police headquarters, waving off the elevator and leaping up the stairs to the second floor, where he would land in his chair, take off his glasses and hat, put on his pince-nez, and start on the first document, either giving it to his secretary or crumpling it to the floor that would soon be littered with snowballs of paper all around his chair. Then if he wanted reporters to come up to his office, he threw up his window and yelled out his cowboy call to the men loitering in front of the stoop. *"Hi yi yi!"*[6]

Roosevelt quickly realized he had to take stock of the rank-and-file policeman, and so he came up with his nighttime journeys into the Heart of Darkness of New York City at the turn of the century. After many nights Roosevelt returned to headquarters in the morning for the day's work without sleep but with no less than seven names in his pockets of officers who had deserted their posts or were found in saloons or sleeping in some restaurant or street corner stoop. "POLICEMAN SLEEP ON POST . . . ROOSEVELT FINDS SEVEN DELINQUENTS IN CAPT. EAKINS PRECINCT"[7] blared an article in the *New York World*. Commissioner Roosevelt made great copy from the start and his nighttime wanderings filled many columns. "President Theodore Roosevelt and Commissioner Avery . . . had just returned from a tour of discovery. Seeking an honest policeman in the Union Market and Eldridge Street stations in the dark hours, they came back happy, for be it said they found an honest man . . . a policeman . . . there was a cloud across the horizon, however, for on the west side they uncovered seven policemen, against whom charges will be made."[8]

The nocturnal patrols continued, with Roosevelt many times not sleeping for forty hours. But in his wanderings in the slums of the Lower East Side, his education of the other side of life continued much as it had out west with the hardscrabble cowboys:

> *Tramping along what must have been hundreds of miles of silent avenues lit only by corner lamps and the occasional flickering torch of an oyster cart, he could sense, if not feel, the ache of homelessness and poverty. In alleys and courtyards to the left and right, he could gaze through open windows at the hot intimacies of tenement life and listen to the bedlam of alien conversation. Italian changed to English, German to Yiddish, Russian to Polish as he moved from block to block as it was relief to hear even a few words of broken English. Sometimes he cast about for pearls of street wisdom as when he asked an Italian fruit vendor what possible "monish" could be made selling his wares on a deserted street at dead of night.*[9]

Roosevelt himself would later write, "These midnight rambles are great fun . . . my whole work brings me in contact with every class of people in New York. . . . I get a glimpse of the real life of the swarming millions."[10]

To New Yorkers, their young commissioner became the teeth-snapping Teddy who would drop in to Mike Lyons's Bowery restaurant in the wee hours, tired and hungry, where he would greet the patrons who shouted, "Hello Teddy. . . . How are you Roosevelt?"[11] The headlines continued: "ROOSEVELT AS ROUNDSMAN . . . POLICEMEN DIDN'T DREAM THE PRESIDENT OF THE BOARD WAS CATCHING THEM NAPPING . . . HE MAKES THE NIGHT HIDEOUS FOR SLEEPY PATROLMEN."[12] Teddy also found conditions of squalor that horrified him. On another night patrol with Commissioner Andrews and Richard Harding Davis, a correspondent from *Harpers Monthly*, he found a sort of Dante's hell. "The three young men entered the Thirteenth Precinct on the Lower East Side soon after midnight and began a systematic search of its clammy caverns. This was distinctly ghetto territory; ill lit, badly sanitized, the air around Union Market heavy with the smells of schmaltz and blood-soaked kosher salt. Roosevelt, who as president of the police board was also a member of the Board of Health, made a note to hasten the closing of the long-condemned slaughterhouse."[13]

The public was taken with their young wandering police commissioner but then like all popular teachers who must give out hard medicine, the goodwill of New Yorkers turned almost overnight. The Sunday Excise Law would be his undoing. The old statute forbade the sale of "intoxicating liquors by saloons on the Sabbath."[14] It was not enforced. Workers were not to be blocked from their weekend refreshment after a six-day work week. It was a necessary safety valve for the sixty-hour work week that left Sunday as a worker's only refuge. And for the large German population it was their right to have a stein or a bucket of lager brought home by tenement kids running down alleys hung with billowing laundry that dried in the hot breeze of long summer nights.

But Teddy Roosevelt felt the law was the law and told his officers to "rigidly enforce" the law and make sure the saloons closed at midnight on Saturday and stayed closed until midnight Sunday. He then called in the reporters with his cowboy yell and let the press know his new policy:

I do not deal with public sentiment. I deal with the law. How I might act as a legislator or what kind of legislation I should advise, has no bearing on my conduct as an executive officer charged with administering the law . . . if it proves impossible to enforce it, it will only be after the experiment of breaking many a captain of the police. . . . I am going to see if we cannot break the license forthwith of any saloon keeper who sells on Sunday. . . . I shall not let up for a moment in my endeavor to make the police understand that no excuse will be

*permitted on their part when the law is not observed . . . this applies
just as much to the biggest hotel as to the smallest grog shop.*[15]

The backlash was swift. The press turned against him with *The World*
and *Herald* devoting pages to "Teddy's Folly." German Americans turned
against the commissioner and demanded his resignation. On August 5,
a postal worker opened a package addressed to Roosevelt. The package
shot out a tongue of flame and smoke. The mail bomb headed for the
commissioner had failed to go off successfully and TR dismissed it as a
"cheap thing." Saloons tried to get around the law by serving beer with
sandwiches but were quickly shut down.

Ninety-seven percent of the city's bars were closed on June 30, voted
The Driest Sunday Seen in Years. From three million glasses of beer,
Roosevelt's enforcement dropped the flow to a trickle. Roosevelt's blue
coats seemed to be everywhere, waving aside bribes with loathing and
writing out summons at the slightest sign of resistance. Sandwiches were
suddenly served all over town as a way to be able to serve beer. Vendors
laced their coffee now with cognac. *The New York Times* reported that the
estimated loss to saloonkeepers was $20,000 each. "In his eagerness to
close the New York saloons," remarked the *Chicago Tribune*, "Mr. Roosevelt has interfered with the hop raisers of New York and Washington
with the corned beef ranchers of the plains, the pig's feet producers of the
West and the barley growers of the North. He is in a fair way to cost the
American people millions."[16]

An enterprising saloonkeeper named Levy found that the hour from
midnight to 1:00 a.m. on Monday was not covered by the law and opened
his doors. Other bars followed and bars opened in the middle of the
night, with *The Sun* claiming "Mr. Roosevelt Is Beaten."[17] But this was
small consolation for the long stretch of dry Sundays for New Yorkers.

Roosevelt anticipated a drop in arrests and disorderly conduct and the
Sunday break from drinking would help families. New Yorkers just went
to Coney Island or Long Island to drink or turned to medicinal liquor
sold by drugstores. The Tammany Hall Democrats swept into power in
the summer of 1895 on the issue of Dry Sundays. Roosevelt, who once
shouted at a crowd of angry Germans, "It is true I may never be heard

of again, but I will have kept my oath of office,"[18] doubled down and the Raines Law was passed, expanding the dry hours. But the saloons soon found a way around the odious law that allowed a hotel with ten rooms to serve liquor with food around the clock. Suddenly, one thousand saloons had little rooms tacked on the back and stayed open all night. The City That Never Sleeps came from the Raines Law that allowed booze to be served all night long.

Still, Roosevelt became a national figure in his crusade even if New Yorkers detested him and he would never win a majority vote in the city again as governor, vice president, or president. You can take away many things from New Yorkers, but never their alcohol. In a strange literary coincidence, Bram Stoker, who wrote *Dracula*, wrote in his diary after meeting TR during the dark days when many had turned against him, "Must be president someday. A man you can't cajole, can't frighten, can't buy."[19] After he left New York, Teddy never did quite understand how people could dislike him for taking a righteous stand that was for their benefit. He never would.

The Lily-Livered Skunk in the White House

1917

THE SUFFRAGETTES LOOKED LIKE BLACK CROWS TO WOODROW WILSON at the White House gates in their long dark dresses with the signs over their heads. Their voices reached him distantly, ineffectually, the chant of the future. They were always there now. Sometimes they lay down in front of his limousine. Sometimes they flashed him and Edith. Sometimes they chained themselves to the White House gates. He had asked them to come in for some hot chocolate on a particularly cold day, but they said they would rather remain out in the cold. In a way, he couldn't help thinking they were like the French, the British, and the Germans. They wouldn't take what he had to offer and persisted in creating havoc.

President Wilson had sent a peace note and proposed what he saw as a way to end war for all time. "A League of Nations to ensure peace throughout the world."[1] Secretary Lansing didn't like the note and blurted out to the press, "The sending of this note will indicate the possibility of our being forced into the war."[2] Wilson sent it anyway and proposed a peace conference. "If the contest must continue to proceed towards undefined ends by slow attrition until the one group of belligerents or the other is exhausted; if million after million of human lives must continue to be offered up . . . hopes of peace and of the willing concert of free peoples will be rendered vain and idle."[3]

The Germans said sure. The British and French had a list of concessions they wanted from Germany before they would even meet. Like the suffragettes, the warring powers preferred to keep fighting even though Verdun and the Somme had proved killing hundreds of thousands of men changed nothing.

Santa Claus read the newspaper at the Cove School Christmas party in Oyster Bay, where Santa appeared every year and seemed with each passing year to be more jolly and more rotund. TR gave out toys, sang out "Merry Christmas," and felt better than he had since the election; he told an acquaintance, "The antics of the last few days have restored what self-respect I lost in supporting Hughes."[4] Wilson was tumbling toward war even as he tried to write it way with peace offerings and speeches to Congress about a peace without victory. In Europe. He then went on and added that an agreement for peace should include "freedom of the seas, general disarmament, self-determination for all nations and common membership after the wars end in a league of nations."[5]

The Germans responded with a declaration of unrestricted submarine warfare on the last day of the year. The Germans had been starved by the blockade by the British and a new faction in the government came up with a plan of Unrestricted Warfare to finally punch the war to a conclusion. The thinking was the war would be over before the Americans could get any soldiers across the ocean. "The key to the success of the plan was the prevention of resupply of Allied positions along the front—the key to prevention of resupply was the severing of the Atlantic link between America and Britain."[6]

Count Bernstorff reportedly wept when he gave the declaration to Secretary Lansing. Wilson for his part found it unbelievable and read what the Germans considered a concession to the Americans. One American passenger liner would be permitted once a week to steam to Falmouth, England, "provided it was painted with vertical red and white stripes, followed a specific course via the Scilly Isles, arrived on Sunday, and departed on Wednesday . . . the stripes were to be one meter wide."[7]

Captain Rose the of the U-53, who was so courteous and pleasant when he pulled up in Newport months before, now got back to work and sank the USS *Housatonic*. Count Bernstorff was handed his passport and Wilson issued a statement. "If American ships and American lives shall be sacrificed. . . . I shall take the liberty of coming again before the Congress to ask that authority be given to me to use any means that may be necessary for the protection of our seamen and our people . . . on the high seas."[8]

Woodrow Wilson responded not with war but with a severing of diplomatic relations with Germany. "He is yellow all through in the presence of danger, either physically or morally," Roosevelt declared to Henry Cabot Lodge. "Of course it costs him nothing, if the insult or injury is to the country, because I don't believe he is capable of understanding what the words pride of country mean."[9]

Still, war was coming. An American submarine in Philadelphia was sabotaged when her scuttling plugs were opened. The sailors aboard an Austrian freighter in New York Harbor wrecked their engine room. The German government ordered the *Konzprinzessin* to be destroyed in Boston. In Oyster Bay, TR had gone from pariah to sage. He had been right all along about the Germans and now the world knew it. In a letter to his son Kermit, Roosevelt wrote, "Even the lily-livered skunk in the White House may not be able to prevent Germany from kicking us into war."[10]

But now TR wanted to get into the line he knew that would form to the White House of men wanting to serve. It was time to organize the Rough Riders and get the wheels in motion. So TR sat down and wrote an immediate letter to Secretary of War Newton Diehl Baker to make his case again for creating a division of men to follow him into battle, which he knew in all probability would be the last charge of the Rough Riders. Baker was a pale, bookish, short man who had only been the mayor of Cleveland for a short time. Strangely, he was also a pacifist who had warned against retaliating for the sinking of the *Lusitania*. Now he had a letter in front of him from one of the most militaristic presidents of the twentieth century:

Sir, I have already on file in your department, my application to be permitted to raise a Division of Infantry with a divisional brigade of cavalry in the event of war. . . . In view of the recent German note and of the fact that my wife and I are booked to sail next week for a

*month in Jamaica, I respectfully write you as follows. If you believe
there will be war and a call for volunteers to go to war, immediately,
I respectfully and earnestly request that you notify me at once so that
I may not sail. Otherwise, I shall sail and in such case I respectfully
request that if or when it becomes certain that we will have war and
that there will be a call for volunteers to go to war you will direct
that a telegram be sent to me at the* Metropolitan Magazine *office
New York from whence a cable will be sent to Jamaica and I shall
immediately return. I have prepared the skeleton outline of what I
have desired the division to be and what men I shall recommend to the
Department for brigade and regimental commanders, Chief of Staff,
Chief Surgeon, Quartermaster General, etc. The men whom I would
desire for officer and enlisted men are for the most part, men earning
their living in the active business of life, who would be glad to go to
war at their countries [sic] call but who could not be expected and
who would probably refuse to drop their business and see their families
embarrassed unless there is war and the intention to send them to war.
So it is not possible for me to do much more in the way of preliminary
actions than I have already done, until I have official directions.*[11]

Secretary of War Baker sent a short, curt response, dismissing
the Roosevelt proposal on February 3, the same day Wilson went to
Congress and announced diplomatic relations had been severed with
Germany. "No situation has arisen which would justify my suggesting
a postponement of the trip you propose."[12] Ex-presidents were such an
annoyance. TR didn't even wait for Baker's telegram and added another
epistle to his letter. "In view of the breaking of relations with Germany
I shall of course not go to Jamaica and will hold myself in readiness for
any message from you as to the division. I and my four sons will of course
go if volunteers are called for against Germany."[13] Roosevelt was almost
jumping up and down in anticipation of Wilson's speech that he was sure
would be a declaration of war. Edith would have to wait for her trip to
the Caribbean.

But Roosevelt was already hedging his bets, writing a letter to French
ambassador Jean Jules Jusserand two weeks after he had written to Baker.

He was already attempting an end run around Woodrow Wilson and Secretary Baker, appealing directly to the allies (France and England) for him to lead an independent force of twenty thousand men:

> *I cannot tell whether we shall have war or not, yet it seems to me almost impossible to avoid it. I have already applied for permission to raise a division. It may be that the government will not intend to send an expeditionary force, it may be that if they do they will not permit me to go with it. In such event, what I should like to do is raise a division of Americans, who would fight in co-operation with the allies either under the orders of France or England. I might be able to make the place of raising it Canada.*[14]

TR was no fool; if he had to bring pressure on Wilson through the allies he would do it. He was essentially going rogue, proposing an independent force that would be trained in Canada and would be under French command. His desperation to serve and lead a division of Rough Riders is evident in the pleading tone of the letter to the French ambassador:

> *Of course, I would not attempt to raise it so far as I can now see, unless the country went to war because I gravely doubt the propriety of an ex-president of the United States attempting to go to war unless his country is at war. But if we were at war, I should be profoundly unhappy unless I got into the fighting line and I believe I should raise a division of 20,000 men even if the government declined to hold out the promise of an expeditionary force of which I should form part, to go at the earliest moment. I believe that in six months I could get this division ready for the trenches. Now I don't want to be a nuisance instead of a help to France and England but it is barely possible that inasmuch as they want men it would be an object to them to have these 20,000 men and that it would be worth their while to have an ex-president with his division in the trenches . . . do you care to inquire confidentially of your Government whether under the conditions above outlined it would be likely that they would care to call upon me and whether I should raise my troops in Canada and take*

them over there for final training in France or whether it would be
better than I should be under the command of English or French Gen-
erals? I shall make some inquiry of England also.[15]

Essentially, Teddy Roosevelt was proposing to hire himself and his
men out as mercenaries who would fight under any flag. This was certainly motivated in part by Secretary of War Baker's response to TR's second letter addressing the colonels "patriotic suggestion that in due time
you be authorized to raise a division of troops for service abroad." Baker
pointed out that congressional approval would be needed and then told
Roosevelt that Congress would provide "under its own conditions for the
appointment of officers and for the higher commands."[16]

In other words, no thank you. One has to wonder why Roosevelt
didn't just get on a ship and go over himself and fight in the trenches.
To make matters worse, Wilson did not ask for a declaration of war but
asked for authorization to arm American merchantmen. Armed neutrality began to creep into Wilsonian patois as the House appropriated a
billion dollars to get the nation ready for war. Roosevelt shook his head
and told Henry Cabot Lodge that Wilson would not go to war unless
Germany "literally kicks him into it." Germany did just that. Arthur
Zimmerman sent a telegram to the German minister in Mexico. The
British intercepted the telegram and sent it to Woodrow Wilson. It
was the bombshell. Germany would form an alliance with Mexico and
declare joint war against the United States and in return Mexico could
recover Texas, New Mexico, and Arizona with the caveat that Japan
might join in the fight. Wilson released the letter to the press overnight
and on March 1 the nation read with shock that not only was Germany
a threat on the high seas, but she had now come to their western border.
Armed neutrality became a reality with the Armed Ships Bill. Roosevelt
was once again vindicated.

On March 5, Woodrow Wilson and Edith Bolling Wilson drove
to his inauguration with thirty-two Secret Service agents around his
carriage and sharpshooters on the roofs of the Capitol with machine
gunners covering the crowd. A gusty rain hammered on the carriage roof
as Wilson spoke in East Capitol Park: "I beg your tolerance, your counte-

nance, and your united aid," [17] Wilson shouted into the wind. Edith stood by him, marking the first time a First Lady had accompanied a president to the Capitol for his inaugural address. There would be no inaugural balls. Only fifty thousand people had gathered for the brief speech of only 1,500 words. He spoke of tragic events that had made Americans "citizens of the world." Then he painted a dark picture of a future world: "The shadows that now lie dark on our path will soon be dispelled and we shall walk with the light all about if we be but true to ourselves. . . . United alike in the conception of our duty and in the high resolve to perform it in the face of all men, let us dedicate ourselves to the great task in which we must now set our hand." [18]

Wilson then got in his carriage with Edith and went back to the White House. He hadn't said it, but Wilson was getting America ready for war. The funereal air of the inauguration "was not a festival," one onlooker observed, "it was a momentary interlude in a grave business and it must be got over with as briefly and as simply as possible." [19] Wilson felt a great weight had descended on him as he stared out at the soggy gray landscape. In Sagamore Hill Teddy Roosevelt felt like he could dance a jig. America was going to war.

Chapter Sixteen

The Brilliant Light of Darkness

1917

THEODORE ROOSEVELT SAT BEHIND A LARGE WALNUT DESK IN NEW York at the Progressive headquarters at 42nd Street and Madison Avenue. Rain drizzled outside and gusted into the open window. War was about to declared any day, he was sure of it, and he had been using the headquarters as a place to organize his Rough Riders. Applications had been flooding in and it was amazing how men all over the country wanted to get in early and make sure they would ride with TR. Newspapers had taken up the Rough Rider cause and produced an avalanche of men looking to join "Teddy." "ROOSEVELT'S MEN READY FOR CALL," blared the *Des Moines Register*.[1] "Entire Division of Trained Soldiers Can Be Mobilized on Short Notice."

The paper went on to explain that "while President Wilson and most of the nation have been preparing for war, secretly, without ostentation, Roosevelt has organized a complete army division, composed almost entirely of men who have already seen active service and who will therefore need none of the months of preparation. . . . My regiment is composed of English war veterans and Texas cowboys, said Colonel Simpson tonight. Every man in it can use a rifle and pistol and ride."[2] TR didn't mind the papers saying he had already organized the division. He planned to organize a division of men once Wilson actually declared war and he got the signoff from Secretary of War Baker. Meanwhile, he would continue to gather applications and sound out men he wanted as officers.

Roosevelt looked up as the door to his office opened and out of the brisk rain stepped an immaculately uniformed German count. Rain beaded on his starched sleeves. He was bearing letters from the German embassy and from the head of one of the great steamship lines. The count stopped in front of Roosevelt and bowed, then stated he bore a message from His Imperial Majesty and that His Majesty wished Roosevelt to know that he always kept in mind the great pleasure it had given him to receive Roosevelt as a guest in Berlin and at the palace in Potsdam. TR nodded and the count continued in perfect clipped English, "And that he felt assured he could count on Roosevelt's sympathetic understanding of Germany's position and action."[3]

Roosevelt stood, bowed, and looked the count straight in the eyes. "Pray thank his Imperial Majesty from me for his very courteous message; and assure him that I was deeply conscious of the honors done me in Germany and that I shall never forget the way in which His Majesty King Albert of Belgium received me in Brussels."[4] The count stared at Roosevelt, clicked his heels together, then bowed and walked out the door. The Germans, it would seem, wanted to make sure there was no hard feelings between Theodore Roosevelt and their country. They would not do the same for Woodrow Wilson.

The inauguration was over and Edith and Woodrow had sat by the fire in the Yellow Oval room to watch the fireworks and invited Colonel House to sit with them. House noticed the president never let Edith's hand go and pressed his cheek against hers for long moments. The fireworks ended and Wilson suggested they take a walk and check out the new streetlights that had just been installed and turned Washington from a town of darkness to the brilliant light of darkness. Wilson at the last minute had the chauffer drive them without a Secret Service agent even though there had been bomb threats. Behind the Pierce-Arrow was a car stuffed with guards who followed closely as the Wilsons made their way toward the glowing Capitol. A crowd gathered and they headed back to the White House.

A few days later, Wilson was laid low with a cold; his personal physician ordered him to bed, where he remained for two weeks. Edith hovered over him and kept as much business away as she could; she had noticed his collapses followed stress "where every nerve was tense with anxiety . . . and the burdens resting on his shoulders were enough to crush the vitality of a giant."[5] The biggest burden that now rested on Wilson was whether to take America to war or not. But during this period where literally the whole world was watching to see if Wilson would commit the United States, he was curiously inaccessible.

Edith Wilson was acting as a cofferdam and directing away problems and when Secretary Daniels and Secretary Lansing needed to see the president, they found themselves going through the First Lady, who carried their messages in to the president and returned with an answer. Edith sat on the end of the bed and read to Wilson the long memorandums that detailed the arming of merchant ships. When he emerged on March 20, he immediately called a cabinet meeting and went around the room to see what the consensus was for war against Germany. "I do not care for popular demand," Wilson said to the gathered cabinet members. "I want to do right, whether popular or not. . . . I want it to be understood we are in the war to the end, that we will do everything we can to aid the Allies and weaken Germany with money, munitions, ships and men, so that the Prussians will realize that, when they made war on this country they woke up a giant which will surely defeat them."[6]

The cabinet was unanimous in its support of declaring war on Germany. All Wilson had to do now was ask Congress. When Secretary Baker returned to his office, there was a telegram waiting for him from Theodore Roosevelt. It was as if TR were in the room during the cabinet meeting and knew Wilson was gearing up to ask for a declaration of war. "IN VIEW OF THE FACT THAT GERMANY IS NOW ACTUALLY ENGAGED IN WAR WITH US I AGAIN EARNESTLY ASK PERMISSION TO BE ALLOWED TO RAISE A DIVISION FOR IMMEDIATE SERVICE AT THE FRONT."[7]

Secretary Baker wrote back and said flatly that no forces could be raised except by an act of Congress and when Congress reassembled the administration would submit a proposal "for a very much larger army than the force suggested in your telegram."[8] Baker was getting irritated by this pesky ex-president and attempted to close the door for good on the Rough Rider. He said there would be no commission for Roosevelt:

"General officers for all the volunteer forces are to be drawn from the regular army."[9]

Roosevelt was furious and fumed to Henry Cabot Lodge over the snub where Baker reduced him to an old man playing at war and it was best left to the professionals: "I shall answer respectfully, pointing out that I am the retired Commander in Chief of the whole Army and that towards the close of the Santiago expedition I actually commanded a brigade—I am a volunteer officer also. Will you tell some of my friends in the Senate and House about the matter and if legislation is passed, try to have it make proper to employ an ex-President—a retired Commander in Chief in such a fashion?"[10]

He then told Lodge he had approached the French with an offer to sponsor him and his division under the American flag. There was an air of desperation in Roosevelt's pleading with Lodge to lobby congress on his behalf. But it didn't end there. The same night as Wilson's cabinet meeting, Roosevelt gave a speech at the Union League in New York, where he endorsed a resolution along with Elihu Root, Charles Evans Hughes, and Joseph Choate stating, "War now exists by act of Germany."[11] The resolution went on to say for two years Germans had been killing Americans on the high seas and "she has proposed to Japan and Mexico an alliance for our dismemberment as a nation"[12] The other Republican endorsees would not have given Roosevelt the time of day in 1912—now he was being seriously considered as a contender for 1920. Roosevelt wound up his speech by saying it was irresponsible to wait another year while a million men were assembled. "We can perfectly well send an expeditionary force to fight in the trenches now . . . within four or five months,"[13] he added.

Then after the speech Roosevelt became the supplicant once again and begged Hughes, Root, and Robert Bacon to convince Woodrow Wilson to let him fight in France. Hughes watched Roosevelt's face turn red as he proclaimed, "I may not come back, my boys may not come back, my grandchildren may be left alone, but they will carry forward the family name. I must go."[14]

It smacked of a grand suicide mission but in Roosevelt's view it was all glory. Still, war had to be declared and to that end Wilson said he would address Congress in two weeks with a "communication concerning grave matters of national policy."[15] And then he retreated once again and let state papers accumulate on his desk while he and Edith went for drives, had social visits, and the president shot pool. This was all in line with Edith's view that stress was the real demon and Wilson's blood pressure could only be relieved through pleasurable activities.

The address was set for April 2. To that end, on March 30 he and Edith worked in the second-floor study to prepare his remarks. On the thirty-first a spring night descended on the White House and Wilson sat outside on the South Portico with his typewriter under the light of an electric lantern strung between two of the columns. Edith stayed upstairs until she thought he might need some sustenance and then brought down crackers and milk on a silver platter, putting them by his typewriter. Wilson continued to work tirelessly while Edith deciphered top secret code for him and then on Saturday they took a break with a drive in the park and then returned for ten hours and finished up his address.

Teddy Roosevelt had decided to go to Punta Gorda, Florida, to reel in sharks and devilfish. He would return for Wilson's address but before he went he couldn't resist jabbing Wilson one last time with a speech to the Union League Club in New York. The barrage began swiftly. "There is no question about going to war," he thundered. "Germany is already at war with us! The only question for us to decide is whether we shall make war nobly or ignobly. . . . Germany despises timidity as she despises all other forms of feebleness . . . let us face the accomplished fact, admit that Germany is at war with us, and in our turn wage war on Germany with all our energy and courage, and regain the right to look the whole world in the eyes without flinching."[16]

Then before he left town, he turned and couldn't resist puncturing the officious Secretary Baker's balloon one more time; he fired off one more letter in response to his telegram. It is the letter of someone who has been told he was not good enough for the team and has to point out his past victories:

I understood sir that there would be a far larger force than a division called out. I merely wished to be permitted to get ready a division for immediate use in the first expeditionary force sent over. In reference to your concluding sentence, I wish respectfully to point out that I am a retired Commander in Chief of the United States army, and eligible for any position of command over American troops, I respectfully refer you to my three immediate superiors in the field, Lieutenant General S. B. M. Young. Major General Samuel Sumner and Major General Leonard Wood. In the Santiago Campaign I served in the First fight as commander first of the right wing and then of the left wing of the regiment in the next the big fight as Colonel of the regiment and I ended the campaign in command of the brigade.

The regiment 1st United States Volunteer Cavalry in which I first served as Lieutenant Colonel and which I then commanded as Colonel was raised, armed, equipped, drilled, mounted, dismounted, kept for two weeks on transport and then put through two victorious fights aggressive fights in which we lost a third of the officers and a fifth of the enlisted men all within over fifty days.[17]

One can see Secretary Baker rubbing his forehead. This was not going away. This man did not take no for an answer. Never mind he is talking about a cavalry operation from twenty years before, where men could charge a hill on horses, take the hill, and end a war. Roosevelt had no idea what mechanized carnage looked like in a twentieth-century war. It was on a scale that few could understand where France and Britain had literally lost a generation of young men. Secretary Baker felt as though he were trying to convince someone that the days of jousting were over and that sadly courage and chivalry meant nothing against the yellow haze of chlorine gas where men drowned in their own mucus.

Secretary Baker sat down and stared out the window. He had been brought up on the Teddy Roosevelt legend as a boy. He knew all about the Rough Riders and the charge up San Juan Hill. He stared out the window at the setting sun over the Potomac and if he said the poor son of a bitch, it would have been in line with his thinking. Some men could never get used to the twilight of a life lived so brilliantly. He couldn't blame Roosevelt. Not many men were able to charge up a hill and single-handedly win an entire war. Baker shook his head—it was an incredible story.

CHAPTER SEVENTEEN

The Great Day of My Life

1898

"THE GREAT DAY OF MY LIFE" DAWNED STEAMY WITH GREEN FOLIAGE slashed from the sunlight perforating the canopy of dense jungle. July 1, 1898, would live forever in Theodore Roosevelt's mind. Early morning mist rose slowly in the jungle as the hills in the east, west, and north emerged while TR walked about his men. He lathered his face and talked in a low voice to those who had "woken afraid." Yellow suspenders slashed his dark-blue shirt, fastened with silver leaves and topped with a stand-up collar with a volunteer insignia. A quick breakfast of beans with bacon fat and hardtack was wolfed down by men not too nervous to eat. Many settled for the scalding black campfire coffee.

At 6:30 a.m. the jungle reverberated with American artillery lobbing shells toward San Juan Hill. The Spanish returned and white plumes of smoke shot up from the forest floor, shrapnel whistling through the trees, raising a shrapnel bump on Roosevelt's wrist. A regular had his legs blown off and a number of Cuban soldiers were killed instantly. Roosevelt moved his regiment into the cover of the jungle until the cannonade ceased at 8:45 a.m.

Roosevelt then led his men up the road toward San Juan. TR rode on Texas as the morning gave way to the intense of heat of a tropical jungle. The one hundred-degree temperature combined with the wet blanket of moisture rising in thick clouds from the foliage. Roosevelt rode on his horse with his blue polka dot scarf dangling from his brimmed cavalry hat. The scarf fluttered and rose behind him as Texas trotted down the road with the increasing whine of Mauser bullets growing all around him and his men. The trees suddenly thinned, and a thunderstorm of bullets descended, ripping through the trees, grass, and bodies where San Juan creek bisected the road. The road turned crimson as the bodies piled up in front of the Rough Riders. The well-hidden Spanish snipers, many up in trees, had a field day as Roosevelt and his men fanned out and plunged across the body-laden water.

Bloody Ford would become legend before the day was done. The water was now blood red as the Rough Riders frantically tried to get across. The snipers had turned their sights to another target, an observation balloon that was glistening in the sun and now sinking lower and lower perforated with holes. They then turned back to the men crouching in a field of waist-high grass in front of San Juan Hill with its blockhouse and breastworks visible to Roosevelt and his men. Roosevelt had orders to move to the right and establish his men in front of a smaller hill. But no one could move under the withering fire now. "There was no hiding from them," wrote Richard Harding Davis. "Their bullets came from every side. Their invisible smoke helped to keep their hiding places secret and in the incessant shriek of shrapnel and the spit of the Mausers, it was difficult to locate the reports of their rifles."[1]

Roosevelt was now a prime target up on his horse with his bright suspenders, his Stetson, his Brooks Brothers khakis now mud splattered, and his eyeglasses flashing prisms of light. The tropical sun had shot the temperature well over one hundred degrees with the men crouched down into the plants while Mauser bullets zinged down from above. This would not do. Roosevelt stared up Kettle Hill to the right of San Juan Hill, sitting on Little Texas, a man on a white horse with a cavalry hat and a bright yellow tunic.

"Boys, this is the day we repeat what we have done before," he shouted. "You know we are surrounded by the Regulars. They are around us thick and heavy." Roosevelt wanted to assure his men they were not alone and had support on both sides. "Don't forget where you belong . . . don't forget what you are fighting for. Don't forget boys, that your reward is not in the immediate past, but think of what will come in the future."[2]

But they couldn't move until the order came.

The Spanish soldiers poured fire down upon their position with bullets zinging past Roosevelt. He saw men below him roll over with bright streams pouring down their foreheads from ruler-perfect shots drilled right between the eyes. Roosevelt was everywhere with his twenty-five-year-old orderly, William Sanders, following him on foot. TR was heard saying over and over, "I wish they'd let us start."[3] He gave orders for men to go back and find General Wood or anybody who could give them orders to get out of the killing field. Casualties among the Rough Riders were increasing by the hour. One messenger Roosevelt sent back didn't go ten feet before falling over from a bullet in his neck. They could not stay here, better to die charging up Kettle Hill than be cut to pieces below. An officer solved the problem, galloping up with orders from General Sumner: "Move forward and support the regulars in the assault on the hills in front."[4]

Teddy Roosevelt needed no more. The red-tiled house on top of Kettle Hill was where he was headed. That was where the majority of the withering fire was coming from. Roosevelt's "crowded hour," which he would write about for the rest of his life, began. He rode up and down the line oblivious to the Cubans shooting at him, shouting for the men to move forward. "Move forward!" One man was lying on the ground and not moving. "Are you afraid to stand up when I am on horseback?"[5] Roosevelt roared. The man began to stand up when he fell over dead from a Mauser bullet that had passed through the length of his body. But the problem was the men were standing but not moving. Roosevelt wheeled his horse around and faced the men. "WELL, COME ON!"

No one started forward. Roosevelt sputtered, "What are you, cowards?"

A trooper grinned. "We're waiting for the command." Roosevelt sat back in his saddle, a grin toying with the corners of his mouth.

"Forward march!" he yelled.[6]

The Rough Riders charged. Some walked, some ran. Some would stop and kneel, fire, then continue. Roosevelt rode back toward the rear of the line to get the stragglers moving; it was where a commander of his rank was supposed to be, but every time he got behind another line, they overtook the line in front of them until TR found himself at the front of the advancing regiment. He came to some men from the Ninth and First Cavalries lying on the ground directly in front of the Rough Riders. Roosevelt told Captain Eugene Dimmick of the Ninth he had been instructed to support an attack on Kettle Hill.

Dimmick shook his head and said he couldn't advance without an order from his colonel. Roosevelt stared at the man with bullets kicking up dust and chewing up the foliage around his horse. Roosevelt demanded to know where his colonel was and when Dimmick couldn't point to him, Teddy nodded and proclaimed, "Then I am the ranking officer here and I give the order to charge!"[7]

Dimmick was a fifty-seven-year-old veteran of the Civil War in the regular army and here was this lieutenant colonel of a volunteer regiment. He could not advance without orders. Roosevelt looked down at the man on the ground, "Then let my men through sir!"[8] Just then Lieutenant Henry Anson Barber of the Ninth rode up and said they were under orders not to advance and he was also carrying orders from First Brigade's Colonel Henry Carroll that the Rough Riders "should be careful of his men, he didn't want them firing into them."[9] Barber then asked what orders he was operating under. Roosevelt replied he was going to charge the hill under his own orders.

Barber raced away to tell Carroll of Roosevelt's planned charge. At this point Theodore Roosevelt didn't care. It was his crowded hour and suddenly an electricity swept the field; everyone knew of the planned Rough Rider charge that was not based on orders but on the man on the white horse. "The cheer was taken up and taken up again on the left and in the distance it rolled on and on," Barber later wrote. "And so we started. Colonel Roosevelt of the Rough Riders started the whole movement on the left, which was the first advance of the assault."[10]

Roosevelt led the charge down into the San Juan River that was at the bottom of Kettle Hill, splashing into the waist-deep water with Little Texas, the water jumping all around him as the Spanish poured down a withering fire. Then began the climb up Kettle Hill. Men fell all around Roosevelt as they ran up the hill. A soldier, Arthur Cosby, would later write, "The top of the hill sputtered like a disturbed volcano and the hail of bullets spattered down on the troops moving upward." The men died, not like in Hollywood, but what a correspondent later described as "little heaps with instant flaccidity of muscles. There was no gradual droppings on one knee, no men who slowly fell while struggling to keep standing. There were no cries. The injured ones did not throw hands up and fall dramatically backward with strident cries and stiffened legs, as wounded heroes fall upon a stage. They fell like clods."[11]

Roosevelt waved his hat, sitting tall on Little Texas "urging the men on—Rough Riders, Buffalo Soldiers, and white Regulars from the First Cavalry."[12] He galloped toward the summit and heard the ringing of a bell and realized it was American bullets hitting large iron kettles. Roosevelt came to a wire fence as the Spanish soldiers were running from the red-tiled house and the trenches from the American onslaught. Teddy leaped out of his saddle and then over the fence and ran toward the house of fleeing soldiers. Two soldiers leaped out of the trench not ten yards away and fired at Roosevelt. The shots went wide and the Spaniards ran. TR raised his revolver, firing on the run. He missed one soldier but the second Spanish soldier crashed to the earth with his face in the dirt. He would later write Henry Cabot Lodge, "Did I tell you that I killed a Spaniard with my own hand?"[13] The Rough Riders and regular troops swarmed over the summit and Roosevelt, collecting his horse with the revolver still in his hand, found himself under fire. Shells and bullets began to land around the men on top of Kettle Hill. Teddy turned and saw some buildings on a long ridge with earthworks and buildings from which the heavy fire was emanating. He stared unknowingly in the smoke, blood, and dust at his high monument, San Juan Hill.

Harpooning

1917

THE PRESIDENT TOOK A LOT OF RIDES WITH EDITH AND PLAYED GOLF. He visited cabinet members. Edith went along. On March 30 he summoned his speech writer and stenographer and then went to the second-floor study with Edith. The president left orders he was not to be disturbed and while he clicked on the keys of his Hammond typewriter after an initial outline, a draft in longhand then shorthand then longhand. Then corrections. Very professorial. Edith meanwhile worked on deciphering top secret codes at a nearby desk. Wilson and Edith lunched then went for a one-hour ride in the park. Then they returned to the study for ten hours and finished after church on Sunday.

President Wilson then summoned Frank I. Cobb, editor of the *New York World*, who said later, "I had never seen him so worn down . . . he looked as if he hadn't slept." Wilson tapped the pages in front of him "and said that he had written a message and expected to go before Congress with it as it stood. He said he couldn't see any alternative that he had tried every way he knew to avoid war." Cobb said Wilson had paused. "I think I know what war means . . . is there anything else I can do?"[1] Cobb told him Germany had forced his hand.

The speech was then sent to the Public Printer and Wilson told Secretary Tumulty to let Congress know that he would appear as soon as the two houses could schedule it. Then he and Edith played golf for the rest of the morning. Monday morning, April 2, seven pacifists stopped in to see Senator Henry Cabot Lodge. They had come from Boston to see their senator and stop the war they knew was surely coming with Wilson's address. They intercepted Henry Cabot Lodge in the hallway of the Senate and demanded he stop the vote to go to war. Lodge looked at the men and told them, "National degeneracy and cowardice are worse than war.... I must do my duty as I see fit."[2] The leader, Princeton graduate and former minor league infielder Alexander W. Bannwart, shouted back at Lodge, "Anyone who wants to go to war is a coward ... you're a damned coward!"[3]

The sixty-seven-year-old Lodge, who was a small man with a Vandyke beard, shouted back, "You're a damned liar,"[4] and he punched thirty-six-year-old Bannwart. The pacifist punched Lodge and the two men fought like pugilists in the halls of Congress until a Western Union messenger, David Herman, threw himself on Bannwart, who was later hauled off to a precinct. Tensions were high to say the least, but President Woodrow Wilson and Edith had managed to play another round of golf in the morning before being driven to the House of Representatives at 8:10 p.m. flanked by two troops of US Cavalry with swords drawn. There was a light rain in Washington, but people lined the streets and cheered as the Wilson carriage passed. Then Wilson entered the Capitol building to make the world safe for democracy. He began in a quavering voice, pale, but gaining strength as he went on:

With a profound sense of the solemn and even tragical character of the step I am taking and of the grave responsibilities which it involves, but in an unhesitating obedience to what I deem my constitutional duty, I advise that the Congress declare the recent course of the Imperial German government to be in fact nothing less than war against the government and people of the United States; that it formally accept the status of belligerent which has thus been thrust upon it and that it take immediate steps only to put the country in a more through state of defense but also to exert all its power and resources to bring the Government of the German empire to terms and end the war.[5]

Wilson then wound up his speech after making a course for war against Germany with a firm declaration that "the world must be made safe for democracy."[6] He and Edith then rode back to the White House in silence with the rain pattering on the roof of their carriage. The world was ignited with the declaration of war, but the one man who had waited the longest, who had yelled from the rooftops, harangued, hurled insult after insult on Woodrow Wilson for not declaring war, was unaware that the president had finally granted him his wish. The country was going to war and now so could he, but he had no idea.

Teddy Roosevelt squinted against the Florida sun reflecting off the Gulf of Mexico. He held a heavy harpoon, ready to attack any shark or devilfish that passed the boat. TR had abandoned Sagamore Hill for a month-long vacation of fishing with a return day in early April when Wilson would address Congress. TR stood in the jumping boat perfectly balanced with his harpoon ready. He had practiced throwing the harpoon in Long Island and he felt invigorated by the violent water, the small boat, the harpoon he would use to impale anything that passed nearby. Roosevelt had gone hunting with a different sort of harpoon before he left New York.

After Germany sank the merchant steamships the *City of Memphis*, the *Vigilancia*, and the *Illinois* with the American flag flying on all three ships and causing the death of fifteen seamen, Roosevelt had not waited for Wilson to ask Congress to declare war on Germany. He put the harpoon right in the president's back:

> *Words are wasted on Germany. What we need is effective and thorough going action. Seven weeks have passed since Germany renewed . . . submarine war against neutrals and noncombatants . . . itself a declaration of war and should have been treated as such . . . she has killed American women and children as well as the American men upon the high seas. She has sunk our ships, our ports have been put under blockade. She has asked Mexico and Japan to join her in dismembering this country. If these are not overt acts of war then Lexington and Bunker Hill were not over acts of war.*[7]

Now Roosevelt stood next to Virginia tobacco planter and noted amateur marine hunter Russell J. Coles in the fishing boat, who ran the boat into a school of eight devilfish. Roosevelt buried his harpoon into the "tough hide, bone and sinew of the fish." Roosevelt and Coles were deluged with water from the fish. "Col. Roosevelt was absolutely cool headed throughout and he did every word I said," Coles wrote later. "He recognized the fact that I knew my work. Finally when I had the boat placed just right I told him to strike and instantly he sent the great spade lance crashing through its vitals and the fight was over."[8]

Coles and Roosevelt chased down another fish and again TR threw his harpoon and then had a long running fight with the wounded fish that towed the boat two miles, leaving a band of blood fifty feet wide. Then the fish turned and in a final death throe the sixteen-foot-wide devilfish rammed the boat, covering Roosevelt with blood and water. When the fish finally died, they towed it back and found it was the second largest ever recorded. They also found out that America was at war and Roosevelt hopped a train for Washington the next day. He had one man he wanted to see and that was the president. It had been a long time since Teddy Roosevelt had occupied the White House, but it seemed like just yesterday. He didn't like to think that if it were not for an assassin's bullet, he might never have been president at all.

CHAPTER NINEEEN

The Accidental President

1901

VICE PRESIDENT ROOSEVELT WAS ON A SPEAKING TOUR OF VERMONT
when he heard the news that President McKinley had been shot by an
anarchist named Leon Czolgozs. McKinley had been shaking hands
in the hot sunshine at the Pan American Exposition when Czolgozs
stepped up, swatted his hand away, and shot him twice, the first bullet
glancing off McKinley's coat but the second bullet burrowing into his
stomach. Roosevelt received the news with stunned amazement as his
first response, writing to Lodge that it was "literally incredible . . . you and
I have lived too long have seen human nature from too many sides to be
astounded at ordinary folly or ordinary wickedness, but it did not seem
possible that just at this time in just this country and in the case of this
particular president, any human being could be so infamous a scoundrel
so crazy a fool as to attempt to assassinate him."[1]

Roosevelt went on to say that McKinley hardly represented the pluto-
cracy; he was not a wealthy man and more a man of the people and he
saw it as a blow more against the essence of America. "It was the most
naked way an assault not on power not on wealth but simply and solely
upon free government, government by the people."[2]

Roosevelt jumped on a train that whisked him to the president's
bedside in Buffalo. The physicians and surgeons meanwhile stabilized
McKinley and looked for the bullet. They couldn't find it, hoping it had
burrowed into some muscle or bone where it might not fester and spread
gangrene through the president's body. His physicians opted not to use

the new technology on display at the exposition, X-rays, and sutured the walls of the stomach. McKinley got better and Roosevelt wrote a friend that "things are now progressing so favorably that I believe the President will be out of danger before you receive this letter" Another letter was even more encouraging, "Thank heaven the President is now out of danger."[3]

On September 10, Roosevelt left Buffalo to join Edith and the children on vacation in the Adirondacks. They stayed at an old mining camp converted into a two-story lodge at Tahawus, but foggy rain kept Roosevelt and his family in the lodge. Physical exercise was TR's greatest tonic for turmoil, and he set his goal and the family's as the ascent of Mount Marcy nearby at a mere 5,300 feet but still the highest in the surrounding area. On September 12, Edith and Teddy and his children set off for the summit.

Halfway up, they spent the night in some cabins along a lake but rain the next day discouraged Edith from taking her children any further and Teddy went on alone. They turned back with a guide while Theodore and some others from the lodge continued climbing. Just before noon the summit was reached with a breathtaking view above the clouds. The group was wet and cold and descended to find shelter and have lunch. Another small lake presented itself with a clearing where the group settled down to lunch when Teddy saw a man coming out of the woods. He did not have the air of a hiker and called to the group, looking for the vice president. "I felt at once that he had bad news," Roosevelt later recalled.[4]

The man handed him a telegram. "The president's condition has changed for the worse."[5]

The Rough Rider Returns

1917

ON APRIL 3, THE DAY AFTER WOODROW WILSON ASKED FOR A DECLA-ration of war, Teddy Roosevelt arrived in Washington. War had just been declared on Germany and he wanted in on the fight. In TR's view the bumbling buffoon in the White House, the spineless Woodrow Wilson, had finally gotten it right with a speech to the combined houses of Congress and had just told them America had to go to war to make the world *safe for democracy*. Roosevelt didn't give a fig about making the world safe for democracy; what he did give a fig about was getting into the fight.

Roosevelt had spent the train ride rehearsing different arguments to use on Wilson. After all, he was an experienced commander of the last major war the United States had been involved in with Spain and he had done very well, essentially winning that war with his charge up San Juan Hill on his big white charger with his handpicked Rough Riders following him up to the top and declaring victory while the Spanish soldiers scattered. Many of his men had died that day, but he had his "crowded hour" and while the nasty Mauser bullets perforated his uniform, cracked around him in the dust, Teddy had managed the day without a scratch. This sent him on a trajectory to the White House as McKinley's vice president and his eventual fate as the youngest assassinated president in the history of the United States at forty-two.

Now time had passed. True. He was fifty-eight. The war against Spain was twenty years ago. But he had the experience and besides, if he were killed by the Germans, well now, that would be in line with a heroe's death and would complete the arc of his life and cement his place in history. He probably would be killed as this was mechanized war with poison gas, tanks, .50 caliber machine guns, and miles of trench where the Germans could obliterate a bunch of old men on horseback charging toward them.

Still, you never knew. He had routed the Spaniards and the Germans might panic. And there was the Roosevelt magic that had allowed him to survive a war, an assassination attempt, a devastating carriage accident, fights with outlaws in the West, surviving falls into the Missouri River, confronting a grizzly bear, going down the Amazon and getting hopelessly lost only to survive a severely infected leg, emerging months later when the world had left him for dead. He had led a charmed life, so it might just hold together for him one last time. And if it didn't, well he "had warmed both hands before the fire"[1] and it was probably time anyway to go out in a blaze of glory.

These were his thoughts as the train rattled into Washington aflame with flags and already on a wartime footing. He had come up from Florida after harpooning one of the largest devilfish anyone could remember, and he now was the returning ex-president coming back in a flash of triumph. He and Henry Cabot Lodge had prevailed. Even the man Lodge had fought, Alexander Bannwart, had joined the fight and after Lodge declined to press charges had stated, "It is a joyous privilege to take part in such a war."[2]

The Princeton president, the egghead, had finally given in to the Rough Rider's demands that he be a man and declare war on Germany. Well, he had, and now Roosevelt was stepping off the train to a gaggle of reporters asking him if he were going to see Wilson:

The President's message is a great state paper which will rank in history among the great state papers of which Americans in future years will be proud. It now rests with the people of the country to see that we put in practice the policy that the President has outlined and that we strike as hard and as efficiently as possible in aggressive war against Germany. We must send troops to the firing line as rapidly as possible. Defensive war is hopeless. We must by vigorous offensive warfare win

the right to have our voice count for civilization and justice when the
time for peace comes.[3]

Butter would not melt in Teddy Roosevelt's mouth now. TR had been eviscerating Woodrow Wilson since 1912 and now believed that was all in the past and some honey liberally applied would catch more flies than vinegar. Whatever metaphor you choose, TR was amazing in his assumption all would be forgiven and that the man he had been smacking with a two-by-four across the back of the head would forget he had been called a coward, a wimp, an egghead, and that his policies had been shredded by the megahorn that was Teddy Roosevelt's mouth. Roosevelt believed that once the battle was over then all was forgotten and forgiven. It is amazing a man who had spent his life in politics should be so naïve as to think a man like Woodrow Wilson, who was known to brood and harbor grudges, would simply allow an ex-president to lead a brigade of Rough Riders and represent America. But that is what TR did believe, never appreciating the political animal that was cagily hidden behind the façade of an academician turned politician.

TR played it loose and said he might drop in on the president and then dropped the real bomb. "I of course very earnestly hope that I may be allowed to raise a division for immediate service at the front."[4] That is what he wanted in the papers. That was his clarion call to men all over the country: now was the time. It was the bugle call of the Rough Riders that it was time once again to mount up and make the world safe, if not for democracy then for Teddy Roosevelt. Were they not the same? And in a sense it didn't matter what Wilson said. He was going over with his men the way he went over with his men to Cuba. One way or another TR was going to go fight the Germans and if he should die, which he fully expected to, then no more of this creeping infirmness of old age. No; better to be cut down on the field of glory.

But first he would go to lunch with his daughter Alice and then drop in on his cohort in crime, Henry Cabot Lodge. Lodge had crowed from the rooftops after Wilson declared war that his will had been done and then afterward knocked a pacifist down for good measure. The truth was, Teddy was just passing through with a few hours between trains on his way east, and Lodge was away from his office. He decided then and there to go see President Wilson at the White House and broach his idea of a Rough Rider brigade led by none other than himself. It was a Rough Rider move to storm the White House after all this dancing around with this man Newton Baker, who was after just a secretary of war. No; the real man he needed to see was Woodrow Wilson, who could give him the nod to start assembling his division.

It would be in the fashion of the Rough Riders of twenty years before, an elite force that would precede the main American force that would take months if not a year to get across the ocean and built up to a point where they could make a difference in the war. Woodrow Wilson was talking about a million men; this would give Teddy and his men plenty of time to soften the Germans up and—who knows—maybe start a rout.

Alice drove her father to the White House in her big car and Roosevelt felt giddy with anticipation. Surely, Wilson would welcome him into the fight; it would be good PR for the White House to have another president crossing the ocean to fight the Boches. Alice's chauffeur drove up to the White House gates, where an armed guard stopped them. The White House had been closed to visitors since 1913, and the guard did not recognize at first the man seated in the back of Alice's car; then he leaned forward and felt something akin to a supernatural event. None other than Theodore Roosevelt was waiting patiently in the back seat. The gates swung wide, and Alice and Teddy were ushered into the White House. Roosevelt allowed himself a trip down memory lane when he had occupied the residence of Pennsylvania Avenue for seven and a half years. The old portico was there and as the doors to the glass vestibule opened, Ike Hoover walked out from the usher's office.

TR greeted Ike and asked to see Wilson. The usher shook his head and said Wilson had gone to the cabinet meeting. Roosevelt nodded slowly and felt the slow burn of the slight. He was not president anymore; in fact, he had been out of the political spotlight ever since the disastrous Bull Moose election of 1912 where he split the ticket with Taft and threw the election to Wilson. It had taken a long time for the Republicans to forgive him for that, and many still had not. Still, he was a man on a mission and when Ike Hoover asked if he might come back later, Roosevelt replied he was short on time and left his card. That turned the tables, he felt, on Wilson. Let him know that he, too, was a very busy man. Besides, his plan for his own division could wait. It would be his present to President Wilson and once he saw the value of his proposal, a division of twenty thousand men to soften up the Germans, he was sure it would be greeted with open arms.

Alice and TR returned to the train station, and she volunteered to ride with him as far as Baltimore. Alice was the daughter he had left behind after his young bride, Alice Lee, died and it was only after he returned West and married Edith Carow that he brought his daughter back from the care of his sister Bamie. Alice grew up and acted out and took her revenge on Roosevelt for his neglect by raising hell during his time in the White House, to the point that an exasperated TR told reporters, "I can either run the country or I can control Alice. I cannot possibly do both."[5] The early flapper, who drank, smoked, wore short dresses, and exulted in a smoldering sexuality made great copy for the newspapers and it was preordained she would marry a much older diplomat who would have numerous affairs.

By the time he reached the station, Teddy was bubbling over with excitement. The war fever had caught him, and he already saw himself leading a glorious regiment of hard-charging men with himself in the lead on a magnificent white charger. The reporters at the station asked him for a statement and he paused before getting on the train.

"I don't know just what I'm going to do when I reach New York," he said mysteriously, and then he let fall his real reason for being in Washington. "I can't say anything more about organizing a division to go to the firing line until I find out something more about the policy of this government. I am sorry not to have seen the President."[6]

TR then boarded the train, leaving Wilson that little grenade to digest over his morning coffee. He would now know why Roosevelt had dropped by the White House. He waved to the reporters and sat back in the train car. An article would appear the next day in the *Star Gazette* under "TEDDY'S CHANGE OF HEART." The Elmira paper would proclaim TR's "Americanism" and describe his call on the White House as "a big and generous thing for him to do." The paper would continue, saying, "He hadn't been there before since he walked out, and Taft walked in 1909 but he remembered about the Presidential 'busy hours' and so refused to disturb President Wilson. He left his card; it was enough."[7]

The *Star Gazette* echoed other papers in laying out the contentious history of the two men and then sounding the gong of nationalism:

> *Roosevelt had been most venomous in his attacks on President Wilson. He had been unreasonable in many of his criticisms. He has been intensely partisan in his attitude. But all that doesn't count now. The country faces a crisis. The President has sounded the call to arms. The Wilson address has been accepted by the world a veritable classic and Roosevelt forget his personal and political antagonisms and gives the President the praise that is due him . . . partisanship is dead. Party lines are wiped out . . . we are all Americans now . . . and our Commander in Chief is Woodrow Wilson.*[8]

TR did believe the past was now behind him, but he was not sure about Woodrow Wilson; the punching bag of his rhetorical boxing for the last five years would be so inclined. In fact, he fully believed the president was capable of snubbing him for past slights and insults. Roosevelt was still breathing hard from climbing aboard the train, and the pain in his left leg was excruciating, a souvenir from the sepsis that had plagued him ever since the streetcar accident when he was president.

The train pulled out into a light rain. TR concentrated on his breathing, getting oxygen down into his lungs. He closed his eyes, the color leaving his face. It was nothing new. He had had acute asthma ever since he was a little boy. He had entered this world knowing that just breathing was going to be a fight. Roosevelt stared out the Pullman window, remembering a boy who had stared out at the rain-slicked streets of New York fifty-one years before.

CHAPTER TWENTY-ONE

Night Rides

1869

TEDDY SHUT HIS EYES AND HEARD THE STACCATO CLACK OF THE STEEL horseshoes on the bricks of New York, his father whipping the horses to go faster past the flickering gaslights on the corner. They had to wait until most people had gone to bed to take these rides and it was exciting to be out in the streets of New York in the middle of the night. Teddy tried to get air. It just wasn't coming yet. He heard the whip snapping on the backs of the horses. He had never gone this fast in a carriage ever. The darkened windows, the smell of coal smoke, hanging on to the carriage rail. Then his father leaning out and yelling back to him, his beard pressed flat with the wind.

"Now Teddy . . . *Now! Now!*"

Theodore Roosevelt then leaned out over the side of the carriage and opened his mouth. People on the streets saw a madman in a carriage galloping full speed through the streets with a boy hanging off the side with his mouth wide open, gulping air like a fish. It was all to push air down into his mucous-coated lungs. Push the air down into the inflamed bronchi. No inhalers. No steroids. People with severe asthma in the year 1869 simple suffocated. Strangling for air, they died in their beds, in their chairs, walking down a street. There were no remedies except for cigars, strong coffee, marijuana, cocaine, smelling salts, castor oil, whiskey, the waters, the beach, anything was better than nothing and of course none of it worked. The asthmatic skinny little boy who couldn't breathe would soon be dead. That's what the doctors thought who examined him around the clock. He was the son of a rich man and that might buy him time, but he was not going to be long for this world.

And so Theodore senior did what he could. He took the boy to Europe. He took him to Hot Springs. He took him out in a boat in Oyster Bay. Catch the breeze. Catch the wind. Infant mortality was off the charts and sickly young people didn't have a chance at a time when the concept of germs was just getting started, people were treated for rheumatism with arsenic, bleeding was still looked upon as a therapy, and amputation was the go-to for infection. No; the boy hanging off the side of the carriage didn't have a chance, but he was the son of a rich man, and a rich man did not take no for an answer or accept there was nothing he could not do for his son.

So they headed out in the carriage for some nineteenth-century respiratory therapy, down the very streets Teddy Roosevelt had seen President Lincoln's funeral pass by just four years before, a moment preserved in a photograph historians would uncover fifty years later: Who is that urchin in the window? Great history had passed by the sickly boy who now was gulping for air like a fish washed up on a beach. Open your mouth to the rushing wind. Teddy inhaled a few bugs with the wind, but the night air was a tonic. At a time when indoor air was polluted with wood and coal smoke, the cool rushing night air did stimulate his airways and for a moment he could breathe—almost like a normal boy. He had been sickly his whole life. Crohn's disease. Unable to sleep. Unable to breathe. A waist that was smaller than a man's thigh. His mother Minnie wrote, "It came to a point where he had to sit up in the bed to breathe. After a strong cup of black coffee the spasmodic part of the attack ceased and he slept . . . had the coffee not taken effect he would have gone on struggling through the night."[1]

But the coffee had not worked this time. Nor the cigar his father had him smoke that sent him hacking so hard he threw up. Nor the whiskey he also threw up. Break the spasms. Stop the attack. So out into the night with the wild horses as the carriage slid around corners and everyone knew that was Mr. Roosevelt taking his sickly son out for a ride again so the poor boy could breathe. Ah me. He would not be long for this world even though Mr. Roosevelt would never accept that—the way he never accepted he would be anything but rich and lesser men could let their sons wither and die but not him. There was a reason he was known to Teddy as Braveheart. *Breathe Teddy! Breathe!*

And the specialists had marched into the mansion on the Upper East Side. Theories abounded. Henry Hyde Salter let go his theory that asthma was not a physical malady at all but a result of the anxiety of the patient brought on by the patient. In other words, it was the fault of the patient and they would have to get over it on their own. Salter pointed to events that kicked off asthma, such as fires or accidents. These proved his theory. It was all in their heads. Tell that to the boy hanging off the carriage in the wet, windy air of a Manhattan night and his father so desperate he had taken his son to Europe and back in search of a cure, a curative spring, a magical wind, anything that might keep his son from turning blue from lack of oxygen, which happened with the worst attacks. Waterboarding would be a modern analogy. Drowning in the mucous of your own lungs.

"The sensation of an acute asthmatic attack is that of being strangled or suffocated, only infinitely more complex. The whole body responds . . . the trouble is not just in the lungs. The central nervous system is involved, the endocrine system, both sides of the brain, possibly the brain stem as well. The agony is total . . . and the largest part of the agony is psychological—inexpressible terror, panic."[2]

So they stayed out into the wee hours. The large man holding the reins in one hand, a whip in the other. The black leather carriage clattering through the empty streets with the lathered horses galloping so hard one would have to be put down from a lame leg. What else could he do? *It was his son.* He had to do something. They were at their wits' end. They had tried everything. How about an enema, or a potion of garlic and mustard seeds, a shot of gin, another cigar, marijuana, smoke from nitrate paper, maybe a bit of opium. Crude chemotherapy to knock the child down and stop the asthma. Sometimes it worked; most of the time it did not. The boy's concept of life was a fight just to breathe. The most basic building block of life—air—he could not have without a fight. Salter then veered and added a corollary that Roosevelt senior grabbed hold of like a drowning man grabbing a life preserver. Salter said that not only was it the patient's fault but the patient had to do something about it himself. "Organs are made for action, not existence, they are made to work, not to be, and when they work well they can be well."[3]

Exercise was the way out. The patient must take control. Theodore senior had taken control of his life and made a fortune; his son must do the same. "Theodore you have the mind, but not the body, and without the help of the body, the mind cannot go as far as it should . . . you must make your body. It is hard drudgery to make one's body, but I know you will do it."[4] Teddy was given his charge for life. Take control. Build yourself up. No one can help you but yourself. At a time when people did not exercise and people who did were looked down upon as strange or middle class, the boy got a personal trainer, a term that would not really get traction until the late twentieth century—a Mr. John Wood, personal trainer to the rich with a pedigree of well-off Victorian clients, the Sloanes, the Goelets, the Vanderbilts.

Teddy's mother Mittie was off to the gymnasium with her son in tow. She sat in a chair while Teddy wrestled with free weights, boxed, swung on parallel bars under the tutelage of Mr. John Wood with his handlebar mustache and short-sleeved shirt. Boxing. Teddy had it out with a punching bag that punched back not a few times and left the skinny boy on the floor. Mr. John Wood would then take him back to the parallel bars, where he would hoist himself up, not able to hold his own weight without assistance while his mother read poetry in an upholstered armchair on the far side of the gym. Underweight, undersized, a skinny weakling, Teddy huffed and puffed and hacked his way through the exercises with many devolving into full-blown asthma attacks.

His sisters watched their younger brother shadow box in the parlor. They watched him jump rope in the foyer. They felt sorry for him. Then he was beat up by two bullies in Maine and when he tried to fight back with his newfound boxing, they put him in his place and knocked him down. Teddy would later reflect how shocked he was they could "handle me so as to not hurt me too much and yet . . . prevent my doing any damage whatever in return."[5]

So the workouts continued under Mr. James Wood and the night rides continued with his father. Teddy kept his mouth open, breathing in the wet night air. In between, he read of great adventures. The boy was a reader. It was all he had really. David Livingstone's *Missionary Travels and Researchers in South Africa* and *Robinson Crusoe* or the books of the Wild West, *The Scalp Hunters, The Hunters' Feast, The Boy Hunters* . . . all took place in the mythical expanse of the unexplored western United States. The great adventures began here with the sickly boy in the overblown Victorian parlor, struggling to take what others took for granted, basic good health, left alone to build his body and his mind, he was that boy hanging off the carriage in the rain-slicked streets of Manhattan. His father admonishing him . . . Breathe! Breathe! *Breathe!*

Theodore Roosevelt sucked in air and woke in the train heading for New York with a start. The rain was streaming down the dark windows, the country lights of distant farms stars of yellow light. Alice was staring at him. TR shook his head as she asked him if he wanted some water. Roosevelt watched the rural countryside outside Washington. His breathing was normal now. The tightness in his chest had subsided. Sleeping was usually a good tonic to the asthma. It would be good to get back to Sagamore Hill and Edith. Yes. There he could plot his next move to get the Rough Riders into the fight, and more than that, convince that dullard Woodrow Wilson he was just the man to lead them.

CHAPTER TWENTY-TWO

The Roosevelt Division

1917

THE MAN WHO HELD TEDDY ROOSEVELT'S FUTURE IN THE PALM OF HIS hand rode back in silence from his congressional address with Edith beside him. Afterward he sat in the cabinet room with Chief of Staff Joe Tumulty. "Think of what they are applauding . . . my message today was a message of death for our young men. How strange it seems to applaud that."[1] Wilson then looked at Tumulty and made a confession that would have floored Teddy Roosevelt: "From the beginning I saw the utter futility of neutrality, the disappointment and heartaches that would flow from its announcement," he confessed. "But we stand by our traditional policy of steering clear of European embroilments."[2] Wilson then read an editorial to Tumulty that empathized with his plight; he paused, mopped his eyes, then laid his head on the cabinet table and sobbed "as if he had been a child."[3]

On April 6, the House and Senate voted on the War Resolution; on the seventh Wilson was informed a printed copy of the resolution was on the way to the White House already signed by Vice President Marshall and Speaker Clark. President Wilson was just finishing his lunch when the resolution arrived. He exited the State Dining Room and went to Ike Hoover's office, where the staff talked about moving to the president's study when he said he would sign it at the usher's desk. Wilson sat down and looked up.

"Stand by me, Edith,"[4] he said as she handed him a gold pen he had given her. His jaw clenched as he affixed his bold signature to the parchment. He rose from his chair, returned the pen to Edith, and excused himself. The executive clerk, Rudolf Foster, let waiting reporters know that Wilson had signed the resolution that marked only the fourth time the United States had declared war on a foreign nation. Wireless operators shot the news around the world. The United States went on an instant war footing with "heatless Mondays" and "gasless Mondays," where Edith and Woodrow would substitute a carriage for their limousine, and the introduction of daylight saving time, which created an extra hour of farm work and saved an hour of electric illumination, saving coal power as well. Edith would do her part by raising eight sheep on the White House lawn and auctioning off the sheared wool for $100,000 for the Red Cross. The world had changed overnight; this change reached all the way to Sagamore Hill, where Edith Roosevelt was worried about a phone call from Quentin. He was leaving Harvard and joining the army as a fighter pilot even though he suffered from a bad back and poor eyesight.

TR was overjoyed at Quentin's decision but neither the ex-president, Edith, Flora, nor Quentin understood what he was undertaking. In World War I, pilots had a greater chance of dying in an accident during training than in a dogfight. Planes were crude and were being rushed into service. They were basically an engine, wire, and cloth—rickety and barely airworthy. Pilots were rushed through training on the unreliable planes and then sent into battle. Frederick Barr Shaw was a cadet in Britain's Royal Air Force who recorded in his diary his training experiences. He had one month of classes on "flight theory, meteorology, wireless telegraphy and engine mechanics."[5] He was then sent to Vendome, a small French town, for flight training. Right away he had his christening.

"A horrible thing happened today. We were all out on the tarmac, having our pictures taken for posterity when somebody yelled and pointed up. Two Avros collided right over the airdrome at about three hundred feet. God, it was a horrible sight. We didn't know who was in either one of them . . . they came down in a slow spin with their wings locked together and both of them in flames. Fred Stillman was in one machine and got out alive but badly burned and Doug Ellis was in the other one and was burned to a cinder."[6]

Pilots literally had to fly by the seat of their pants, a phrase founded in the fact that many times, especially in clouds, early aviators could only tell if they were ascending or descending by feeling if they were floating in their seat when going down or pressed down by going up. There were few instruments, if any, except for a compass for navigation and eyesight was regarded as keenly important to see from dead reckoning if a plane was on course.

But no matter, Sagamore Hill was alive with the excitement of a military recruiting station. All four Roosevelt boys were headed for the war. Ted and Archie aimed for appointment as officers with Quentin already determined to make it as a pilot, declaring he would go north to the Canadians if the Americans disqualified him. Kermit, who had accompanied Roosevelt down the Amazon and suffered from the same recurring malaria, was a bit more difficult to place. Roosevelt believed Kermit's wanderlust and his eccentricities might be best served in the foreign service; perhaps the British could use him in Mesopotamia.

President Wilson may have been sobbing on the cabinet room table at the prospect of thousands of young men facing death in the trenches of France, but Theodore Roosevelt could not have been happier. War had finally come. The crowded hour would return. What he had been preaching for three years had come to pass and he had been vindicated. He had switched from an antagonistic dog nipping if not biting at the president every chance to full blown proselytizing cheerleader recruiter. In a speech on April 9 in Manhattan, he blared, "The soldier who breaks regulation yet is found on the firing line in the hour of battle is better than the God-forsaken mutt who won't enlist and does all he can to keep others from enlisting. In these days all are patriots or traitors to your country and the cause of Jesus Christ."[7]

The press had picked up on Roosevelt's visit to Washington to get the nod of the administration to raise a division. On April 5, an article picked up by the *Des Moines Register* appeared: "ROOSEVELT'S MEN READY FOR CALL. Entire Division of Trained Soldiers Can be Mobilized on Short Notice. . . . NO TRAINING NECESSARY. . . . Prepared for duty in France or Elsewhere the Moment Word is Given." The newspaper then went on: "The Roosevelt division for foreign service is organized and ready for war. This was stated here today by Colonel Sloan Simpson close friend of Roosevelt and colonel commanding the Texas Oklahoma regiment.... 'My regiment is composed of Spanish war veterans and Texas cowboys,' said Colonel Simpson. 'Every man in it can use a rifle and pistol and ride. They need very little drill. We are ready to mobilize within ten hours after receiving the call.'... Colonel Simpson said that he inferred that the Roosevelt division would be accepted within a week by the President and would be sent at once to Europe probably to fight side by side with Belgian troops."[8]

Colonel Simpson then cited a letter that Roosevelt had sent around to various commanders, recruiting soldiers for his division:

> *If I go into this division I mean business. I expect no mercy myself and I shan't show any mercy. If I don't produce results I expect the department to scrap me and if my own men don't produce results I shall scrap them. Make everybody to whom you speak know that accepting a commission under me will be no holiday and if the man isn't going to give the best possible service he had a great deal better not come with me at all. I shall as you know is my habit, recognize good work and I shall not pardon bad work.*[9]

Sloan was then quoted as saying that members of the old Rough Riders are "overjoyed at the chance of getting with Teddy again."[10] Sloan then speculated the difficulty of getting sufficient horses but was confident this could be overcome. One has to wonder if Sloan or Roosevelt had read the papers at all; tanks were now being used to advance on the Western Front and the prospect of cowboys charging on horses into the teeth of flamethrowers, .50 caliber machine guns, and gas would be almost comical were it not so tragic. But Roosevelt wanted a one-way charge against the Germans and that matched the way he had lived his life. Roosevelt had proclaimed at the Union League Club in New York that he hoped to fight and die in France. Afterward, Elihu Root asked him if he really meant that.

"Yes," Roosevelt answered.

"Theodore, if you can convince Wilson of that I am sure he will give you a commission," Root quipped.[11]

Even as far back as 1912, TR had made it known his preferred death was to die in battle and Jack Greenway, a former Rough Rider working with Roosevelt on the campaign trail, said, "Colonel, I've long wanted to ask you something."

"Go right ahead," answered TR. "What is it?"

"Well colonel, I've always believed that it was your ambition to die on the field of battle."

Roosevelt slammed his fist upon a nearby table.

"By Jove, how did you know that?"

"Well colonel . . . do you remember that day in Cuba when you and I came upon that soldier propped up against a tree, shot through the abdomen? It was evident that he was done for. But instead of commiserating him, you grabbed his hand and said something like, 'Well, old man, isn't this splendid!' Ever since then I've been sure you would be glad to die in battle yourself."

TR grew solemn.

"You're right, Jack," he answered. "I would."[12]

But before the Roosevelt division could be launched and Roosevelt could have his glorious death in battle, he had to return to the White House and sit down with Woodrow Wilson.

CHAPTER TWENTY-THREE

The Brooding Professor

1917

PRESIDENT WILSON HAD REALLY THE SAME PROBLEM AS TEDDY ROOSevelt, except on a much bigger scale. How do you get a million men trained and over to Europe to turn the tide of battle against the Germans? A volunteer army would not do. Only thirty thousand would sign up voluntarily by the end of the month. The very heart of the Roosevelt plan was built on men willing to go and fight of their own volition, but for war on an industrial scale Wilson knew the only way was through a draft, a conscription bill. The days of the volunteer army were long gone, but here was a fifty-eight-year-old ex-president barnstorming the White House again. One can only see Wilson rolling his eyes when he was informed on April 7 that Theodore Roosevelt was on the way to see him.

It was three days after President Wilson signed the declaration of war that Roosevelt had taken it upon himself to assault the White House again. There was just too much electricity in the air, too much to be done to let the biggest moment of his life hang fire. No. It was time to put into action what he had been thinking about, planning, dreaming: the formation of a second division of Rough Riders. And now he had his war and now he would leave just as he had before left for Cuba. Yes, it would be tough to leave Sagamore Hill and Edith and all he had known, but he was not a well man anymore. He was suffering from malaria, yellow fever pathogens, strange heart palpitations, severe rheumatism, a lingering infection in his ankle, high blood pressure, gout, he was blind in one eye from a boxing match, his left shoulder hurt where he broke it out

West, he suffered from a hacking pleurisy from the assassination attempt that left John Shrank's bullet in his chest, he was severely overweight, he could not stop gorging on five-course meals—and he was a year and half from sixty, which he had always declared would be his end date to stop working.

It was time to go and that meant it was time to confront the man himself head-on and settle the question of taking a division of Rough Riders to France to fight the Germans. TR had written an article over Easter weekend for *Metropolitan Magazine*, and while not apologizing to Wilson for years of intemperate speech, he did throw him a bone. "Of course when war is on, all minor considerations, including all partisan considerations, vanish at once."[1] Maybe that was so for Roosevelt, but for the brooding moody professor, Woodrow Wilson, it was another matter.

TR picked up his daughter Alice and stopped off at Henry Cabot Lodge's home, where he beat his chest and proclaimed that even though he was not calling ahead to the White House, he dared Wilson to not see him. "I'll take chances on his trying to snub me. He can't do it. I'd like to see him try!"[2] Somehow Joseph Tumulty heard Teddy was on the way and when Alice dropped him off at the White House the next morning at 11:00 a.m., Secretary Tumulty was waiting. TR followed him into the Green Room, and he must have realized everything depended on this moment. Roosevelt had for months communicated with men all over the country, sending out the letter that stated plainly this would be a danger-ous feat they were undertaking and many would not come back. Many troops of men had already organized and were waiting for the word from their commander, who was now meeting his commander in chief.

President Wilson greeted TR coldly, and one could hardly blame him. He had been bruised and battered by the Rough Rider ever since their lemonade meeting and now all was expected to be forgiven? Not a chance. The two men were temperamentally opposites. One might be considered a braggart—an extrovert who bullied his way through life. The other was a reticent, retiring man with a steely protective shell that few besides his wife penetrated. An aide, Thomas Brahany, later wrote of the meeting: "The President doesn't like Theodore Roosevelt and he was not one bit effusive in his greeting."[3] The conversation, by all reports, was stiff and one sided in the beginning. TR complimented Wilson on his address and his bill for the selective service and then talked about the division he would like to lead. Woodrow Wilson didn't let down the gates and spoke defensively about his policy of neutrality for the last three years, feeling the arrows once again that the archer in front of him had slung. Teddy, never liking anything better than smoking someone out and risking all on a single roll, sat forward and opened his arms as he thew down the gauntlet.

> *Mr. President . . . what I have said and thought and what others have said and thought is all dust in a windy street, if now we can make your message good. Of course it amounts to nothing if we cannot make it good. But if we can translate it into fact then it will rank as a great state paper, with the great state papers of Washington and Lincoln. Now all that I ask is I be allowed to . . . help get the nation to act so as to justify and live up to the speech and the declaration of war that followed.*[4]

Woodrow Wilson, who was no stranger to flattery, began to thaw. Roosevelt really was incorrigible and there was something warm and charming about the man he found very hard to resist. Thomas Brahany was amazed to hear Wilson laughing as the two men found common ground. "The interview lasted twenty-five minutes and before it closed the President had thawed out and was laughing and talking back."[5]

During that twenty-five minutes, Roosevelt brought up his division and stressed the need for America to get into the war right away. "I told him we should hit at once and hard," he later recounted. "The next several months would be crucial."[6] American soldiers must get into the field as soon as possible. This was where the volunteers would come in. Roosevelt explained how he had already done much research and planning. The Allies had plenty of weapons; what they needed was men. A division of highly motivated volunteers training with English and French rifles could be ready for combat months before a larger expeditionary force of regular recruits. Nor would the volunteers steal resources from the regular army. "I explained that all the necessary expense could be provided out of private funds. I also explained to him that I would not take a man the draft might get."[7]

Wilson asked questions and Roosevelt the boxer felt he had him on the ropes. "The fact that I proposed to use material that otherwise would be unavailable seemed new to him. He seemed interested and he asked many questions."[8] Before he left, Roosevelt asked Wilson if he might see Secretary Tumulty again in the executive office, where there were handshakes and backslaps and TR greeted some of the old household staff. "You get me across and I will put you on my staff and you may tell Mrs. Tumulty that I will not allow them to place you at any point of danger,"[9] TR said jokingly to Wilson's chief of staff.

When he finally left, Wilson and Joe Tumulty stood watching him walk out the front door to a crowd of reporters. Woodrow asked his chief of staff what he thought of Roosevelt. Tumulty replied that he had overwhelming personality. "I was, as formerly, charmed by his personality."[10] Teddy for his part held court with the reporters outside the White House, noticing the suffragettes down by the White House gates. "The President received me with upmost courtesy and consideration."[11] Then Roosevelt dictated a terse statement he later released to the press, stating he has asked authority to "raise a division of volunteer soldiers many of them already trained and available . . . such a division to be sent as part of any expeditionary force sent to France at an early moment." He then said the president had neither accepted nor rejected his request and would come to a decision "in his own good time." He then said his division would not interfere with the draft or regular conscription by the war department. "I have been in communication with Secretary Baker but do not intend to call on him."[12]

He didn't have to. Roosevelt held court that evening in Representative Longworth's townhouse and Baker attended. When he arrived he found the townhouse full of "British, French, and Japanese ambassadors and a long list of legislators and policymakers, including the chairmen of the House and Senate military commanders and officers of the National Defense Council, . . . being briefed on the Roosevelt Division." Roosevelt took Baker upstairs, where he declared, "I am aware that I have not had enough experience to lead a division myself . . . but I have selected the most experienced regular officers from the regular army for my staff."[13] Secretary of War Baker replied he was taking the proposal "under advisement. . . . The Colonel must appreciate that mobilization was a hugely complex process that could not be swayed by personal considerations."[14]

By the time Roosevelt returned to New York, the best he could say was he had good talk with Wilson and Baker but beyond that little had changed. The press got hold of the Roosevelt visit and sang the praises of TR throwing in with Wilson and how the administration was looking to him for advice. "The appearance of Secretary Baker there was alone enough to show that the wholehearted support offered to the democratic president by the republican ex-president was accepted in the same full way in which it was offered. The sight of the ex-president losing not a moment after his visit to the president in taking his coat off to work for the president's policy is a thing to fill the hearts of Americans with pride."[15]

Editorials appeared urging Wilson to approve the Rough Rider division. "Nothing the United States could do quickly would be more effective than to accept this offer of Colonel Roosevelt's. Give him every facility to raise his little army and expedite their journey to the trenches of Belgium and France . . . the announcement that Roosevelt and his Rough Riders were getting ready to go to Europe to settle the war would strike more terror into the hearts of the Germans and their allies than any other announcement."[16]

Letters to the editor flooded in from Americans all over the country urging Wilson to give Roosevelt his commission. Although the war had been reported on, most Americans' concept of war had not changed since the Spanish-American War. Even though trench warfare seemed very different, the average American still believed a man on horseback could make a difference, especially out West. An article from *The Washington Post* but picked up by papers all over the West proclaimed, "WESTERN ROUGH RIDERS READY MEN OF THE CATTLE COUNTRY WAITING FOR THE CALL." A sheep and cattle rancher of Wyoming, William C. Irvine, was quoted:

The most popular action the federal authorities could take in our Western country would be to authorize some man of force and energy with military training and experience to raise a cavalry division to be made up of men who served in the Rough Rider regiments of the Spanish-American War . . . a cavalry division of Western men would require but brief training to make them effective. They are hardy, vigorous and courageous, skilled in the use of firearms, expert horsemen and fearless riders . . . if Colonel Roosevelt were given the authority to organize such a division of Rough Rider cavalry it could be raised . . . almost overnight.[17]

These articles believing in Roosevelt's ability to make a difference were a tonic to the old Rough Rider, but other papers took a more realistic view and clouded the sunshine that TR supporters saw. An article on April 13 pointed out that "President Wilson is against the proposition. He does not like Roosevelt, and he does not like what he thinks would be the effect of such an expedition . . . those who oppose his going say frankly that the effect of such an expedition might be to make Roosevelt a 'war hero.' The administration is not aiding the manufacture of war heroes out of other than democratic material."[18]

Still, the same paper pointed out that some in the administration did support sending Roosevelt for the exact opposite reason of stirring up support for the war. They believed that sending Roosevelt would "arouse enthusiasm for the war and stimulate enlistments."[19] The article got one thing right, that "it may be safely predicted that Roosevelt will not submit quietly to a Presidential refusal."[20] But TR was once again forced to wait to hear—something that Teddy Roosevelt did not do well, but then again, waiting to hear had made him president in 1901.

CHAPTER TWENTY-FOUR

The Odd New President

1901

THAT TEDDY ROOSEVELT WAS IN THE MIDDLE OF NOWHERE WHEN HE
became president of the United States is fitting. He now sat in an old
buckboard wagon and hung on while the wagon rolled down the dirt
road of the Adirondacks. He had just become president, although he
didn't know it yet. He was four hundred miles away from where President
McKinley lay dying in Buffalo, New York, from an assassin's bullet. The
telegrams had been relayed by phone, telegraph, riders, and boys who
had run up to his camp breathing hard with the news that the president
was dying from gangrene from the bullet's infectious journey into his
abdomen.

"THE PRESIDENT IS CRITICALLY ILL. . . . HIS CONDI-
TION IS GRAVE. . . . OXYGEN IS BEING GIVEN. . . . ABSO-
LUTELY NO HOPE."

Then a final telegram reached TR's cabin in Upper Tahawus.

"THE PRESIDENT APPEARS TO BE DYING AND MEM-
BERS OF THE CABINET IN BUFFALO THINK YOU SHOULD
LOSE NO TIME IN COMING"[1]

Roosevelt didn't lose any time and left at midnight; after kissing
Edith and his children goodbye he began the seven-hour journey down
to North Creek station. The buckboard bounced down the road for three
hours and now he was halfway there, with a borrowed raincoat and a
slouch hat pulled low against the rain that fogged and blurred his glasses.
But there was nothing to see anyway beyond the circle of lamplight. His

mind raced. Leon Czolgozs had changed the nation by firing a bullet into President McKinley's abdomen and made Theodore Roosevelt the youngest president ever at forty-two.

"If it had been I who had been shot, he wouldn't have got away so easily. . . . I'd have guzzled him first,"[2] he shouted into the night. Three hours later they reached Aiden Lair Lodge where Mike Cronin held the reins of another rig. "Any news?" Roosevelt asked, jumping down from the buckboard.

"Not a word," Cronin replied. "Jump in right away, and we'll be off."[3]

He tried to hold a lantern, but Roosevelt took it and joined him on the seat. "Here, give it to me." The two black Morgan horses knew every bit of the sixteen mile road in the darkness, but the rain continued and more than once they slipped with Cronin pulling back on the reins. "Oh that doesn't matter, "Roosevelt exclaimed. "Push ahead!"[4]

Log bridges drummed loudly as the wagon sped along. The horses stumbled again. If they slipped off the road, they would tumble into the bogs below. Teddy looked at his watch by the lantern and shouted, "Hurry up! Go faster!" The horses skidded around a curve and Cronin looked at the man who would become president before the end of the day. "If you're not afraid I am not," was all Roosevelt said.[5]

The speeding rig plunging through the night was very different from his life as vice president. It had been a political stasis for him where men were put into the vice presidency to be sidelined, or worse, put into political oblivion. Roosevelt had his fair share of enemies and they had relished the gag enforced by the office of second in command. VPs just didn't do very much and what they did didn't matter at all. But now they were passing a cemetery with the glow of dawn on the horizon; they stopped two miles outside of North Creek to let the horses rest and Roosevelt was able to compose himself. Then came a final gallop into the darkened town past houses and stoops with people shouting as they passed.

The special train stood waiting along with Roosevelt's secretary, William Loeb Jr. He handed TR a telegram: "THE PRESIDENT DIED AT TWO-FIFTEEN THIS MORNING."[6] Roosevelt took the telegram and jumped into his private car; the fastest locomotive of the Delaware and Hudson Railroad began its puffing journey, getting up to speed quickly, whisking the president-in-waiting along at sixty miles an hour. News flashed around the world of President McKinley's death while Roosevelt cruised toward Buffalo. An old newspaper editor in South Dakota recalled Teddy's lack of surprise when he told him that one day he would be president. Henry Adams, in arctic Norway, read the wires and nodded. "So Teddy is President! Is that not stupendous! Before such a career as that, I have no observations to make!"[7]

The train reached the Exchange Street Station in Buffalo at 1:30 p.m. and then proceeded to the Terrace Station, where a carriage and twelve mounted policemen waited. Roosevelt jumped down from his car before the train even stopped, with his eyes dark from fatigue. A crowd of onlookers shouted "*Hurrah for Teddy*," but he ignored them, climbing into the carriage when a policeman reached after him. "Colonel, will you shake hands with me?"[8] Roosevelt turned and then embraced the man quickly and then he was away, leaving the Rough Rider staring after his old commander, tears welling up uncontrolled.

By the time he reached Buffalo, President McKinley was dead. Teddy Roosevelt was now president at age forty-two. The youngest president ever. He immediately summed up his youth and compared it to the country. "Is America a weakling to shrink from the world work of the great world-powers? No. The young giant of the West stands on a continent and clasps the crest of an ocean in either hand. Our nation, glorious in youth and strength, looks in the future with eager eyes and rejoices as a strong man to run a race."[9]

Theodore Roosevelt would never be assassinated. He was too strong. The winter before, he had jumped off a horse and kicked a pack of hounds aside to knife a cougar to death. His 185 pounds, superb reflexes, and uncanny luck would keep him safe. Besides, if he died, he died and he would "go down into the darkness,"[10] which was his image of death and not some heaven ringed by angels. So there was work to be done.

Twenty years later he would return to the White House in 1917 to see President Wilson as a political outsider, but even when he was president he was an outsider. When he took office in the White House in 1902, the capital city never quite knew how to take him. Some said he lacked decorum. Some said he was crazy. There were reasons for this. On a day in late May he was seen hanging from a cable over the Potomac. He later said he wanted to improve the strength in his wrists. Owen Wister saw him tiptoeing behind John Jay like a panther. White House guards often saw him standing under trees for long periods of time not moving, not understanding he was a published orchidologist. People strolling through Rock Creek Park learned to get behind trees or rocks when the president galloped past with a pistol in his hand, taking potshots at stumps. People never were quite sure they had his attention as he read often while carrying on a conversation in the Oval Office. Or when he demanded his entire cabinet go for a swim with him in the Potomac in the nude. In winter.

Then the odd new president decided the White House and the presidency should be more regal and put on order three black glossy carriages, five horses, and new patriotic livery "consisting of blue coat, white doeskin trousers, high boots, and top hat with tricolor cockade."[11] Gone was the gothic script of the White House stationery, replaced by the block letters THE WHITE HOUSE in sans serif. There was a new sheriff in town, but nothing prepared the Washington establishment for what came next.

On October 16, 1902, Theodore Roosevelt heard the great African American educator Booker T. Washington was in town and invited him to dinner at the White House. Roosevelt felt guilty about a momentary hesitancy about being the first president to have a Black man dine in the White House,[12] then was more determined than ever to break precedence. Booker T. Washington, who had come to national prominence since the 1895 Cotton States Exhibition in Atlanta, had invited Roosevelt to the university he founded, the Tuskegee Institute, in 1901 but McKinley's assassination had caused the plans to be canceled.

Theodore Roosevelt now felt it was "natural and so proper" to have Washington to dinner. His own views had evolved concerning race. "Here, dark and dignified among the paler company, was living proof of what he had always preached: that Negroes could rise to the social heights, at least on an individual basis . . . a black man who advanced faster than his fellows should be rewarded with every privilege that democracy could bestow."[13]

So on October 16, 1901, at 7:30, a well-dressed Black man was shown into the White House accompanied by Roosevelt, who introduced him to Edith. The other guest was family friend Philip B. Stewart. A disapproving Black butler served Washington while TR and the renowned educator discussed the South, race, politics, and the state of the country. Roosevelt, who had seconded the nomination of the first Black chairman for the 1884 Republican convention, saw "that Washington's race was merely adolescent, as his own had been in the seventeenth century. Negro advancement must 'necessarily be painful'... but equality would come."[14]

The night ended and an AP reporter stopped by at 2:00 a.m. to inquire about the guest list for the day. A one-sentence line lit up the telegraph lines overnight: "Booker T. Washington of Tuskegee, Alabama, dined with the President last evening."[15] By morning the firestorm had begun. The Black newspapers congratulated Roosevelt and telegrams poured in. "Greatest step for the race in a generation,"[16] a Black man telegraphed from Memphis. The liberal papers of the North were supportive of the dinner, but all hell broke loose in the South. The *Memphis Scimitar* led the way:

> *The most damnable outrage which has ever been perpetrated by any citizen of the United States was committed yesterday by the President when he invited a nigger to dine with him at the White House ... it is only very recently that President Roosevelt boasted that his mother was a Southern woman ... by inviting a nigger to his table he pays his mother small duty. .... No Southern woman with a proper respect would now accept an invitation to the White House nor would President Roosevelt be welcomed in Southern homes.*[17]

Other papers followed suit with bold headlines.
"ROOSEVELT DINES A DARKEY"
"A BANK NEGROPHILIST"
"OUR COON-FLAVORED PRESIDENT"
"ROOSEVELT PROPOSES TO CODDLE THE SONS OF HAM"[18]

Hate mail and death threats poured into the White House when it was also discovered Roosevelt had Black people dine at the governor's mansion in Albany and at Sagamore Hill. Senator Tillman of South Carolina endorsed revenge: "The action of President Roosevelt in entertaining that nigger will necessitate our killing a thousand niggers in the South before they will learn their place again."[19] The *Richmond News* declared Roosevelt had "destroyed the kindly warm regard and personal affection for him which were growing up fast in the South."[20]

TR was accused of nothing less than promoting a "mingling and mongrelization" of the Anglo-Saxon race.[21] Roosevelt was stunned at the reaction in the South and by mutual agreement he and Washington agreed not to discuss their dinner with reporters. But in private letters he let his feelings be known. In a letter to Lucius B. Littauer he stated that he

> *had no thought whatever of anything save of having a chance of showing some little respect to a man whom I cordially esteem as a good citizen and good American. The outburst of feeling in the South about it is to me literally inexplicable . . . as far as I am personally concerned I regard their attacks with the most contemptuous indifference . . . there are certain points where I would not swerve from my views if the entire people was a unit against me and this is one of them. I would not lose my self-respect by fearing to have a man like Booker T. Washington to dinner if it cost me every political friend I have got.[22]*

When Roosevelt was scheduled to march in academic procession with Booker T. Washington in attendance, the South went wild again. The Secret Service swarmed around the president on October 23 as he traveled through Connecticut and the two men were kept far apart in the march to the Hyperion Theatre. Awards were given to honorees Mark Twain, Woodrow Wilson, John Hay, and Elihu Root. Yale president Arthur Haley then paused. "One name yet remains."[23] The house came down and the cheering went on for ten minutes for President Roosevelt. Twain would later show his own shallow view of the president's action by saying Roosevelt should "refrain from offending the nation merely to advertise himself and make a noise."[24]

So says the man who was never seen in public without being carefully attired in a white suit. As late as November, Roosevelt was still brooding over the problems of race in America and could only conclude that the only "Christian thing to do is treat each black man and each white strictly on his merits as a man . . . of course I know that we see through a glass dimly, and after all, it may be that I am wrong, but if I am then all my thoughts and beliefs are wrong and my whole way of looking at life is wrong."[25] In this instance, Theodore Roosevelt was not wrong.

Booker T. Washington wrote a letter to Roosevelt while the storm raged around him:

> *My dear Mr. President, I have refrained writing you regarding the now famous dinner which both of us ate so innocently until I could get to the South and study the situation at first hand. Since coming here and getting into real contact with the white people I am convinced of three things: In the first place, I believe that a great deal is being made of the incident because of the elections which are now pending in several of the Southern states and in the second place I do not believe the matter is felt as seriously as the newspapers try to make it appear; and in the third place I am more than ever convinced that the wise course is to pursue the exact policy which you mapped out in the beginning; not many moons will pass before you will find the South in the same attitude that it was a few years ago.*[26]

Roosevelt read the letter and later told friends that he had only wanted to show "some little respect" for an esteemed fellow American. Regarding Booker T. Washington, the Rough Rider charged right ahead, declaring, "I shall have him to dine just as often as I please."[27]

CHAPTER TWENTY-FIVE

Want to Go with Teddy

1917

ALL OVER THE COUNTRY FORMER ROUGH RIDERS WERE GOING UP INTO attics, opening old trunks, and taking out swords and dusty uniforms. Brimmed hats hardened from sweat, dust, and time were now being fitted on heads mostly smooth, while blue polka dot neckerchiefs were tied around necks now lined. The Rough Riders of 1898 were older men now—forties, fifties, sixties—but it didn't matter. Boots were being tried out and pistols taken down from hooks for target practice. Some had not mounted a horse in years, but they could get back in riding form once the call came. And the call was coming soon.

The press couldn't get enough of the idea of TR's resurrected Rough Riders heading over to France to take on the Germans. Local papers were alive with regiments forming up and waiting for Teddy's call. "OKLAHOMANS WANT TO GO WITH TEDDY," blared the *Daily Oklahoman*:

> *Col. Theodore Roosevelt will be swamped with fighting Sooners if he is authorized to form an army division to go to France. An offer of a regiment of Oklahomans has already been made to Roosevelt by Orval Johnson of Oklahoma City . . . action by President Wilson on Roosevelt's offer is being watched with keen interest by Spanish-American War veterans here. The Colonels well known liking for mounted troops makes it probable that his division would be one of cavalry should it be organized and horseman from all over the state are anxious to serve with Teddy.*[1]

If the federal government did not want to give TR the nod, then the state government would. Governor Whitman in Albany, New York, gave out a statement to the press saying he would be "glad to give a commission to Colonel Roosevelt to command New York State troops. . . . I have not asked Colonel Roosevelt to accept a military commission . . . nor has he made such a request. I am ready however to give him any military commission within my power which his own judgment would permit him to accept. I think that no other living America would attract by his leadership so many men to the colors." Another article stated that all through the ranch section of southwest Texas recruiting had been going on with "more than 3000 cowboys and cattlemen signing preliminary papers."[2]

America had accepted Teddy Roosevelt once again as their leader to go over and whip the Germans with cowboys, pistols, horses, and good old American grit and toughness. All Roosevelt needed was a nod from Wilson. On April 12, having not heard from the administration, he went directly to Congress to pass legislation allowing volunteer regiments, thereby leaving Wilson's approval as something he wanted but did not need. Roosevelt knew a general army could not be mustered into service before 1918 and he knew as well that the French and British were desperate for American troops; they needed them now. Britain had sent Lord Balfour to plead with Wilson to speed up troop deployment and Roosevelt saw that as his opening. What better way to stop the British and French bleeding than with a tourniquet supplied by the Rough Riders.

He dashed off a letter to George Chamberlain, chairman of the Senate Military Affairs Committee:

> *Let us use volunteer forces, in connection with a portion of the regular army, in order at the earliest possible moment, within a few months, to put our flag on the firing line. We owe this to humanity. We owe it to the small nations who have suffered such dreadful wrong from Germany. Most of all we owe it to ourselves, to our national honor and self-respect. For the sake of our own souls, for the sake of the memories of the great Americans of the past, we must show that we do not intend to make this merely a dollar war. Let us pay with our bodies for our soul's desire.*[3]

After leaving this little bomb for Secretary Baker and the president to deal with, TR rushed off to the wedding of his son Archie to Grace

Lockwood on April 14. This was the last time the Roosevelts would assemble as a family. The war was already tearing them apart. Quentin, who was headed for the nascent air force, was best man with Ted and Kermit as ushers. It was a war wedding. The bride, Grace, had recently graduated from a female training camp in Chevy Chase, Maryland. Patriotic bunting and flags were de rigueur as the Roosevelts entered the war phase of their family life. If everything went according to plan, all the Roosevelt men would soon be in France fighting the Germans. But things did not go as planned.

Secretary Baker had his marching orders. On April 15, Roosevelt got the letter he didn't want from Newton Baker. He was not going to France. Secretary Baker turned down his request to be a volunteer commander in the war for "purely military" reasons. Baker put it all on the War College:

The War College Division earnestly recommends that no American troops be employed in active service in any European theatre until after an adequate period of training, and that during that period all available trained officers and men in the Regular army or National Guard be employed in training the new levees called into service. It should, therefore, be our policy at first to devote all our energies to raising troops in sufficient numbers to exert a substantial influence in a later stage of war. Partially trained troops will be entirely unfit for such duty and even if our regular troops and national guard could be spared from training duty their number is too small to exert any influence.[4]

Baker then further explained: "This policy does not undertake to estimate what if any sentimental value would attach to a representation of the United States in France by a former President of the United States."[5] Baker then shot out the last card Roosevelt had to play, the pressure of the allies to get troops to France ASAP. If the Allies did bring pressure then that American Expeditionary Force would be commanded by "the most experienced professional military men in our country and that it be officered by and composed of men selected because of their previous military training and as far as possible actual military experience ... who have devoted their lives exclusively to the study and pursuit of military matters and have made a professional study of the recent changes in the art of war."[6]

In other words, Woodrow Wilson and Newton Baker did not need an ex-president from the nineteenth century playing cowboys and Indians while men were being annihilated by machine guns, poisonous gases, and tanks. The message was loud and clear. You have no idea what war is, and we don't want you to be killed on our watch. And politically, Woodrow Wilson did not want the specter of Roosevelt somehow becoming a national hero again if he should somehow survive. And besides all that, Roosevelt had not made but a few enemies.

The regular military had a long memory, with many of the same men still holding commissions since the war with Spain. Army Chief of Staff Tasker Bliss gave Wilson an eight-page letter on why a Roosevelt division was a bad idea. Joseph Leiter angered Roosevelt as president of the Army League when he opposed him. After Roosevelt resigned from the league, Leiter responded, "I am now constrained to believe that your own schemes of personal and political aggrandizement lie at the bottom of the agitation."[7] Many of the older officers remembered Roosevelt as self-promoting and lacking respect for army regulations. And the election of 1920 was not that far off and now that the love fest between TR and the Republicans seemed to be growing it was not unreasonable to think he might be the standard bearer once again. And what if he went over there and survived . . . *my God!* And the Germans happened to throw in the towel in the next year. It would be San Juan Hill all over again, where many in the military community believed Roosevelt's charge up San Juan Hill was ill-conceived, that he had stumbled into an ambush, and that it was only through sheer luck he and his men had lived to see another day. Many believed it was the Rooseveltian bluster, his shameless self-promoting, that had turned a charge up a hill into presidential gold. And if Roosevelt somehow was not killed, if somehow he crossed no-man's-land and reached the German trenches, and if somehow the Germans retreated, left their trenches, they would never hear the end of how Teddy Roosevelt and the Rough Riders *had won World War I.* Impossible. Unthinkable. Unbelievable—still, the man did seem to defy death and had an uncanny knack for ending up on top. No. Best not to even go there. As far as the Wilson administration was concerned, the issue was closed. Of course, Theodore Roosevelt had other plans.

CHAPTER TWENTY-SIX

Three Cheers and a Tiger
for Teddy and His Division!

1917

EDITH WILSON ROSE EARLY WITH THE KITCHEN STAFF TO CHECK PRESident Wilson's agenda and approve his diet. If his agenda was too busy, she suggested to Joe Tumulty that some down time be inserted. His high blood pressure was a constant problem, and Wilson complained of headaches that centered in his forehead and felt like someone was driving in a nail. Now with the war the stress had increased tenfold and Edith had to be more vigilant, more obsessive, over enforced leisure to lighten the load. That might be golf. A drive in the Virginia countryside. Going horseback riding. Reading poetry by the fire in the presidential residence. Or taking the yacht out for a spin down the Potomac.

Wilson had just had Secretary Baker give Roosevelt the bad news and the papers were alive with the opinion he should have given his assent. "It may safely be predicted that Roosevelt will not submit quietly to the Presidential refusal. There are still the committees of congress to whom he can appeal against the executive orders," the *Chattanooga News* blared on April 13. "Even the administration opinion is divided as to the wisdom of refusing to let Roosevelt raise a division and take it to war." The paper went on to speculate Wilson was driven by politics not to make Roosevelt a "war hero."[1]

Woodrow Wilson read the papers over coffee, making a clicking noise with his tongue, shaking his head. "While in Washington Roosevelt had talks with Senator Chamberlain of the senate committee on military affairs . . . and a dozen other members of congress of both parties."[2] Wilson rubbed his forehead. A real throbber was coming on. It was just like 1912 when Roosevelt split the Republican Party, which was a good thing for Wilson, but it showed the man could not take no for an answer. Woodrow sipped his coffee, lifted the paper, and continued reading. "If Col. House or some other good political adviser gets Wilson's ear, the latter is very likely to change his mind and give graceful assent to Roosevelt's requests. If he is dominated by the narrower councils of Secretary Baker and the war department clique the refusal will continue to stand. What Roosevelt will do then will be an interesting news development. . . . I might risk a guess that Roosevelt will somehow or other at no very distant date, go to the front."[3]

President Wilson snapped the paper shut and shook his head, muttering. Just what he needed. Teddy Roosevelt going to the front on his own and getting killed and then becoming a martyr. The problem was *he might really do it!* Wilson rubbed his eyes under his pince-nez; the headache was becoming excruciating. The Rough Rider had been driving up his blood pressure for years, really since 1912. He picked up the paper again and turned the page. The headline was in bold type: "GIVE TEDDY HIS COMMISSION AND LET HIM GO TO IT."[4]

Wilson stared in wonderment. It was as if Roosevelt had just walked into the room. Here he was in the paper. Wilson read as if the article were talking directly to him:

President Wilson has under consideration Roosevelt's earnest request that he be permitted to raise a volunteer division of troops for service in France. Roosevelt urged the matter on the president in a personal interview at the White House, Tuesday. We hope the president grants the request and gives the colonel his commission at once. It would not only be a graceful thing to do, but it would be an effective thing as well. Roosevelt is one of the greatest driving forces in America. He is without question the most popular private citizen in the United States and has the largest personal following.[5]

Wilson slapped the paper down again. The pain was right behind his eyes. He took off his pince-nez and closed his eyes. The paper was arguing for Roosevelt! The Rough Rider was right in front of him, making his case. Wilson adjusted his pince-nez and picked up the paper again. "Nothing that the president could do at this time would so challenge the imagination of the nation as this. It would enthuse the middle west and the far west. . . . Roosevelt raising a division would be more effective in arousing the patriotism of the nation than a thousand recruiting sergeants. Roosevelt and his division on the firing line in France would be the best guarantee that we could give our allies of the earnestness of our purpose to go through with them to the finish. Three cheers and a tiger for Teddy for his division!"[6]

Wilson slammed the paper down again, muttering to himself, rubbing his forehead. The man was incorrigible. He must have had that article planted. Edith watched her husband rubbing his forehead, glaring at the paper, and that's when she suggested they go for a nice long cruise in the yacht down the Potomac.

The presidential yacht provided just the relief Edith hoped. It was a beautiful spring day and the Potomac sparkled green in the brilliant sunshine. They passed a small island and decided to go exploring. Germany, Teddy Roosevelt, and the war were now distant. Edith just had to keep the president's mind off of anything that stressed him, and the truth was Theodore Roosevelt stressed him greatly. The small launch of officers, the president, and Edith approached the island. They could see a group of people that immediately dispersed into their homes when Woodrow and Edith approached. Wilson remarked that it was strange. They walked around some more and then went back to where the launch was docked.

They turned around the people scattered back to their houses except one man. He shut one eye as Wilson approached.

"You wouldn't be the president, would you?"

Wilson nodded.

"I have that honor sir."

The man grinned. "Phew, we thought you were the Germans come to invade."[7]

Woodrow Wilson stared at the man. It wouldn't have surprised him if the man had suggested he send Theodore Roosevelt over to fight the Germans. He just couldn't escape. Edith eyed the president uneasily as they made small talk and then returned to the yacht. Wilson's face had darkened again as the yacht turned and headed back up the river. Edith realized then the war would not be so easily left behind, and Teddy Roosevelt would not be left behind either for that matter.

CHAPTER TWENTY-SEVEN

The Countercharge

1917

ROOSEVELT'S COUNTERCHARGE BEGAN WITH AN EIGHTEEN-PAGE LET-
ter outlining why he should be made commander of a volunteer division.
Secretary of War Newton Baker had to wade through page after page of
Rooseveltian military accomplishments. "My dear sir, you forget that I
have commanded troops in action in the most important battle fought
by the United States army during the last half century"[1] He then pointed
out that other military commanders with half his experience were being
appointed. He then attacked the war department's preparedness and
pointed out that Baker should have started manufacturing rifles two years
ago and that if he had, "we would now be a million rifles to the good."
TR then pivoted to lambasting the bureaucrats of the war department as
"well-meaning men of the red-tape and pipe-clay school . . . hidebound
in the pedantry of that kind of wooden militarism which is only one
degree worse than its extreme opposite, the folly which believes that an
army can be improvised between sunset and sunrise."[2]

Then Roosevelt proposed soldiers under him would be better served
than those in the army. "As for the young American who you feel should
have better guidance and protection than I can give them, my dear Mr.
Secretary why not let them judge for themselves? The great majority
of men who were in my old regiment will eagerly come forward under
me, in so far as they are fit. I believe I can appeal to the natural fighting
man of this country." Roosevelt then proposed he could put captains
or young majors of the regular army into his division to command the

soldiers and pointed out that his division would be ready to go quickly. "In four months, the division would have been seasoned under the thorough training which you rightly demand. Most of the men would come forward would be seasoned already exactly as was the case in my regiment nineteen years ago."[3]

Roosevelt then showed tragically that his view of warfare had not changed much since 1898 and that he thought cavalry could still win the day.

Cavalry should be able to act as a mass together. I therefore very earnestly recommend that in connection with each division we raise a three-regiment brigade of cavalry. As long as the fighting is in the trenches, this cavalry will be used dismounted and will represent an addition to the infantry. As soon as we begin to fight outside the trenches, the two brigades could be joined together and could be used as a small cavalry division under the direction of the corps commander.[4] *TR incredibly saw divisions of men on horseback descending on the Germans in their trenches. One can only imagine Secretary Baker wading through the single-spaced dissertation of eighteen pages covering everything from logistics, army composition, strategy, assessing the state of the regular army, history of volunteerism in the United States, and winding up with the same request to head a division. It was as if Baker had not written a letter at all to Roosevelt. So much for Wilson and Baker's refusal to let Theodore Roosevelt command a regiment. The press certainly did not believe he wouldn't prevail. The New York* Times *on May 8 led with a front-page article:* "NEW RUSH SETS IN TO JOIN ROOSEVELT. *Predicted that 250,000 will be enrolled for Division by End of Week.*[5]

The paper went on to say that "recruiting for an overseas force for early service at the front in France went on with renewed vigor yesterday at the headquarters of the Roosevelt Division, 753 Fifth Avenue. About 200 men, 90 percent of whom were college graduates, applied in person at the office; more than 1,100 applications were received by mail or telegraph." Other newspapers were not so sanguine about the Roosevelt division and the editorials of the day would have given Woodrow Wilson and Secretary Baker heart. The most interesting editorial against Roosevelt's leading of a division of Rough Riders in France comes from a Mrs. Annie Riley Hale, a Southerner who had written a book, *Rooseveltian Fact and Fable*. The *Times* gave wide play to her editorial with a leading headline, "Mrs. Hale Believes Roosevelt Would Make Atonement. Alleges Colonel Would Repay for San Juan Affair." Mrs. Hale's book and her editorial questioned if Roosevelt ever charged up San Juan Hill at all. "Pretty nearly everybody in this country knows that so far from leading the famous San Juan Hill charge Colonel Roosevelt bore not even an inconspicuous part in it. That he was not within a third of a mile of the hill when the charge was made by the infantry of Kent and Hawkins."[6]

Mrs. Hale then postulated that Roosevelt's desire to lead the Rough Riders in the new war was to atone for his lies in the old war. Even though she cites Roosevelt's own writing as evidence that he was watching from Kettle Hill as her smoking gun, her book is more of a polemic against Roosevelt for having a "negro" in the White House. If nothing else, the prominent placement of her editorial shows the powerful forces allied against Roosevelt that Mrs. Hale, a known White supremacist, should be given so much play. Clearly for Hale, there was nothing worse than Roosevelt's breaching the White House by dining with Booker T. Washington.

Other editorials that did not come from the deep wellspring of unreconstructed Southerners, such as the *St. Louis Dispatch*, made the case that the days of the volunteer army were over and that international conflicts required large armies not dependent on the inspirational leadership of a man on horseback. "If Mr. Roosevelt intends to command an expeditionary army, made up of new Rough Riders or Roosevelt followers, he will have to enlist under some other flag than the Stars and Stripes. There will be but one army, it will be the American army. Independent commands are inconsistent with modern warfare and the day of the Ellsworth Zouave, the Louisiana Tigers, and the Roosevelt Rough Riders has passed."[7]

Still, Rough Rider fever was sweeping the country along with the wave of patriotism, and even popular boxers wanted to join with Teddy. "THE BATTLER PREFERS TO HELP TEDDY ROOSEVELT OVERTHROW THE KAISER" ran the headline in the *St. Louis Dispatch*.[8] Apparently, a rival band of Rough Riders called the Ozark Rough Riders had approached boxer Bat Nelson to join them, but Bat declined, citing his desire to join up with TR. "Bat Nelson is some fighter. Also he is fortunate in that his country knows about it. Bat's fighting prowess is in such demand that his friends are quite prepared to see R. P. Dickerson of Springfield MO and Col. T. R. Roosevelt scraping vigorously to decide which is entitled to have the battler enlist in the regiment each hopes to organize to overthrow Germany." Bat decided on Teddy. "Teddy gets my assistance when it comes time to go to the front."[9]

So America was going to war with boxers, cowboys, Ivy Leaguers, ranchers, frontiersmen, ex-presidents, bankers, businessmen, and weekend warriors of all stripes. There was not a soldier among them ready to fight the battle-hardened Germans using poisonous gas and flamethrowers to annihilate human beings. And this is what worried Secretary Baker and Woodrow Wilson as they pored over Roosevelt's eighteen-page diatribe on the deficiencies of the war department, if not Baker and Wilson themselves. The twentieth century wasn't even twenty years old, and one could make a case that the two oceans had kept America in a time warp where the West was still wild and individuals could control their own destiny and affect the destiny of nations. Clearly, Roosevelt still believed this, and he was not alone.

Secretary Baker did not respond directly to the Roosevelt missive. He told a friend he hoped to avoid "a repetition of the San Juan Hill affair with the commander rushing his men into a situation from which only luck extricated them."[10] Clearly he was in the Annie Riley Hale camp on this one. He finally responded to TR on May 5 with a letter saying that "for obvious reasons I cannot allow myself to be drawn into a discussion of your personal experience and qualifications. This is a subject upon which my personal opinion would be of little importance . . . nor can I undertake a general defense of Regular Army officers and particularly of my associates in the General Staff against your suggestion that they may be possibly 'of the red-tape and pipe-clay school.' They are after all that part of our professional army of longest experience and by our law are my constituted military advisers."[11]

Clearly Teddy had hit a nerve with Secretary Baker by attacking the military establishment. Baker then swung off and tried to bring some reality to the issue of a volunteer army in a mechanized twentieth-century conflagration. "The war in France is confessedly stern, steady, and relentless. It is a contest between the morale of two great contending forces."[12] Should the United States jump into a struggle with a division of "hastily summoned and unprofessional volunteers," the Allies would be depressed and disillusioned, "deeming it an evidence of our lack of seriousness about the nature of the enterprise." Baker then wound up and tried to push through the Rooseveltian barricades once more.

> *Thus, upon every consideration, my mind justifies the conclusion expressed to you in my letter of April 13th. This reasoning quite frankly eliminates the consideration of personality, but, upon that subject, there is so much uncertainty of judgement that I do not feel that I could with confidence elect a course at plain variance with every other consideration in order to satisfy a personal conclusion based wholly upon a personal consideration.*[13]

So, Secretary Baker would like to say yes, but the evidence against it was too strong. He knew he who he was dealing with and try as he might to remove "the consideration of personality" it was all personal to TR. Roosevelt read Baker's response and then threw the letter aside. Bureaucrat. He knew nothing about waging war. He was the type of man Roosevelt loathed, a Washington insider who was the opposite of the man of action. The Wilson administration was full of them. TR had launched his counteroffensive and he would have to take his triumphant moment not in the White House but in the halls of congress. There would be sharks swimming all around him there too, but he had shown before he could swim among the sharks and be just fine. It seemed the whole world wanted to join Teddy Roosevelt on his next charge with the Rough Riders if he could only get through the Washington bureaucracy. Roosevelt understood why thousands of applications were pouring in to Rough Rider headquarters if nobody else did. There was nothing in the world like the moment when "the wolf rises in the heart,"[14] and a man had his "crowded hour." Twenty years before he had had his.

Chapter Twenty-Eight

San Juan Hill

1898

Roosevelt stared into the harsh sunshine at San Juan Hill, hearing his own labored breathing as he fired round after round into the far hill of Spanish soldiers. The Rough Riders were under heavy fire from snipers, men in rifle pits, and shells that arced down, blowing men into the air. Roosevelt and his men tried to support the American soldiers who were rushing up San Juan Hill and getting cut down by the Spanish. TR and the Rough Riders had taken Kettle Hill and had a bird's-eye view of the battle; now they tried to support the assaulting troops rushing up San Juan Hill any way they could. Then came *BOOM BOOM BOOM* and the men thought they were being assaulted by Spanish machine guns. Roosevelt turned and thought it was coming from the left side and then realized it was their own Gatling guns. "It's the Gatlings, men! It's our Gatling guns!"[1]

The Gatlings were ten barrels that rotated on a central shaft and fired one at a time. The guns sprayed bullets at the Spanish in the rifle pits until the soldiers began to stand up and run. Roosevelt ordered a cease-fire so his men wouldn't shoot the Americans just reaching the pits. Still the bullets sprayed around the Rough Riders, the Mausers killing men to right and left of Roosevelt with deadly accuracy. The men were crouched down, but many were shot anyway.

Roosevelt had enough. The Mauser bullets cut the air around him as he stepped in front of the line and raised his pistol high into the air and shouted, "Now, by God men! Let's charge em, God damn em!"[2] He then jumped over a wire fence and sprinted down Kettle Hill toward the shallow lake and grassy clearing separating the two hills. Up above was a wooden house with earthworks built by the Spanish where the fire had been pouring down on Roosevelt and his men and the assaulting regular army soldiers. Roosevelt was now running by himself; in the heat of battle with the screaming, shouting, the bullets zinging, and the cheers no one heard him give the order to charge.

Trooper Oliver Norton shouted, "For God's sake, follow the colonel,"[3] and as he rose was shot dead with a bullet into the brain. By now Roosevelt, after covering a hundred yards, realized he only had five men with him and two of them were cut down by the Spanish. He shouted at the remaining men, "Lie down boys . . . and wait here until I return."[4] Then Roosevelt returned to the rest of the men on Kettle Hill. Later he would realize the folly of leaving men behind.

"There was really no possible point in letting them stay there while I went back," he later wrote, "but at the moment it seemed perfectly natural to me and apparently so to them for they cheerfully nodded and sat down in the grass, firing back at the line of trenches from which the Spaniards were shooting at them."[5] Every man lying in the grass would be shot but would survive to tell the story. "Well, it was a ticklish place, but we'd have lain on a gridiron of hell if he'd given the order," one man later recalled.[6]

Roosevelt's own orderly, Henry Bardshar, had not heard Roosevelt's charge order either. A shell had exploded nearby and left him momentarily deaf and covered with blood from other men. He thought he was dead because he could hear nothing and saw Roosevelt run up to him and lean forward. "Didn't you hear me call for a charge?" Bardshar heard that as the concussion from the shell wore off. Roosevelt asked the same question of the Rough Riders with many expletives. "Even while I taunted them bitterly for not having followed me," he later wrote, "it was all I could do not to smile at the look of injury and surprise that came over their faces."[7]

But Roosevelt wanted other regiments with him; he ran over to General Sumner and asked permission to assault the trenches. The general gave the order to his men and now when Roosevelt jumped the fence, buffalo soldiers, Rough Riders, and regulars all followed in a charging mass that the Spanish concentrated their fire on. A buffalo soldier, William B. Applegarth, later wrote his brother, describing the charge:

> *We pushed forward to within 1000 yards of their firing line, which was on a hillside. They were in trenches about six feet deep and I should judge by the size of these that they outnumbered us nearly two to one. Before us lay an open field about 750 yards wide and beyond that a hill about 1000 yards long and forty yards high and very steep with a battery of artillery on the summit in our front and a blockhouse at the right . . . we could hear no commands on account of the heavy firing, so we advanced in skirmish lines and squads to the edge of the thicket, where we got the order to charge.*[8]

Five troopers from Troop D were cut down instantly. The charging men were now a running, stumbling juggernaut with men passing Roosevelt, some going into the lake, and some going around it. Then it was a dead run up the hill into the teeth of Spanish fire, a mob of men shouting, yelling, and heading straight for the rifle pits. "It was the grandest sight I ever saw,"[9] wrote Second Lieutenant John Greenway to his mother. Another Rough Rider would later write that it was "just a mob that went up a hill. If the Spaniards had been able to shoot, we'd have never made it to the top."[10] The rifle fire from the trenches came down in volleys and men fell, with other men jumping over them.

William Applegarth described the open field charge to his brother:

> *Away we went out across the open on the dead run with the Spaniards peppering us for fair and right here we struck one of the toughest propositions yet encountered by the American troops—a creek about four feet deep with a high barbed wire trocha on either side of it . . . at the foot of the hill we encountered another double line of barbed wires which we had to stop and pull down . . . they killed us off like sheep.*[11]

Some of the soldiers returned fire but kept moving all the time. Roosevelt heard William Pollock, a Pawnee Indian in Troop D, let out an "ungodly war whoop." Roosevelt himself was somewhere in the ether, high on adrenalin; he turned to Henry Bardshar, his orderly, as they climbed the hill, shouting "Holy Godfrey, what fun!" William Applegarth described the final charge to his brother: "If I should live a thousand years I'll never forget it. Right up in the face of a storm of bullets that seemed to sweep the hillside like a shower of hailstones. It was here that the boys began to yell 'Old Glory,' 'Dixie,' 'Uncle Sam,' 'Remember the Maine,' and with yells and cheers we dashed straight up and over their entrenchments to the top."[12]

With just a hundred yards to go, the Spanish jumped out of their rifle pits and earthworks and began to run. One of the first men to reach the trenches was Rodger Fitche, who later wrote, "There was a good many dead and wounded Spaniards in and about the trenches . . . we also captured one playing possum in the trench. He was nearly scared to death and piteously begged for mercy."[13]

Many of the men had to catch their breath while Roosevelt and other men inspected the house and the rifle pits. TR noticed quickly most of the Spanish dead had blood and brain oozing from their heads. It was all the men had to shoot at. Roosevelt looked down the hill he had just run up and realized then what he had just accomplished. The Spanish counterattacked later with cannon fire and volleys of rifle fire. The men hugged the ground while Roosevelt remained standing. "We lay in the intrenchments and exchanged shots with them until 12:30 July 3rd when they shoved up a white flag and firing ceased. There has been no firing since." Robert Ferguson, Roosevelt's old ranch partner and a sergeant in K Troop, wrote that "Theodore preferred to stand up or walk about snuffing the fragrant air of combat. I really believed firmly now, they cannot kill him."[14]

Theodore Roosevelt, standing in the smoke among the dead and the dying in the heat of the Cuban sun with his Rough Riders all around him, never took cover. He had seen the white flag and he realized that his great adventure, his crowded hour was at an end. He looked out from Santiago Hill at the spreading dense green foliage and realized then he was standing on the mountaintop of his one true desire. All his life he had wanted to conquer, to lead men, to test himself in battle. Ever since his father had sent a substitute to the Civil War there had been a sense of opportunity missed. He looked around the smoking battlefield, strewn with lifeless bodies, hats, rifles, canteens, bayonets, and bleeding men. He turned slowly in the stifling heat now broken by a far seaborne breeze, fixing the image in his mind for all time. This was the high point. He knew this. Never again would he be so intensely alive as he was now. Leading men into the jaws of death, the young American cowboys of a young nation and then emerging on the top of the contested hill victorious. He had just won the Spanish-American War. One man. It had the ring of great mythology of all the stories of knights of old he had nourished his young asthmatic soul on. It already had become legend, although he didn't know it. Teddy Roosevelt and his Rough Riders charging up San Juan Hill. A million schoolchildren would read of his exploits for all time in the history books, the writers and poets would relive the miracle of Roosevelt's Rough Riders over and over and hand it down to the ages to haunt the old men they would all become.

CHAPTER TWENTY-NINE

Swimming with the Sharks

1917

ROOSEVELT WAS NOT ONLY PETITIONING TO GET HIMSELF SENT OVER TO France to fight the Germans but he was working just as hard to get his boys, Archibald, Ted, Kermit, and Quentin into the front lines of France; to that end he went right to the top with a letter to General Pershing:

> *I very heartily congratulate you and especially the people of the United States upon your selection to lead the expeditionary force to the front. When I was endeavoring to persuade the Secretary of War to permit me to raise a division or two of volunteers, I stated that if you or some man like you were to command the expeditionary force I could raise the divisions without trouble. I write you now to request my two sons, Theodore Roosevelt Jr., aged 27 and Archibald B. Roosevelt, age 23, both of Harvard, be allowed to enlist as privates under you, to go over with the first troops . . . they are keenly desirous to see service and if they serve under you at the front and are not killed, they will be far better able to instruct the draft army next fall or next winter or whenever they are sent home.*[1]

That left Kermit and Quentin. TR had already thought about getting Kermit over as an aide to a general. Quentin was a little trickier. He was not straight Roosevelt material. More sensitive, more attuned to the nuances of life, he was as much his mother's son as his father's. Knowing only the privileged life of growing up in the White House, his every move was reported by the press. "A REAL BOY. Quentin Roosevelt

Shows His Mischievousness"[2] was a front-page headline in the *Akron Beacon Journal* in 1902. "The youngster discovered the switch controlling the electric lights of the state dining room and turned it on and off to the consternation of the guests, who were at times in utter darkness and again in the full blaze of the chandeliers."[3] He brought his pony up the back freight elevator to visit his sick brother and ran with other boys called "the white house gang." He walked through the White House garden on stilts until his father told him the gardener objected. "I don't see what good it does for you to be President," he told his father. "There are so many things we can't do here. I wish I was home again."[4]

He was the youngest son and in 1903 made news again with an attack of the measles followed by malaria. His recovery was duly noted. A manufacturer of toys sent him a wagon to go with the pony he was requesting from his father. He had his father's bad eyesight and a bad back. Edith hovered over her youngest and Teddy had a hard time denying him anything. Now that he had dropped out of Harvard to join the air corps, TR had to go back, hat in hand, to the man whom he had been besieging with letters to let him go to France. Now he had to ask for a favor for his son from Secretary of War Baker.

Quentin's eyesight could keep him from ever ascending to the skies over France and to that end Roosevelt requested help for getting Quentin into the flying school at Fort Monroe, Virginia. He was essentially asking the war department to look the other way and put his son up in skies in a rickety plane with bad eyesight, a clear disadvantage when going up against experienced German fighter pilots. But while Secretary Newton would not give TR the clearance to take a division to France with the Rough Riders, he cleared the way for his son.

"It will give me pleasure," Baker replied, "to think that your boy is there and a part of our establishment."[5] Secretary Baker did not bear any ill will toward Theodore Roosevelt, or at least he didn't take revenge against him through his son. Quentin was summoned to Washington for flight training. "Doctors at Walter Reed Hospital poured hot and cold water into his ears, dropped belladonna into his eyes, made him hop along blindfolded and then conveniently ignoring his short sightedness declared him fit for service."[6] He was billeted to Hazelhurst Field, Mineola, Long Island, just a motorcycle ride away from Sagamore Hill.

Roosevelt might have considered that Quentin's vision would put him at a disadvantage and could well get him killed, but TR had come through war without a scratch and undoubtedly he assumed his sons could do the same. But destiny is a singular tap on the shoulder and that shoulder belonged to the father, not the sons. All his life Teddy Roosevelt had skirted death. Even after the suicidal charge up San Juan Hill where men to the right and left of him fell as he sat exposed on a horse, Teddy had to prove the Gods favored him one more time. And so his sons should also have their own moment to prove they were men, to live life on that higher plane where "the wolf rises in the heart."

Roosevelt had proved there was no better way to advance in life than to prove oneself on the battlefield and then broadcast that feat all over. It had carried him to the vice presidency and then of course the presidency. This had been an American tradition going all the way back to George Washington. Advancement in the military translated to advancement in life. This notion would die hard in the twentieth century, even though Dwight Eisenhower would prove once again there was a through line from military heroics to the White House. But for the millions who would serve in World War I and World War II, service in the military would be something to survive and then forget. The swashbuckling glory of charging up a hill had been left in the last century along with horses, sabers, and cowboys, but no one told Roosevelt and he wouldn't have believed it anyway.

Quentin and Flora Whitney picked up where they left off when Quentin returned from Harvard to enlist. The young couple spent time reading poetry together, going on drives, attending the social events of Newport. If TR was concerned about the safety of his sons in the coming war he hid it well; in fact, he encouraged all of them to get into the action as soon as possible. This might have been related to the fact he had come through war unscathed and literally could swim with sharks and live to tell the tale.

In July 1898, many of his Rough Riders were sick with malaria or yellow fever in Cuba, but TR had remained strong and healthy and one day proposed swimming in the Caribbean with Lieutenant Jack Greenway. They had been invited to Morro Castle by General Fitzhugh Lee and Roosevelt stared out into the bay at the wreck of the *Merrimac* some three hundred yards distant. Colonel Roosevelt immediately proclaimed they would go investigate the wreck and began pulling off his clothes. Lieutenant Greenway had no choice to but to accompany the colonel and began pulling off his clothes as well. He later wrote about what would become legend:

We weren't out more than a dozen strokes before General Lee, who had clambered up on the parapet of Fort Morro, began to yell.

"Can you make out what he's trying to say," the old man asked, punctuating his words with long overhand strokes.

"Sharks," says I, wishing I were back on shore.

"Sharks," says the colonel, blowing out a mouthful of water, "they" stroke "won't" stroke "bite" stroke "I've been" stroke "studying them" stroke "all my life" stroke "and I never" stroke "heard of one" stroke "bothering a swimmer" stroke "Its all" stroke "Poppycock."

Just then a big fellow, probably not more than ten or twelve feet long, but looking as big as a battleship to me, showed up alongside us. Then came another, till we had quite a group. The Colonel didn't pay the least attention.

Meanwhile the old general was doing a war dance up on the parapet, shouting and standing first on one foot and then on the other and working his arms like he was doing something on a bet. Finally we reached the wreck and I felt better. The colonel, of course, got busy looking things over. I had to pretend I was interested but I was think-ing of the sharks and getting back to shore. I didn't hurry the colonel in his inspection either. After a while we had seen enough and we went over the side again. Soon the sharks were all about us again, sort of pacing us in, as they had paced us out, and while the old general did his second part of his war dance. He felt a whole lot better when we landed and so did I.[7]

Theodore Roosevelt assumed his sons would enjoy the same protec-tion in World War I that he did when dodging Spanish bullets, facing down grizzly bears, getting lost in blizzards in the Badlands, or swim-ming with sharks. Roosevelt didn't know it, but he had the myopia of the blessed and would realize too late that what was good for the father was not necessarily good for the son.

CHAPTER THIRTY

The End Run

MAY 1917

THE ROUGH RIDER WAS FEELING PRETTY GOOD. ON MAY 3, 1917, *THE Oklahoman* led with a front-page article, "WILSON MAY APPROVE ROOSEVELT WAR MOVE."[1] The sprawling article, which also featured illustrations of Roosevelt as a Rough Rider in 1898 and as he was today, with a summary of his charge up San Juan Hill, went on to say, "The Roosevelt division issue again was the most interesting if the most important question before the house and senate conferees on the army bill today. All other differences are expected to be settled quickly. Since the bill passed the Senate late yesterday strongest pressure has been brought to bear on those opposed to permitting Roosevelt to plant the Stars and Stripes on battlefront."[2]

This was amazing news. In April it looked like the Roosevelt amendment attached to the conscription bill was in trouble. Henry Cabot Lodge had been lobbying hard and pushed it through under the name of Senator Warren Harding of Ohio. Harding, who had blocked Roosevelt's nomination in 1916, was no fool; he saw a clear runway to 1920 if he pleased the party bosses. Harding added to the amendment the ability of Wilson to create four volunteer divisions of men "not subject to conscription." This would satisfy those who saw the volunteer divisions as muddying the waters for straight conscription. Roosevelt was not named in the amendment, but Lodge went all in for his friend.

"He is known in Europe as no other American. His presence there would be a help and encouragement to the soldiers of the allied nations...."

For heaven's sake is there any reason why he should not be given the opportunity if he desires to give his life for what he regards as the most sacred of all causes."[3] Lodge wanted Roosevelt to have his kamikaze mission. He understood there was little chance of Roosevelt surviving the war, but he also agreed it would be a brilliant capstone to an amazing career. "What is that is asked? It is asked only by a man who is now readily in the twilight of his life that he may finally lay down his life for the country that has been his."[4]

The debate raged on, with newspapers throwing in behind Roosevelt and the Rough Riders. *The Oklahoman* was the first to proclaim victory. "Those opponents are known to be wavering today, many having taken the stand they did against it solely because they thought that to inject the Roosevelt idea into selective service would weaken and perhaps kill the bill. . . . Roosevelt proponents declared today they even believe President Wilson will come out in favor of authorizing Roosevelt to raise and lead a fighting force to France."[5]

Meanwhile, Roosevelt was receiving two thousand applications a day to join his division. As the debate raged on, the issue of other militias demanding to be sent over became a hot point of contention. On the front page of *The New York Times* a boxed-in article dead center in the middle proclaimed, "DEADLOCK ON ARMY BILL OVER ROOSEVELT DIVISION. AGE LIMITS OF RECRUITS ARE ALSO NOT SETTLED."[6]

The amendment had broken down in conference over "the Senate amendment to the Draft bill to raise a division for early service in France . . . the points at issue are prohibitions in and around camps, tribunals for passing on questions of exemptions from the draft, designations for troops drafted from the states, volunteer divisions to give Colonel Roosevelt his opportunity."[7]

Just below on the front page of *The New York Times* was another headline: "NEW RUSH SETS IN TO JOIN ROOSEVELT PREDICTED THAT 250,000 WILL BE ENROLLED FOR DIVISION BY END OF WEEK."[8] The article described men flocking to join TR. "Recruiting for an overseas force for early service at the front in France went on with renewed vigor yesterday at the headquarters of the Roosevelt Division . . . about 200 men, 90 percent of whom were college graduates, applied in person at the office and more than 1,000 applications were received by mail or telegraph . . . by the end of the week at the present rate more than 200,000 having been previously enrolled."[9]

A deluge of young men seeking to serve with Teddy Roosevelt had descended, looking for the Great Adventure they had grown up hearing about. Clearly the tide, for the moment, had shifted to the Rough Rider. Secretary Newton Baker's letter telling Roosevelt his services were not needed was essentially dead. The momentum was too strong and what had been a wild fantasy by an ex-president was now being taken up by Congress and the actual details were being hammered out to bring a division of Rough Riders to face the Germans in the trenches of France.

Roosevelt surely was dancing a jig at Sagamore Hill; if he wasn't then, he had a reason to on May 12. The *York Dispatch* led with the headline, "HOUSE FOR TR GOING TO FRANCE."[10] On May 13, the *Democrat Chronicle* announced in bold letters, "HOUSE VOTES FOR ROOSEVELT'S DIVISION."

> *The way was cleared in Congress today for Colonel Roosevelt, if he is given authorization by the Administration to raise a division of volunteers for service in France. After stormy debate led by Republicans, Votes to Restore Senate Clause. The vote had stood at 170 to 106 against Roosevelt's army but Lodge and others put on the pressure and the vote turned around to 215 for the Roosevelt Division with 178 against.*[11]

The Wilson administration had been completely bushwhacked by the former president. The paper saw it as a complete win for TR.

"By a vote of 215 to 178 the house today after stormy debate voted to instruct its conferees on the army bill to restore the senate amendment to permit Colonel Roosevelt to lead a division to France." Readers in 1917 believed the government had just given Teddy Roosevelt the go-ahead to lead a division of Rough Riders and head to France. The pace of applications became a hurricane as Roosevelt gave an interview to *The Washington Times*, which resulted in the headline, "TR TO MARCH UNDER OLD ROUGH RIDER FLAG . . . GIVEN CHANCE HE'LL CARRY TO FRANCE, HE TELLS SCOUTS."[12]

"I am exceedingly pleased at the wise and patriotic action of the house," said Colonel Roosevelt when informed that the war bill had been referred back to committee with instructions to include an amendment which make the Roosevelt Division possible. Three hundred boy scouts marched to Roosevelt's home at Sagamore Hill and cheered the colonel after word of the House action was received. Roosevelt addressed the boys then led them into his trophy room where he pointed out the Spanish war battle flags carried by the rough riders and the revolver he used in Cuba. "If they give me a chance," he declared, indicating the relics, "I will carry them to France."[13]

Even the Boy Scouts were on the side of the old Rough Rider. *The New York Times* sent a small cloud of doubt into the sunshine with the subheadline, "Ex Rough Rider Promises Horses Within Twenty-Four Hours." While other nations were scrambling for planes and tanks and high explosives shells along with mustard and chlorine gas—America was scrambling for horses. Still, Roosevelt now saw only an ocean between him and the last glorious charge of the Rough Riders. Even an egghead, his favorite term, like Woodrow Wilson had to see now that it was a matter of his destiny. The last charge of the Rough Rider would not and could not be denied.

CHAPTER THIRTY-ONE

House Votes for Roosevelt Division

1917

WOODROW WILSON READ THE SAME NEWSPAPERS THAT ALLOWED Teddy Roosevelt to crow from the rooftops that he was headed for France. Wilson had the papers spread over his desk while Edith worked on ciphers from the code book across the room. The papers were more balanced than TR wanted to believe. Further down, some reality crept into the articles. "Whether the necessary authority will be given Colonel Roosevelt by the Administration is problematical. The army general staff whose advice President Wilson has followed closely in the conduct of the war, is strongly opposed to such a plan, declaring volunteer units of that character no place in the great war army."[1]

Wilson then read of men rushing to sign up with the old Rough Rider and the papers criticizing Wilson for standing in the way. "Roosevelt is tremendously eager to do this job. He has a strong bent toward the military and his sentiments have been strongly enlisted on the side of the allies. Moreover, he feels that the United States is bound by all the obligations of patriotism to take a fighting part in the struggle against autocracy . . . if nobody else in this country will go to the front he will go alone."[2]

Woodrow put the paper down. It was amazing. It was as if he were a bad cold that kept coming back or an old lover who never quite went away. It was like those damn letters he had written to Mary Peck. Wilson looked over at Edith. They continued to haunt him. It had almost cost him his marriage, twice. She smoked. She was erudite. She walked down a beach and looked like a million bucks. He had come to Bermuda to get over a ministroke where he had trouble holding a pen. He had come alone and left Ellen Wilson at home.

Mary Peck had left her husband at home as well. Her husband was a rich socialite who allowed Mary to travel at will. Mary had the rapid-fire repartee that Woodrow Wilson liked in his women. They took long walks on the beach, and he speculated about running for president. Mary Peck said he should do it. No one knows if they had sex, but Woodrow Wilson did what he did with all his women . . . he began writing Mary Peck love letters.

Ellen Wilson would later write, "The only unhappiness he ever caused me was the Mary Peck affair."[3] But their marriage continued and the love letters continued to circulate. During the 1912 campaign against Teddy Roosevelt and William Howard Taft, the letters surfaced. It was a tight race even though Roosevelt had split the Republican Party. TR now had in his possession a way to knock Woodrow Wilson out of the race. Woodrow Wilson had an affair while married to his first wife. Death in 1912. TR evaluated the letters with his advisors telling him to go directly to the press.

Teddy Roosevelt shook his head. He was not going to the press. He would not use the love letters to win the election. He added that most people thought of Wilson as a druggist. He didn't want them to think he was a passionate man. Roosevelt lost and the letters disappeared until the election of 1916, when they reappeared on the horizon. Colonel House, Wilson's campaign manager and political advisor, was nervous about Edith Wilson. She was young, from the trades, a bit common, and she had ensnared the president, who planned to remarry with Ellen Wilson barely a year in the ground. Not good news for a presidential campaign.

House hatched a plan. He told the president the Mary Peck letters had surfaced and were going to be published. Wilson had already asked Edith to marry him, and she had accepted. But now—now he had to tell her about the Mary Peck affair. Wilson sent Dr. Grayson to her apartment with the bad news. Edith said she would take the weekend to think about it. She did and wrote Wilson a letter saying the past is the past. She then gave the letter to Grayson and didn't hear from the president for three days.

Finally, Grayson came to her apartment and said she must go to the White House immediately. She found the president still in his bed and she asked him if he had received her letter. He nodded but confessed he did not have the guts to open it because she might turn him down. They opened it together. Now Wilson had the equivalent of the Mary Peck letters back in his lap. Every time the letters went away, they seemed to surface somewhere else. It was the same with this damn Roosevelt division. The world now seemed to want Roosevelt's division in France.

Ambassador Arthur Balfour had come over from Britain pleading for money, troops, and Teddy Roosevelt. Balfour wanted TR's division even though he had been told by his top military advisor, Lieutenant General George Bridges, that the situation was "too serious . . . for untrained men or amateur of any sort."[4] Bridges had also telegraphed Baker to warn against any form of volunteer group from America. Marshal Joffre, though, pled for Roosevelt's division to be attached to his troops further south. He had just lost another 120,000 men in the Soissons-Reims sector and had replaced his commander in chief, General Robert Nivelle with General Henri Philippe Petain. Joffe wanted Roosevelt and his division for the men, yes, but also for morale.

On May 9, Joffe was able to put his case in front of Roosevelt at Henry Frick's mansion. The Wilson administration knew what Joffre wanted and made a point of excluding Roosevelt from a city reception for the French mission before the dinner at Frick's mansion. The rapprochement between Wilson and TR that ended with laughs in the White House had turned to two weary boxers eying each other once again. But like the missives of love that kept popping up, Roosevelt managed to see Joffre anyway and during the dinner the two men got along well. TR spoke the whole time in French and Joffre walked away from the dinner with a new word, "Bul-lee."

Roosevelt later wrote, "He did not tell me anything I did not know or suspect. . . . France does want our men. She wants them badly, more than she wants supplies."[5] Then another dinner for the French and British missions was held at the Waldorf with Roosevelt seated strategically away from Balfour and Joffre. But it didn't matter. Wilson later heard that Balfour had quietly gone out to Sagamore Hill on Sunday, May 15, for high tea. The state department was alerted by the deployment of Secret Service agents out to Sagamore Hill, but they couldn't stop the former British prime minster from seeing the man he once knew as president.

This was all happening as bold headlines broke out all over the country like the one in the *Democrat Chronicle*: "HOUSE VOTES FOR ROOSEVELT'S DIVISION."[6] To Balfour and Joffre, it would seem the road to France had been cleared if they read the article in Washington's paper, the *Evening Star*: "ROOSEVELT ARMY ORDERED BY HOUSE. Theodore Roosevelt broke up the House of Representatives today just as if he and his big stick had been there to cause ruction and turmoil. In the last final struggle to enact a military law which would allow the colonel to lead a division to American adventurers to France, the House divided itself into frenzied friends or howling opponents of the idea of a 1917 edition of Rough Riders, and despite the pleadings of the chair, the galleries could not refrain from an occasional 'whoop' at the mention of the colonel's name."[7]

But after four hours at Oyster Bay, Balfour realized there were still hills to climb. Balfour complained of Wilson's administration lacking urgency in getting relief to the Allies, and Roosevelt complained of being blocked by Wilson. The only other two men in the room were Balfour's parliamentary assistant Sir Ian Malcom and "a rookie pilot from Mineola, Private Quentin Roosevelt."[8] The Europeans were all for the Rough Rider division, and this put more pressure on Woodrow Wilson, but Secretary of War Newton Baker was still holding the line and fired off another letter to Roosevelt:

> *It does not seem to me that the considerations urged affect in any degree the soundness of the conclusions stated in my letter of the fifth. . . . Since the responsibility and decision in this matter rests upon me, you will have to regard the determination I have already indicated as final, unless changing circumstances require a restudy of the whole question. I appreciate your willingness so thoroughly to discuss this important subject and have read with interest your suggestions for organization and action. It is, of course, unpleasant to find myself at variance with you in a matter of opinion of this sort, but the earnest-*

ness with which you have pressed your views is a comforting assurance of the zeal with which you will cooperate in carrying forward unitedly, whole heartedly and effectively the operations determined upon, now that this particular phase of the question is finally disposed of.[9]

Bones for the dog. Roosevelt read the letter that meant nothing to him. Who was he fooling? It was all up to the man in the White House now and TR felt the people were with him. If Woodrow Wilson empowered the clause in the draft amendment and summoned up the 500,000 volunteers, then Roosevelt's division was a fait accompli. Teddy felt he alone could supply half that number after the applications he had received. All Wilson had to do was give him the nod and activate the volunteer divisions of the draft act.

The author of the Mary Peck letters had the weekend to ponder. Wilson was due to sign the draft bill that week and then it would be upon him to either give Roosevelt his command or not. Their dance starting back in 1912 was coming to an abrupt end. The world wanted the Rough Riders to ride again, but actions have consequences. Wilson knew this of all people. Should he give Teddy Roosevelt his wish? To die in glorious battle. Should he make him a national hero? Should he give the man who never missed an opportunity to attack him, to assail his decisions, his character, his policies, who had done everything he could to defeat him except publish the Mary Peck letters, give this man his last will and testament to go out in a brilliant charge and if he survived, give him the presidency back in 1920? He would take the weekend to think about it, much as Edith had taken the weekend to think about their future together. Actions have consequences.

Woodrow Wilson rubbed his forehead. Another throbber was coming on. His blood pressure was peaking. Why shouldn't it be? He turned and stared out the window. He felt like telling Roosevelt he should be careful what he asks for; he might just get it. Mary Peck came back one more time when he was president and met with Edith. She had fallen on hard times. Her husband had divorced her, and she was trying to raise her son. She was about to be evicted and needed help with her mortgage. Edith's impression of the young socialite who had bewitched Woodrow

Wilson was she was a faded, common woman. President Wilson quietly paid the mortgage and Mary Peck went away again.

Wilson looked at the newspaper proclaiming that Roosevelt's Rough Riders were eager to get to France, then read about the debate on the floor of the House.

> *Representative Anthony of Kansas a Rooseveltian started the merry row when he declared that 'there are thousands of Americans whose hearts are bursting with patriotism eager to serve under the one great American capable of leading such a force to France.' 'Is the general staff in favor or the idea? asked Representative Bitten of Illinois. 'I do not know what the general staff wants,' said Anthony, 'but I do know that the American people want him.' The answer was a volley of the wildest cheers. 'Does the proposed amendment name Roosevelt?' 'No,' answered Representative Anthony, 'but there is only one American capable of such leadership.' Another wild burst of cheering greeted this sally.[10]*

Wilson shook his head. He just didn't share Roosevelt's love of death. He saw nothing glorious in war, ever since he was a boy when he saw Jefferson Davis parade through Staunton, Virginia, in handcuffs at the end of the Civil War. That is why this must be the war to end all wars. He already had in mind a League of Nations that would essentially outlaw war by ensuring all nations would confront any aggressor. But Roosevelt saw only glory in death. There was no glory in death. None. There was only death. This was the essential difference. Wilson saw war as a last resort; Roosevelt saw it as a first choice, and he had heard TR was already pulling favors to get his boys into the frontlines. Wilson shook his head. To lose a child would be more than he could bear. He wondered how Roosevelt might bear it and then remembered a story from almost twenty years before when Roosevelt's son had pneumonia.

CHAPTER THIRTY-TWO

Hell

1902

PRESIDENT ROOSEVELT SHOOK HIS SON. HE WAS STILL BREATHING hard from running into the college infirmary at Groton. It was freezing out, but he was sweating like a man who had just run a marathon. There was his son Ted Junior, pale in the small bed. Roosevelt hit his knees and began to shake him. He had been unconscious most of the day. There were no antibiotics. People with pneumonia died by the thousands. The flu was oftentimes a death sentence. He was president of the United States and he could do nothing. He shook the young boy again and again, speaking his name over and over. He began to sob, his shoulders shaking, his breath gasping. He shook his son again but he could not rouse him. He was dying like his wife Alice Lee and then his mother Mittie on the same day. And before that his father, who had died suddenly from stomach cancer. And now his son, his namesake, was dying in front of him and there was nothing he could do.

The press had started a death watch: "PRESIDENT'S SON IS WORSE AND MAY DIE. . . . YOUNG TEDDY ROOSEVELT'S ILLNESS HAS REACHED THE CRITICAL STAGE AND PHYSICIANS FEAR RESULT MAY BE FATAL. PARENTS WATCHING AT BEDSIDE."[1]

Theodore Roosevelt Jr.'s classmate Hodges had died days before at Groton. Pneumonia. It was a killer. The death angel was in the room. Teddy could see her. She was above the bed—a spirit that hovered with death, and death was close as the president bowed his head and held his son's cold hand. The tracks had been cleared from New York to Boston and a special train whisked President Roosevelt to Groton in four hours and seventeen minutes. He reached the bedside of his son Theodore Roosevelt Jr., who had come down with pneumonia and had taken a turn for the worse. The black headlines that evening in the *Pittsburgh Press* told the story:

> *Theodore Roosevelt Jr., who is suffering from pneumonia, took a turn for the worse this morning. At 9:15 it was announced the disease had spread to the other lung. The temperature increased and respiration became less favorable. The pulse was a little better. Young Roosevelt is now nearing the critical stage of his disease. The youth had grown much weaker in the last 24 hours and any complications now would be highly dangerous . . . the unconscious spells began on Saturday afternoon and were the cause of Mrs. Roosevelt sending for her husband to come from Washington to Groton.*[2]

No ventilators. No respiratory therapy. Just the luck of the draw as to who would die and who would live. The special train that brought Roosevelt was now on a sideline, ready to go at a moment's notice, but TR couldn't move, staring at his son suffering from a raging pneumonia infection without antibiotics, a disease that proved fatal often where the patient's lungs filled with fluid.

The papers reported "the trip from New York to Groton was made in record time, President Roosevelt through his secretary having urged the railroad companies to get him to Groton as quickly as possible . . . the trip from New York to Boston was made in four hours and seventeen minutes."[3] Literally the president had dashed away and left papers on his desk, meetings unattended. "Business at the White House is practically at a standstill. The only callers are those who drop in to inquire for the latest from Groton and the telegraph and telephone wires are heavy with messages of inquiry and information regarding the condition of the President's son."[4]

Things took an ominous turn when Ted Junior passed out and "the physicians in attendance seem to be very anxious,"[5] the Pittsburgh paper noted. "They have noticed with no small degree of alarm symptoms almost exactly like those of young Hodges, another student at the school, who died from the disease a few days ago."

Roosevelt had left Washington and "nobody not even the President knows when he will return . . . the President certainly will not leave until the critical stage of the disease is passed." Roosevelt had broken down and the press reported that "he shook with convulsions when he failed to rouse the boy from the unconscious spell in which he had been lying. Finally Mrs. Roosevelt led the father away and he trembled all over as he realized the possibility that his boy would never arise from his sick bed."[6]

TR believed his son was dying. He had seen it with his first wife and his mother. They just passed out and never woke up. He had left the White House in the hands of his daughter, Alice Roosevelt, until he returned. The press reported that "Mrs. Alice Roosevelt is the mistress of the White House. She will have very few social duties to perform however . . . there will be no dinners or luncheons given at the White House."[7]

Roosevelt had sent for Dr. Alexander Lambert from Cornell University Medical College to come at once on the train. Beyond that, all they could do was wait. "The critical period will be reached within the next 24 hours, the attending physicians say."[8] TR stayed by his son's bedside while doctors and nurses did what they could. He would not let his son slip away. This he would not do. There were three other boys in the Groton infirmary suffering from pneumonia as well. On February 13, an article appeared in the *San Francisco Examiner*: "YOUNG ROOSEVELT IS MUCH IMPROVED.[9] If the President's Son Holds His Own for Twenty-Four Hours the Probabilities are That He Will Recover." The news had come in after a long twenty-four hours that "there is a marked improvement in the condition of Theodore Roosevelt Jr. His left lung has cleared considerably and temperature, pulse and respiration show improvement." Secretary Cortelyou gave out a statement that told "what a favorable night the patient had passed, that liquid food had been greedily taken and that if improvement continued for forty-eight hours the sick boy would be beyond the point of grave danger."[10]

Edith had personally approved the statement that "her son was much better. She spoke with cheerfulness and joy."[11] The Reverend Dr. Charles

H. Parkhurst of New York spoke to reporters as he left Groton. "The parents of the sick boy are much encouraged, indeed are quite hopeful. They have suffered great anxiety."[12] The president the next day left Groton much relieved. The railroad had a train standing by and he jumped on board and headed back to Washington. As he rode, Roosevelt looked out the window and knew one thing: there could be nothing worse than losing a child. He had lost his wife, his mother, his father, and thought he had lost his son Theodore Jr. No. There was nothing in comparison to losing a child. He had come close, and he hoped never ever to come that close again.

CHAPTER THIRTY-THREE

Rough Rider Down

MAY 18, 1918

THE WASHINGTON POST LED WITH THE HEADLINE, "PERSHING TO LEAD US FORCES TO FRANCE; WILSON TURNS DOWN ROOSEVELT'S ARMY; DRAFT REGISTRATION IS SET FOR JUNE 5TH."[1] And just like that the Rough Rider Division of Teddy Roosevelt headed for France was shut down. The subtext of the *Post* laid out the president's case against TR's independent force.

> *Col Roosevelt will not be permitted to raise his volunteer expedition to carry the American flag against the Germans to France. On staging the war army bill last night President Wilson issued a statement saying that acting under expert advice from both sides of the water, he would be unable to avail himself at the present stage of the war of the authorization to organize volunteer divisions. There was talk in army circles last night of the possibility that a way could be found to use the former President's services in another way, but official comment on the subject was lacking.*[2]

Woodrow Wilson then zeroed in on Teddy's Rough Rider fantasy with a direct statement. Secretary Baker and Wilson had realized that nothing short of a direct statement would stop the Roosevelt juggernaut.

"I shall not avail myself, at any rate at the present stage of the war, of the authorization conferred by the act to organize volunteer divisions. To do so would seriously interfere with the carrying out of the chief and most immediate important purpose contemplated by the legislation—the prompt creation and early use of an effective army—and would contribute practically nothing to the effective strength of the armies now engaged against Germany."[3]

There was no doubting the meaning of Wilson's statement. The old man playing at cowboys and Indians proposing to fight modern war of tanks, flamethrowers, high-explosive artillery shells, .50 caliber machine guns, and poison gas with the nineteenth-century cavalry tactics was not going overseas to fight anyone. TR's Rough Riders would "contribute practically nothing to the effective strength of the armies now engaged against Germany."[4] Brutal. Woodrow Wilson had left Roosevelt in the dusty past by signing the conscription bill that required ten million men between the ages of twenty-one and thirty-one to register for the draft. He was now the most powerful commander in chief in US history.

But then came another accompanying statement to the press that took direct aim at Theodore Roosevelt's Rough Rider division by name. In this, Wilson anticipated the arguments that would be made for Roosevelt going overseas as a morale booster for the allies.

I understand that the section of this act which authorizes the creation of the volunteer divisions in addition to this draft was added with a view to providing an independent command for Mr. Roosevelt and giving the military authorities an opportunity to use his fine vigor and enthusiasm in recruiting the forces of the western front. It would be very agreeable to me to pay Mr. Roosevelt this compliment and the Allies the compliment of sending to their aid of our most distinguished public men, an ex-president who has rendered many conspicuous public services and proved his gallantry in many striking ways. Politically too, it would no doubt have a very fine effect and make a profound impression. But this is not the time . . . for any action not calculated to contribute to the immediate success of the war. The business now at hand is undramatic, practical, and of scientific definiteness and precision.[5]

Woodrow Wilson was blunting the Roosevelt advance on every front. He anticipated the twists and turns of the wily Rough Rider who had managed to duck all of Secretary Baker's missives and essentially taken his case to the public. Wilson now blocked the idea of TR's advance force with brutal honesty.

*The advice is that the men most needed are men of the ages contem-
plated in the draft provisions of the present bill, not men of the age
and sort contemplated in the section which authorizes the formation of
volunteer units and that for the preliminary training of the men who
are to be drafted we shall need all our experienced officers.*[6]

After telling Roosevelt that he and his men were too old to go to
Germany as advance force, Wilson then pivoted and used TR's words
against him:

*Mr. Roosevelt told me, when I had the pleasure of seeing him a few
weeks ago, that he would wish to have associated with some of the
most effective officers of the regular army. He named many of the most
effective officers of the regular army. He named many of those whom he
would desire to have designated for the service and they were men who
cannot possibly be spared from the too small force of our officers at our
command for the much more pressing and necessary duty of training
regular troops to be put into the field in France and Belgium . . . the
first troops sent to France will be taken from the present forces of the
regular army and will be under the command of trained soldiers only.*[7]

The door to interpreting the president's meaning as anything but an
unequivocal NO to Roosevelt's plans was fast closing. But Wilson was
not finished; he twisted the knife a little more. "The issues involved are
too immense for me to take into consideration anything except the best
most effective, most immediate means of military actions. What these
means are I know from the mouths of men who have seen war as it is now
conducted, who have no illusions and to whom the whole grim matter is
a matter of business."[8]

No illusions. Those two words were the shot between the eyes for
TR. Teddy Roosevelt's heroic ideal, his very charge up San Juan Hill, was
built on illusions. Woodrow Wilson had finally slammed the door on the
nineteenth-century mode of warfare. Charging cavalry and heroics were
all well and good in the last century, but we are in a different world now
where science, mechanization, and megadeath are preeminent. The quaint

notion that one man and a group of cowboys, patriotic bluebloods, and prize fighters could turn the tide of battle in the Valley of Death horrors of trench warfare was absurd and everyone knew it. With the coldness of a professor grading an errant student's term paper, the old schoolmaster had not only given Teddy Roosevelt an F for his thesis, his reasoning, and his approach, he had then expelled him from the university. There would be no playing soldier at Woodrow Wilson's school of twentieth-century warfare. Of course the French and the British wanted Teddy Roosevelt and his Rough Riders to come over and get obliterated. It was the surest way to ensure America was in the war. But Woodrow Wilson was not in the business of sacrificing ex-presidents as tripwires.

Still, Roosevelt held his hands over his ears and like the bad student merely played hooky. *The Washington Post* reported "ROOSEVELT SILENT ON WILSON'S STAND." "Theodore Roosevelt declined tonight to comment on President Wilson's refusal of his offer to raise a volunteer army for immediate service in France. 'I have nothing to say tonight,' said the former President. 'I wired to President Wilson this afternoon offering to raise two divisions for immediate service and if he so desired, two others.'"[9]

The words of Woodrow Wilson simply bounced off the Rooseveltian skull. TR had four divisions ready to go. That was his response. Wilson must have read the front-page article in *The Washington Post* and shaken his head. The man could not take no for an answer. It was worse than that; he couldn't even acknowledge someone had said no. The student was not to be redeemed. Better to kick him out altogether. Wilson sent a follow-up telegram to Roosevelt explaining that his statement had been based on "imperative considerations of public policy and not upon personal or private choice."[10] TR wasn't buying that. James Amos was with TR when he received the telegram and said later he had never seen the president so cast down. "He was truly in a black mood."[11] Wilson, by declaring there was nothing personal in his decision, tipped his hand. To think that years of castigating acid flung from Sagamore Hill and other quarters at the president would not influence his decision to send his old antagonist into battle is naïve and Wilson was a political animal at heart who saw all downside to Teddy Roosevelt riding high again in the Hearst newspapers as he did in Cuba. And really did he want a dead ex-president on his hands?

Roosevelt would later complain to a friend, "I could have raised four divisions of the finest fighting men . . . could have put them into the fighting line at the earliest moment long before we had even begun to prepare our army here."[12] But the real blow was that he was denied the hero's death. "For Roosevelt, France offered a last chance for heroism. He wasn't exactly the suicidal type . . . and yet the romantic notion of death in battle held an irresistible appeal for him—the more so as he felt old age coming on and the prospect of increasing enfeeblement."[13]

Teddy Roosevelt would never forgive Wilson for denying him his chance to go fight in France. "I cannot overstate how bitterly I regret that the President refused my offer to raise troops," he wrote Georges Clemenceau and then he pulled out the knife once again. "Of course the fundamental trouble with Mr. Wilson is that he is merely a rhetorician, vindictive, and yet not physically brave; he cannot help believing that inasmuch as sonorous platitudes in certain crisis win votes they can in other crisis win battles."[14]

Roosevelt cautioned Clemenceau this was for his eyes only, but Wilson was flinging his own arrow as well. John M. Parker, a former Rough Rider, had been in Woodrow Wilson's company when he said that "Colonel Roosevelt is a splendid man and patriotic citizen as you say but he is not a military leader. His experience in military life has been extremely short. He and many of the men with him are too old to render efficient service and in addition to that fact, he as well as others have shown intolerance of discipline."[15] Parker later quoted the exact words back to Roosevelt.

In other words, Theodore Roosevelt was a person with whom the established army did not want to deal. He belonged to the time of the Plains Wars in America, when men on horseback made a difference, and he could charge up a hill in Cuba and proclaim battle won. TR belonged to the dusty pages of history that produced Geronimo and Buffalo Bill, and beyond that he was a man who could not follow orders and could not take no for an answer—in short, Teddy Roosevelt was a pain in the ass with whom Wilson no longer wanted to deal. And besides all that, he and his men were now historical. The frontier was closed, Geronimo now marched in parades, and Roosevelt's days as a Rough Rider belonged to the textbooks of history. The future was not his.

Still, TR hoped for a miracle from the Allies that they might pressure Wilson into sending him over. A week later, Georges Clemenceau published an open letter to Wilson putting the case forward for sending Roosevelt to France. "It is possible that your own mind, enclosed in its austere legal frontiers . . . has failed to be impressed by the vital hold which personalities like Roosevelt have on popular imagination . . . the name of Roosevelt has this legendary force in our country at this time . . . send them Roosevelt. I tell you because I know it—it will gladden their hearts."[16]

Woodrow Wilson never replied to the letter. Roosevelt later told the Harvard Club that Wilson was a "jealous rival determined to deny him the right pro patria mori. . . . I told Wilson that I would die on the field of battle, that I would never return only if he would let me go!"[17] Which of course was what Wilson feared most.

On May 21, 1917, an article in the *El Paso Morning Times* proclaimed, "VOLUNTEERS AWAIT TEDDY'S NEXT MOVE FOR TRIP TO FRANCE. PROMINENT MEN WHO HAVE ENLISTED WITH ROUGH RIDER HERE A BIT DISMAYED BUT HOPEFUL."[18] The press had carried Wilson's decision, but TR had yet to issue a statement to his defector army. Speculation was rampant. "A bit dismayed but none the less determined to keep up the fight in some manner, not yet decided upon, prominent men in all parts of the country had offered their services to the Roosevelt division of volunteers are awaiting today Mr. Roosevelt's next move in his fight for a chance to go to France."[19]

The hot air rushing out of the balloon that Roosevelt had been blowing up for years was now sputtering and the balloon was sinking fast. If Teddy was going to throw a Hail Mary, it had to be now. There was the possibility of going anyway, a mercenary force unsanctioned under the flag of the United States. This idea, though, seemed to be gaining no traction. "There is no intention of the part of Mr. Roosevelt or any of his associates of going to France to fight without the sanction of the President, though it has been declared this could be legally done."[20]

The same day the article appeared in the *El Paso Morning Times*, Roosevelt released a statement saying that while the aims of the Rough Riders were noble and would serve the national interest, "as good American citizens we loyally obey the decision of the Commander in Chief of the American army and navy."[21] The game was finally over, and for now Woodrow Wilson had checkmated the last Roosevelt move in the game of political chess. All that was left for Teddy Roosevelt now was to live through his boys heading over to France. It was all about getting his sons into the fight now. "I don't care a continental whether they fight in Yankee uniforms or British uniforms or their undershirts, so long as they're fighting."[22] On this—TR would have his wish.

Roosevelt returned to Sagamore Hill and the quiet of the house had the feeling of dejection of when he first left Washington all over again. It was almost summer in Oyster Bay, but the feel of Siberia, of leaving, was the same as 1909.

CHAPTER THIRTY-FOUR

Cold, Violence, and Iron Cruelty

1909

THE ARTIC WIND BLEW THROUGH WASHINGTON. THE SNOW PUMMELED the horses pulling the inaugural carriage to the Capitol. The inauguration was supposed to be outside, but the ice that had snapped telephone and telegraph wires and hung from trees like daggers of glass had coated the roads and sidewalks with carriages sliding sideways, horses falling, people falling, automobiles slipping off roads into ditches, and streetcars screeching to a halt on tracks coated with ice. The wet, thick snow of March blew sideways; top hats were brimmed with cotton-like snowflakes and mustaches frosted. William Howard Taft had never seen such a winter storm and the last time TR could remember such a storm was in the Badlands.

But that would not stop the succession of power as Taft and Roosevelt entered the Senate Chamber and then through a solemn swearing in with Roosevelt staring stonily on, William Howard Taft took up the mantle of power. Then Teddy bounded out of his seat and shook Taft's hand, the two men embraced, TR spoke to him with his hands still on his shoulders. "There was not a dry eye in the place," Bamie wrote, "and everyone's throat contracted as he said goodbye. Before anyone realized what was happening, he went down the steps from the speaker's desk and, bowing and smiling, went out the little side door.[1]

Theodore Roosevelt broke out into the fresh cold air. The snow had stopped, and a crowd held back by police shouted out and roared, "Goodbye Mr. President!" Roosevelt waved and then was escorted to the train station by an honor guard of a thousand Republicans. A special train was delayed two hours, but TR finally left Washington, DC, at 3:26 p.m. A picture taken from a caboose during one of Roosevelt's famous whistlestop speeches shows people of all walks of life running after the receding train car that had brought the comet of life into their world.

And keeping with his own philosophy that "black care rarely sits behind the rider whose pace is fast enough"[2] he is off to Africa on a massive safari, even for an ex-president. He rides above the cowcatcher of the train pushing into darkest Africa and it is only April. Two months before he was president; now he was stalking a lion that he has fired at with his .405 Winchester but has gone into the tall grass. TR walked slowly with his son Kermit, who has come with him on the great adventure into the heart of Africa. Teddy hears grunting ahead of him, then "right in front of me, thirty yards off, there appeared, from behind the bushes which had first screened him from my eyes, the tawny, galloping form of a big maneless lion. Crack! The Winchester spoke and as the soft nosed bullet ploughed forward through his flank the lion swerved so that I missed him with the second shot, but my third bullet went through the spine and forward into his chest. Down he came."[3]

Then an elephant nearly ends it all when Roosevelt runs out of bullets and dodges behind a tree. While he is trying to eject the shells and slam in new ones, J. R. Cunningham, one of the trained guides, fires off two shots that brings the elephant down. Now the dead elephant is gutted and flayed by the porters, gunbearers, and Ndorobo guides in the field.

Soon they were all splashed with blood from head to foot. One of the trackers took off his blanket and squatted naked inside the carcass, the better to use his knife. Each laborer rewarded himself by cutting off strips of meat for his private store, and hung them in red festoons from branches round about. There was no let-up in the work until it was stopped by darkness. Our tents were pitched in a small open glade a hundred yards from the dead elephant . . . fires were speedily kindled and the men sat around them feasting and singing. . . . I toasted slices of elephant heart on a prolonged stick before the fire and found it delicious, for I was hungry and the night was cold.[4]

Eating the heart of an elephant, killing the creatures of Africa in an orgiastic bloodbath, the ex-president is far from the world but he observes the unbridled Darwinism of life in the wild and writes, "Life is hard and cruel for all the lower creatures and for man also in what the sentimentalists call 'a state of nature.' The savage of today shows us what the fancied age of gold of our ancestors was really like. It was an age when hunger, cold, violence and iron cruelty were the ordinary accompaniments of life."[5]

Letters reach him from the other world. Henry Cabot Lodge writes that "President Taft is proving an inept executive and that Republican insurgents now pose a serious threat to the unity of the Republican Party."[6] Taft has fired the ambassador to France and Teddy writes Henry White a letter of sympathy. In it there is the restlessness no amount of killing can cure. "He said without any qualification that he intended to keep you," Roosevelt tells the ambassador. "It was of course, not a promise any more than my statement that I should not run again for President was a promise."[7]

At the end of his safari, he has killed 9 lions, 8 elephants, 6 buffalo, 13 rhino, 7 giraffes, 7 hippos, 2 ostriches, 3 pythons, 1 crocodile, 5 wildebeest, 20 zebras, 177 antelope of various species, 6 monkeys, and 32 other animals and birds.[8] His son Kermit has bagged 216 creatures.

And while he sits around the campfire where "the night was clear, stars shone brightly, and in the west the young moon hung just above the tree line of tall tree tops,"[9] Roosevelt eats the heart of the elephant on a stick, resting in the bloody flickering darkness that will one day engulf him.

CHAPTER THIRTY-FIVE

Over There

1917

AMERICA WAS SMITTEN WITH WAR. GEORGE M. COHAN PENNED A ditty, *Over There*, that went viral for its time and was the most played song in 1917. F. Scott Fitzgerald marched off to training camp in Montgomery, Alabama, where he bumped into a young southern belle, Zelda Sayre, whom he would use as a heroine over and over in his *Saturday Evening Post* short stories and novels. Young men couldn't sign up fast enough and flooded recruiting offices. Quick wartime weddings and engagements heightened by looming departures to France made young love more vital, tragic, and certainly more romantic. Quentin Roosevelt was one of those young, tragic wartime figures whom Flora Whitney had fallen hopelessly in love with.

Between flying biplanes into the clouds over Long Island with a bad back and poor eyesight, learning the tricks of aviation where a faulty rudder, a sprung connecting wire to an elevator, or a jammed aileron could mean a tail-spinning death, Quentin would hurry over to the Whitney estate at Old Westbury, near enough to Hazlehurst Field for the young couple to have evenings on wide porches in the porch swing and then to Sagamore Hill for weekends when Edith and TR had vacated the premises. TR was genuinely fond of the young beauty, as was Edith, and they looked the other way as the couple got in as much time as possible before Quentin went overseas.

"Ah Fouf," Quentin wrote from camp, using Flora's family nickname. "I don't see yet how you can love me—still I feel as though it were all a dream from the which sometime I shall wake . . . with nothing left to me but the memory of beauty and the wonder of it all."[1] The beauty and wonder of it all had pushed the couple into a secret, hurried engagement. Quentin was a year and a half younger at nineteen than the twenty-one-year-olds signing up for the draft, and in the one picture in his flight gear he looks like a boy headed for Scout Camp. He was the youngest, and like most parents Teddy and Edith held him close as the days of parenthood drew to a close; they wanted to squeeze every last bit of halcyon days from their child-raising years and with Quentin around during his training at nearby Hazelhurst field, father, mother, and son could pretend there was not a war that would tear them apart, possibly forever.

Quentin was being hurried through his training with the French calling for five thousand pilots, and it was hard to believe young men who had never sat in a plane before would be flying solo in less than a month. There were fewer than a hundred trained pilots in the United States, and Quentin was caught in the early vortex of young men pushed through quickly and then shipped to France to face experienced German pilots who had months, if not years, of experience in dogfights. Like all wars, there was the months before it actually happened and then horrific speed in which people's lives were changed forever. An article appeared in *The New York Times* citing seventy-five British planes shot down in one dogfight. The news was that it was even more dangerous to be aloft than down in the trenches.

TR had his wish. All of his sons were heading over there. Ted and Archie arrived at Sagamore Hill on June 17 and told the ex-president and Edith under secrecy dictated by the new Espionage Act that they would be shipping out in three days. Grace, Archie's wife, gave birth the same day, adding to the drama that there was a good chance the father might never see his new daughter grow up. With all this wartime pathos, Flora and Quentin revealed they were engaged. Even the staid Roosevelts could not argue with the reality of a soldier leaving who might never come back and see his fiancée again, and Edith gave the young couple her blessing.

Flora, for all the flamboyance of her red roadster and her gin-packing crowd and the cigarettes she smoked with mints at the ready for her breath-sniffing mother, her bobbed hair, galloping horseback rides under moonlight—was actually insecure around the Roosevelts. Her family was fabulously wealthy—much more so than the Roosevelts—but Quentin's father was a famous ex-president and she could never get used to the famous people who would drop by Sagamore Hill or appear at the dinner table. The same way the Roosevelts recited poetry, sang songs, went on ankle spraining hikes daunted her, she could never get used to the sheer energy the clan emanated around the nucleus of energy that was Teddy Roosevelt. Her own father, Harry Whitney, was a globetrotting man of the superwealthy who rarely saw his daughter, and her famous mother (the sculptor) had the strange distance of the artist. But here were the earthy Roosevelts and it seemed to Flora there was so much love around and she wanted to be part of that love.

And now that love was being scattered by a war that would destroy families for the next three years. On June 20, TR had his long-time wish fulfilled that his sons would get into the fight early. Ted and Archie sailed for France under orders from Pershing's headquarters that attached them to the general's staff. Kermit was in Boston enjoying the good life and was sitting for a portrait by John Singer Sergeant when he received a telegram informing him that his father had secured a position for him in Mesopotamia by pulling strings through Lord Northcliffe, New York's roving ambassador. Kermit, who would have been quite fine to sit out the war, was shipped overseas by mid-month. On July 18, a small article appeared in the papers: "QUENTIN ROOSEVELT BREAKS INTO SERVICE. Quentin Roosevelt, a son of the former president, was among forty aviators who received commissions yesterday as lieutenants in the aviation section of the army signal reserve corps . . . owing to poor eyesight he was rejected at the officers' training camp at Plattsburg [*sic*] where Theodore Jr. and Archibald received commission before joining General Pershing's troops in France."[2]

The fact that poor eyesight had been the grounds for denying Quentin a commission at Plattsburgh and now he was going to fly biplanes in France in arial combat where keen eyesight is critical, was ignored.

Quentin had graduated as a first lieutenant in the Flying Corps and then assigned to the Ninety-Fifth Aero Squadron and had orders to ship overseas as soon as possible. The young lovers now had their wartime parting looming as they tried to spend every moment together. A childhood friend, Fanny Parsons, had an eerie sick feeling when she saw Quentin come out of Christ Church with Edith and thought they would never share sacrament again. The date was set for Monday, July 23. Quentin told his mother he wanted to spend his last night on the Whitney yacht with Flora, and so on Saturday night his mother came up to his bedroom with the crickets outside the open windows and looked around the room with the trophies of a boy still on the shelves. The summer breeze touched mother and son as she tucked him in to bed one last time.

On Monday, July 23, 1917, the Roosevelts trooped down to the docks in Manhattan to see their youngest child ship out on the SS *Olympia*. It was a brutally hot day with the smell of dead fish wafting up from the water slopping between the troop ship and the dock. Flora came to the dock as well along with the Whitney family, who knew nothing of their secret engagement. The *Olympia* had been painted troopship gray and like most departures involving troops, logistics, orders, she was delayed. Quentin sat on some bales of hay holding hands with Flora and under the broiling heat his parents finally decided to give the young lovers their final moments. Flora gave Quentin a farewell letter he carried onto the troop ship to be read once the Statue of Liberty was behind him, becoming a silhouetted torch of liberty.

"Dearest . . . with every breath I draw there will be a thought of you and a wish for your safety and success and good luck. . . . All I can do now will be for you. . . . There is nothing in me that could make you care for me as much as I care for you . . . and you couldn't anyway, because its absolute worship on my part. And be careful and don't take any unnecessary risks or anything solely for bravado . . . please please dear?"[3]

One can imagine the utter feeling of loss that overwhelmed the young soldier now alone on a ship and heading into Armageddon. Strangely, the man who was denied that same passage across the ocean felt the same utter desolation as he rode back to the empty house that was now Sagamore Hill. Teddy Roosevelt now had to contemplate the lonely life in front of him he had tried so hard to avoid.

CHAPTER THIRTY-SIX

An Elderly Male Cassandra

1917

THE SUMMER LASSITUDE LAY ACROSS OYSTER BAY AND SWEPT UP IN long, hot breaths to Sagamore Hill, passing into the wide screened porches that was usually so invigorating to TR but now had the quiet of a past life. There were no longer the quick steps of Quentin coming down the stairs and chatting with Teddy and Edith on the piazza while they drank their coffee. The sons were all gone now and the silence of the warm months so pregnant before with possibility now had the tang of lives lived. A strange loneliness had crept into Roosevelt's world.

TR was not sleeping well at all. Tossing and turning from severe rheumatism, neuropathy, high blood pressure, pain from his leg, his shin, his chest, his back, all testaments to past wounds, he felt his age. In October he would be sixty. As July gave way to August, Teddy had not heard from his sons and in the middle of the night he felt the real implication of his push to get his sons into a world war. How would he tell Edith one of her sons had died, should it come to that. Then Cuban fever attacked him and at the same time his leg, which had been infected in Brazil, was inflamed once more and red streaked with a possible infection. "He sat around the house with his head and back throbbing and his thigh done up in a moistened clay poultice."[1] There was one man who had done this to him, allowing the ravages of old age to attack all at once. The man whom he now denounced as "an absolutely selfish, cold blooded, and unpatriotic rhetorician,"[2] was probably golfing, riding horses, taking the Pierce-Arrow for long drives in the country. They might have even been making love. Woodrow Wilson was a sensual man, and it is not for nothing his career was nearly derailed several times over a woman to whom he wrote two hundred love letters and nearly destroyed his marriage. They might have taken the presidential yacht for a cruise down the Potomac. It didn't matter what they were doing. Woodrow Wilson was at the seat of power, and he had just banished an old political rival for good. Teddy Roosevelt wasn't going anywhere but home and that was a ghastly place now that only the echoes of his four children remained. His four sons were not just gone; they were overseas in a war he had not been allowed to join and they would soon be in danger that he was powerless to control. His children had always been passing through or retreating from life to Sagamore Hill or returning from college like Quentin. There was always someone there along with the political aficionados, strategists, secretaries, consultants, lawyers. Now—now there was the ticking silence of time gone by. The whole world was focused on the conflagration across the ocean and the ex-president was literally on an island unto himself.

Archie's and Kermit's wives, Grace and Belle, had crossed the ocean to be with their husbands in France and Eleanor, Ted's wife, brought her daughter and son to see their grandfather or Flora Whitney would drop by to commiserate with Edith on how much she missed Quentin and talk with his father about what a great and brave man Quentin was. A letter left with TR for Flora was given over on one of these visits. Quentin had written it just before he left. "I love you dearest and always shall, far, far, more than you will ever know of believe, . . . ah sweetheart war is a cruel master to us all."[3]

But he was gone and TR had heard nothing from him even though he wrote to him on July 28, "Flora came over for dinner with mother and me. So darling and so pretty. . . . I cannot overstate how fond I have grown of her and how much I respect and admire her—so pretty and young and so good and really wise."[4] Flora would pour out her innermost feelings to Ted's wife, Eleanor, feeling it would be too much for his mother or father to hear: "If the fates can be so cruel as to take him from me, I need all the courage I can get from him and his influence now, while he is concretely mine, so that my life has to be lived for him and now not with him . . . it was hard during the last day but toward evening

I got to the point I couldn't cry. I felt as if the tears of the centuries had amassed themselves somewhere between my throat and my stomach and intended to remain there."[5]

Edith had her own inner hell. Her youngest child had gone over to a war with his bad back and poor eyesight; it was as if she had sent over a kitten that could barely walk and barely see. Flora picked up on this and told Ethel, "I am so sorry for your mother that when I am with her . . . I almost forget my own troubles."[6] The veil of secrecy over troop moments and agonizingly slow ships kept Roosevelt and Edith in suspense until August 9, when he received a letter from Major Theodore Roosevelt Jr. He had no news on Quentin or Kermit, but Ted had been appointed commander of the First Battalion, Twenty-Sixth Infantry, AEF First Division—it was the only war-ready unit that was ready to deploy to the front and brother Archie was scheduled to join soon.

TR immediately wrote back: "I had no idea that you could make a regular regiment in a line position. . . . I am busy writing and occasionally speaking. I have had several offers which are good from the financial side but my interest of course now lies entirely in the work of you four boys for my work is of no real consequence . . . what I did was in the Spanish War."[7] Roosevelt was still smarting and never missed an opportunity to refer back to his glory days. Then insult was added to injury. Secretary Baker made William Howard Taft a major general. It was really only a "certificate of identity" with no real command, but to the man sitting in the big drafty house on Sagamore Hill it was another slap in the face. The thought of Taft parading around in khaki drove the former Rough Rider crazy. Roosevelt later lampooned Taft to a friend, but the wound was still fresh: "Major General Taft! How the kaiser must have trembled when he heard the news!"[8] Finally, the Roosevelts heard news of Quentin and TR dashed off a letter on September 1:

> We were immensely pleased to get a note from Miss Emily Tuckerman saying that you and the blessed Hurrahs, were all in Paris together. I hope you saw Eleanor. Miss Given Wilson is just leaving for six months in France with the Red Cross; she is immensely pleased. The other evening she and darling Flora came over to dinner. Really, we

*are inexpressibly touched by Flora's attitude towards us; she is the
dearest girl; and the way that pretty charming pleasure-loving young
girl has risen to heights as soon as the need came is one of the finest
things I have ever seen. By George you are fortunate. I suppose you are
hard at work learning the new type of aircraft. My disappointment
at not going myself was down at the bottom chiefly reluctance to see
you four in whom my heart was wrapped, exposed to danger while
I stayed at home in do nothing ease and safety. But the feeling has
now been completely swallowed in my immense pride in all of you.
I feel that mother and all of you children have by your deed justified
my words.[9]*

Roosevelt then laid out the life in front of him with uncharacteristic
gloom: "I hope to continue earning a good salary until all of you are home
... then I intend to retire. An elderly male Cassandra has-been can do
a little, very little, toward waking the people now and then ... I make
a few speeches, I loathe making them, among other reasons because I
always fear to back up the administration too strongly lest it turn another
somersault."[10]

The house at Sagamore Hill was becoming more oppressive to the
Roosevelts. Edith imagined she heard Quentin's steps on the piazza as if
he were about to show up for dinner and Teddy found himself on long
walks staring at the autumn leaves and feeling a dark foreboding of the
approaching winter. They were snatched out of their torpor by an invitation to write for the *Kansas City Star*. Teddy needed the money and the
$25,000 a year would come in handy. Flora Whitney's father also offered
the former president $5,000 for a monthly article on whatever he felt like
for *Metropolitan* magazine. The Roosevelts left for Kansas City, where
they were treated as returning royalty.

Ten thousand citizens cheered Teddy as he rode to the newspaper
office. Roosevelt had already written several articles for the newspaper
using the *Stars'* style rules: "Use short sentences. Use short first para-
graphs. Use vigorous English."[11] A new reporter hired around the same
time Roosevelt would go on to literary fame using these simple rules on
writing: Ernest Hemingway.

Roosevelt needled Wilson whenever he stopped and spoke. In Chicago he attacked pacifists, noticed soldiers in the crowd, and wistfully said he would give anything to accompany them to war: "I greet you as comrades, you with the white faces and you with the black faces."[12] At Camp Grant, he wryly pointed out that the troops had one rifle for every three men and added that he "had seen camps on Long Island where recruits were still drilling with broomsticks."[13] Edith was concerned, though, about Roosevelt's health as they moved on to speaking engagements in Illinois, Wisconsin, and Minnesota. "He is in good spirits with his head up," she wrote to Corinne Roosevelt Robinson. "But at times the horrid futility of beating the air comes up in a great wave."[14] He admitted on more than one occasion to his audience that he felt "blackballed" by the Wilson administration. Indeed he was.

Woodrow Wilson had shot the one arrow that could bring down a man of action: stasis. Theodore Roosevelt was psychologically incapable of dealing with his demons without the balm of action. Action cured him when his wife and mother died. Action cured him when he lost the 1912 election for the Republicans. Black care could never quite catch him and now, like an old horse that had run many races and had finally been put out to pasture, the scars began to show. "He was graying fast now, his mustache almost white, his belly and buttocks massive."[15] He was still energetic in his speeches, but the force of his oration would suddenly leave as current fading from rural circuits until only a dim glow remained. And still there was no real news from Quentin. TR didn't sleep anymore; he lay awake wondering what his youngest son was doing up among the clouds.

CHAPTER THIRTY-SEVEN

Where Angels Freeze

1917

IT WAS SO UNBELIEVABLY COLD. QUENTIN ROOSEVELT FELT AS THOUGH he were inhaling ice into his lungs. The high-altitude flying in his little French Newport was brutal on his back. The cold went right through his flight suit, his goggles, helmet, and gloves and centered in his back, where knives tortured his spine. He never should have been given the approval to fly. His eyesight was appalling, and it was hard enough to see with oil blowing back from the engine and the exhaust blasting back and the clouds that seemed to go on forever. And now they were training in high-altitude flying where the air was so thin it was hard to breathe and so cold his nose froze and frost accumulated over his mouth from breathing. He had already developed a cough from the freezing cold flights that was threatening to get worse. This is when he felt most alone and saw his death clearly. He could not escape the feeling he would never see Sagamore Hill again, or more than that, he would never see Flora Whitney again.

When he had arrived in Paris, he had only stayed in the city forty-eight hours before taking a train to Issodun in central France, where a large aviation instruction center was being built. "I confess I'm sorry," he had written to Flora, "for I wanted to get started flying and have it over with, I knew my back wouldn't last very long."[1]

Quentin pulled back on the control stick and went even higher. His back had not lasted long. In fact he was in excruciating pain a lot of the time, but he told no one. It had taken a few months to get into the air, but he was shocked at the war's effect, even in Paris:

> *For it is not the Paris we used to love, the Paris of five years past. The streets are there, but the crowds are different. There are no more young men in the crowds unless in uniform. Everywhere you see women in black and there is no more cheerful shouting and laughing. Many, many of the women have a haunted look in their eyes, as if they have seen something too terrible for forgetfulness . . . there is a sobering like no other feeling I know in the sight of a boy my age helped along the street by someone who takes pity on his poor blind eyes. It all makes me feel older.*[2]

Quentin had lived the life of an American president's son with the pursuit of pleasure his chief goal, and now he knew he was in something that could well snuff out his own life. He wrote Flora that he felt it was his fate to participate in war that would change the future of the world: "The thing that it brings home the most is the fact that it has got to be fought to a decision. For if there is no decision, we will go through it all again in fifteen years. That would be about the time we settled down."[3]

Amazing prescience in someone so young but he was looking down the barrel of a gun, which had given him insight that his father was lacking. It was an existential war for national survival. It was total war. It was mechanized dehumanizing mass extinction. This was all before he had even flown. Now he was in charge of a fleet of fifty-two trucks and since he spoke French fluently, he was called upon to mediate between American officials and local officials. He had started to smoke a pipe and had made friends with a wealthy family nearby with a daughter Flora's age. Going to get some supplies from a nearby town, Nevers, he was involved in a motorcycle accident. "We were passing a truck, with him in the lead, for some unknown reason, he slowed up. I was coming up on him, so I slammed on my brake which jammed and I started on down the road skidding side and every which way . . . the next thing I remember is lying on the bank with Cord and the truck driver pouring water on me . . . a couple of deep cuts on my face, some loose teeth and some hands with not much palm left."[4]

Another motorcycle accident soon follows with a deep cut on his hip. Quentin seems to be already tempting fate. He manages to go over to a French school and fly and says of the French planes, "They are not much different from the Curtis. They are as safe as an auto, as safe really as the old Curtis."[5] In a letter written in August he was filled with a troubling foreboding: "Ah dearest, if I have to pay the price of war, yet I am happy, in that earth has no higher blessing than the knowledge of a love that fills one heart and soul."[6] This was too much for Flora, and at Roosevelt's urging she considered going over to France to marry him before he was sent into combat on the front line. In October Quentin wrote Flora, "The autumn is well here, often two weeks of dismal, chilly rain and mist and the country side [sic] is bright with its brave resistance to the frosty nights."[7] In December he is flying the French Nieuports regularly. "These fast little machines are delightful. You feel so at home in them, for there is just room in the cockpit for you and your controls . . . it's not like piloting a great lumbering Curtis, for you could do two loops in a Newport [sic] during the time it takes a Curtis to do one."[8]

But there is increasing mention of pain in his back and the freezing cold of the high-altitude flying: "It's frightfully cold now tho. Even in my teddy-bear, that's what they call those aviator suits . . . if it's freezing down below it is some cold about fifteen thousand. Aviation has considerably altered my views on religion. I don't see how the angels stand it."[9] And then a near disaster when he is taking off when some mud was thrown into his propellor and it splintered. "One of the pieces went thru the gasoline tank and before the wheels were really down on the ground again or before I even had a chance to cut the switch, the whole thing was in flames. I made a wild snatch at my safety belt, got it undone, and slid out of the plane on the doublequick time. It can't have taken more than thirty seconds and yet when I got out, my boots and pant legs were on fire."[10]

These alarming letters had Flora write Quentin and propose the idea of her going over to France immediately so they could marry. The letter that came back could have not been more funereal. The man with whom she had just parted did not have the faith he might return, much less survive. "He dreaded temporarily marrying her only to be killed a month later, or becoming one of the war's many paraplegics . . . a useless chain to which you were tied."[11] Then in a another letter he seemed to be more sanguine about his chances for survival and proposed a wedding next summer after he had completed his duty at the front and might be able to get leave.

And then he was flying, trying to cram into a few months a lifetime of experience that might allow him to survive against the battle-hardened Germans. Flora for her part wrote him often and with a sense of desperation she might never see him again: "Oh Quentin . . . I want you so desperately and the hollow blank feeling that is a living nightmare almost kills me at times."[12] The debutante whose only care was how many parties she could attend in her red roadster had disappeared and left a young woman in love with a man in danger of being obliterated by a nameless pilot over a nameless town in France. The world had flipped on its head and dragged the innocent into the conflagration. Quentin was not one of those rushing to join the Rough Riders to get in on the fun. Even though he believed in his father's credo of pursuit of the crowded hour, he would have been content to live out his life in the shadow of Sagamore Hill, having children with his wife Flora and launching into the stream of domesticity and bliss.

Now she was receiving letters stamped with censor's ink, postmarked weeks if not months before from a downcast man who saw only "endless gray vistas of war."[13] Even though he had started flying, he was pulled back into logistical duties. His engineer's nature, loving coordination, was outraged by the reshufflings and reversals that kept the Aviation Service in a state of perpetual organizational flux. At any given moment he was truck officer, groundskeeper, pilot, purchasing agent in Paris, or recalled to Issodun to fly again.

But he had received some good news. He had been notified he would be a "fighter up in the ceiling" and not used to drop bombs over the trenches. If there was any romance in flying, it was in being a fighter pilot, but that was because like the gallant knights of old, there was a high probability of death. This he did not tell Flora, or anyone for that matter. He does tell her that "two fellows in the last week have gone straight into the ground in vrilles, totally wrecking the plane, and yet neither one is seriously hurt." Then in eerie prescience he adds at the end of his letter,

"I've decided that nothing short of shooting a man or breaking a control is fatal!"[14]

And now it was time to return to the field at Issodun. They had said he would not go to the front for at least three months, but Quentin knew that timeline could be moved up any moment. He was living day to day now, a fantastic, horrible way of living that no one except maybe his father might understand. And Quentin wondered now, coming down from the freezing high altitudes and seeing Issodun field spread out below him in late golden October light, if his father would even understand this impersonal new war where people simply ceased to exist. There seemed to be no gallantry in this war, no honor, no charging up a hill by men on horseback to save the day. To Quentin, floating down from the heavens, there seemed to be only death now in this new world.

CHAPTER THIRTY-EIGHT

Jack Cooper's Health Farm

1917

TEDDY ROOSEVELT CHARGED ACROSS THE FIELD OF CABBAGES, A FAT man running ahead of other men struggling to keep up. He was running in long pants with suspenders and hard shoes. He was not running up San Juan Hill or charging the Germans. He was leading the fat brigade and he was winning. The young reporters were falling away and then the mayor of New York dropped out. That left just him to cross the finish line, and even though he thought his chest might burst he kept up his pace until he made it back to where they had started.

Roosevelt turned around hands on his knees watching the reporters in dusty jackets and black shoes trudging in. They all were smokers and that is one thing he didn't do. They were probably drinkers too; even though he had been on trial for being a drunk, he rarely took a sip. TR was twice their age and twice their weight, but he had willed himself to win even though he could easily fall down and collapse. He pushed himself up and went to shake the reporters' hands. It would make a good story he thought. It did.

Two weeks before he had been on the Reducycle. The reporters didn't go on that with him. The Reducycle was sheer hell. Roosevelt didn't think he could keep pedaling. The steam coming out of the two nozzles facing the bicycle was scaldingly hot and made it hard to breathe. The sweat was a river collecting into a lake below him. Twenty-five minutes. That was all he had to do, but it was agony. He just loved to eat. His breakfasts were prodigious. Five eggs. Two chickens. Cream on strawberries. Muffins. Bacon. Coffee by the buckets. Milk. He ate and ate and ate. And then it was time for lunch. Another meal of turkey or beef or more chicken. Peaches and cream. Biscuits. Pies. Cakes. Then it was time for dinner, but he dressed for that. His pants had been let out and let out by his tailor and still buttoning that last button was like a dike holding back a mighty river—a mighty river of fat.

After he nearly passed out in Madison Square Garden, Edith had had enough. The presidential girth had grown beyond impressive—more like monolithic. And he had high blood pressure. He ate salt with no regard to hypertension. Salt was good. Meat was good. Milk and cream were better. This was the year 1917, and eating right was not a concept that had come into popular parlance. If you were successful you ate, if you were poor you starved. Look at William Howard Taft. A very successful man and what a monster. Big capitalists were big men. TR was no exception, but it was killing him.

Teddy Roosevelt had been cutting edge when as a boy he had taken on a personal trainer and begun to build up his body. Now he was headed for a fat farm at a time when fat farms did not exist. They were not needed. Most people in America in 1917 were underfed and malnourished. The Wilson administration was finding this out as a million men lined up for service overseas and many were too unhealthy for service. Many were malnourished, many were starving. Small men whose bodies just didn't seem to grow because as children they did not get the necessary vitamins or nutrients. So for the 1 percent there might have been fat farms but for the general populace there was not an obesity problem . . . there was a starvation problem.

But TR was headed for Jack Cooper's Health Farm, outside of Stanford, Connecticut. Jack Cooper was an ex-boxer who had other famous clients looking to reduce their waistlines; Roosevelt was to be at his spa for two weeks. The press was all over it. "TR HOPES TO SEE LESS OF HIMSELF. . . . Colonel Roosevelt is reducing. The colonel is what is technically described as a patient at Jack Cooper's health farm at Stanford, Connecticut. There is absolutely nothing the matter with him, except the extent of his girth."[1]

The press seemed more concerned with saying Roosevelt was absolutely fine and just wanted to cut a few pounds. But on the same page that reported Roosevelt had gone to Jack Cooper's spa was an article: "431,800 RECRUITS NOW IN TRAINING."[2]

No reporters saw the irony that a man who had taken the extreme step of going to a health farm was just months before heading for France to head a division of Rough Riders. Roosevelt arrived on October 10 as the only patient of the health camp. He soon wrote Eleanor, "The men are professional athletes touching the underworld on one side and gilded youth and frayed gilded age on the other."[3] Cooper was an old-time skin fighter, one of those men with the handlebar mustaches with fists raised circling another man with fist raised. His staff was another retired boxer and an overweight Hungarian cook. After examining the former president, he informed him he was thirty-five pounds overweight and suffering from high blood pressure.

"What's the matter, colonel?" he asked.

"Well, I feel myself slipping a bit mentally and physically. I'm an abnormal eater and I can't see how you are going to do much good . . . but I'm told you can."[4]

Jack Cooper then told Roosevelt that he could eat as much as he liked, "providing he consented to a daily routine of long hikes, gym exercise, massage, and sessions on something called 'the Reducycle'"[5] It was Cooper's own invention, a souped-up Peloton in what was essentially a steam room that Roosevelt had to grind out twenty-five minutes, which supposedly would cut two pounds a day. Half charlatan, half consultant to the stars, Cooper charged a hefty sum to take pounds off ex-presidents, silent film stars, political heavyweights. And so Roosevelt was now on the Reducycle, breathing like an asthmatic (he was), his heart pounding like a heart patient (he was), his face cherry-red like someone who was hypertensive (he was), his left leg aching, and his joints on fire like someone who had rheumatoid arthritis (he did), squinting like a man who could barely see (he couldn't).

The reporters showed up daily, but Jack Cooper was unforthcoming on his most famous client: "He's very spry and responds quickly to treatment. But just what his schedule is I am not at liberty to say now. Next week he'll be ready to see you."[6] So Roosevelt began a series of hikes, working with weights, and sessions on the Reducycle while reading to keep himself mentally sharp. In a sense he had come full circle. As a boy he had to build himself up just to survive, now he had to take himself down to just survive. In both instances few understood the benefits of exercise. His father had spurred him on the first time and now Edith had given him his marching orders the second time.

Roosevelt plodded through the grim routine like a soldier, but he didn't believe in exercise for the health benefits. That would belong to later generations. He believed in exercise though action, and yet the action had been denied him and he could find no replacement when the whole world had gone to France. The only action, the only balm for his torment, was the total immersion into danger by charging toward the Germans at the head of a division of men. Instead, he found himself on the Reducycle, sweating like a fat man in a sauna in the sloth of old age. It was what he feared and detested the most. Slow disintegration.

The biggest revelation of the Jack Cooper sojourn was when the press found out that Roosevelt was blind in one eye. At the end of his two weeks, one paper proclaimed, "ROOSEVELT LOSES 14 POUNDS; SAYS HE'S HIS BLIND IN ONE EYE."[7] This had been carefully concealed from the public while he was president; it was the result of a boxing match with a young officer in the army when a blood vessel burst in his eye. When asked by the press how he lost weight, Roosevelt produced his daily schedule for Jack Cooper's Health Farm:

7 a.m.—Shower bath.

7:15 a.m.—Breakfast.

8:15 a.m.—Opening mail and reading newspapers for an hour and three-quarters.

10 a.m.—Four-mile walk around the lake at a fast clip, followed by gymnasium work until noon.

12, noon—Bath. Rub down. One hour rest. Reads volume of original Greek.

1:15 p.m.—Lunch.

2 p.m.—Receives callers and writes letters.

4 p.m.—Villagers and reporters arrive to see the Colonel walk a mile.

4:30 p.m.—Walk finished. Resumes work in gymnasium.

6:45 p.m.—Dinner.

8 p.m.—Parlor games and reading. Latin and Greek in the original.

9 p.m.—Two-mile walk.

10 p.m.—Good-night.[8]

Roosevelt then challenged the reporters to run with him through cabbage patches to see "how he did it." The reporters took up the challenge. "At the finish those who also ran were convinced that the Colonel was just as young as he used to be."[9] The papers reported Roosevelt was now a slim 202 with a forty-three-inch waist after he had completed his two weeks at Cooper's Health Farm. When he returned to Sagamore Hill, Edith noted he was thinner but exhausted. She wrote later in her diary, "Cooper's not a success."[10]

Teddy returned to Sagamore Hill in winter and suffered terrible reviews for the book *Foes of Our Own Household*, a polemic against those who were against war with Germany. Besides ripping the literary quality of the book, the critic singled out the "pervasive and sustained ugliness of the Colonel's personal campaign against Wilson and his love of war for war's sake . . . apparently he cannot contemplate with equanimity a future in which our children shall be deprived of the glory of battle with their peers."[11]

And now the winter had set in. Sagamore Hill was a house of fireplaces for heat and Edith and TR shut off several rooms to try to stay warm. Flora was no longer coming over. Quentin had mysteriously stopped writing to her, and she slipped into despair. Teddy and Edith faced a winter as cold and brutal as they could remember. The temperatures before Christmas dipped below zero and TR shivered. The only advantage of his extra weight had been insulation and now he didn't even have that. He brooded over the man who had kept him from his destiny in the trenches of France. The critic of his latest book was right. He did hate Woodrow Wilson. No. He loathed him.

In December TR wrote Quentin a parental letter. They had not heard from him for over a month.

> *Mother, the adamantine, has stopped writing to you because you have not written to her—or to any of us—for a long time. . . . Flora spoke to Ethel yesterday of the fact that you only wrote rarely to her. She made no complaint whatever. But she knows that some of her friends receive three or four letters a week from their lovers or husbands . . . if you wish to lose her, continue to be an infrequent correspondent. If however, you wish to keep her write her letters—interesting letters, and love letters . . . write no matter how tired you are, no matter how inconvenient it is; write if you're smashed up in a hospital; write when you are doing your most dangerous stunts . . . write enough letters to allow for half being lost.*[12]

Roosevelt took out his frustration on Wilson with the assumption that since being blocked from leading the Rough Riders he had nothing to lose. He had a deal with Flora Whitney's father to provide articles for the popular magazine *Metropolitan*. The vitriol spilled over into articles that made the editors of *Metropolitan* uncomfortable. TR declared Wilson's pledge to "make the world safe for democracy" was a "rhetorical sham" and assailed his "broomstick preparedness" that resulted in the president and the war department being unprepared to go to war. When Roosevelt attacked Wilson's peace plan, some said he should be prosecuted under the sedition act.[13]

Woodrow Wilson replied to the suggestion the justice department go after TR by saying that "the best way to treat Mr. Roosevelt is to take no notice of him. That breaks his heart and is the best punishment that can be administered." Wilson then added, "While what he says is outrageous in every particular, he does, I'm afraid, keep within the limits of the law, for he is as careful as he is unscrupulous."[14] In private, TR massacred Wilson with letters to friends, calling him "a wretched creature" and stating that "fundamentally our whole trouble in this country is due more to Wilson than any other man."[15]

TR's utter frustration at not being allowed to go to France had turned into a blind rage. He saw Woodrow Wilson's blocking of his Rough Riders as nefarious, venal, and coldly political. "He has no convictions . . . he has no convictions at all; although he has opinions and coldly malicious hatreds."[16] To Roosevelt, Wilson was nothing more than an evil master intent on his own private designs apart from the country. When people pointed out to him that he was being overly critical of the president, Roosevelt lashed out.

The gravest damage that can be done to the cause of decency in this country is to stand by Wilson in such a way as to imply that we approve or condone his utterly cynical disregard of considerations of patriotism and national efficiency and his eagerness to sacrifice anything if to do so will advance his own political interests. He has just one kind of ability; a most sinister and adroit power of appealing in his own interest to all that is foolish and base in our people. He not only appeals to base and foolish men, he appeals also to the Mr. Hyde who, even in many good and honorable men, lurks behind the Dr. Jekyll in their souls.[17]

It was Roosevelt's firm belief that he had stopped him from going to France for one reason and one reason only: "His eagerness to sacrifice anything if to do so will advance his own political interests."[18] To TR it was clear that had he survived the war he would have been a hero, and that was something Wilson could not stand. In the final analysis, Woodrow Wilson had stopped him not only from going to France, but from becoming president again. This, Teddy Roosevelt firmly believed.

And during all this there was the incessant worry over his boys. Quentin had not written for some time and Flora was beside herself, as was Edith. The 1917 Christmas had an oppressive pall that TR could not shake. He was very worried about Quentin, well aware of the high mortality rate of pilots. He lay in bed with the moon on the snow lapping up against the creaky old house moaning in the winter wind, wondering if his youngest son was still of this earth.

CHAPTER THIRTY-NINE

The Stranger Side

1917

LIEUTENANT QUENTIN ROOSEVELT BURST INTO THE OFFICE OF THE quartermaster captain. His men had been standing guard in rain and cold and issued no rubber boots because of bureaucratic red tape. Quentin wanted to know why, but the captain refused to tell him and ordered him out of his office. Lieutenant Roosevelt refused to leave until he had boots for his men. The captain stood up from behind his desk and stared at the insubordinate officer. Rain was pooling just outside the door.

"Who do you think you are? What is your name?"

"I'll tell you my name after you have honored this requisition, but not before."

The captain again told him to get out of his office. Quentin stared at him.

"If you take off your Sam Brown belt and insignia of rank I'll take off mine, and we'll see if you can put me out of the office. I'm going to have those boots for my men if I have to be court-martialed for a breach of military discipline."

Just when it seemed a punch was going to be thrown, two officers pulled the men apart. Quentin left the office and told his battalion commander what happened and his effort to get his men boots. He left and then the captain burst in, complaining and demanding Quentin be court-martialed.

"Who is the lieutenant?" the major asked.

"I don't know who he is, but I can find out."

"I know who he is. His name is Quentin Roosevelt and there is no finer gentleman nor more efficient officer in this camp and from what I know if anyone deserves a court-martial you are the man. From now on you issue rubber boots to every cadet who applies for them, army regulations be damned."[1]

Quentin had adjusted to military life, but there was a far stranger side to the young man that even Flora knew nothing of. He had a strange obsession with death. "At one time," his brother Kermit noted, "he was greatly interested in demonology and witchcraft and combed the second-hand bookstores for grimy tomes on this subject."[2] Historian Edward J. Renehan noted how Quentin "tended to churn out macabre tales of madness, desperation and suicide that he did not dare to show his parents. . . . Every hero was a tragic, thoughtful, existential intellectual, brave but doomed."[3]

In France he wrote another short story about a U-boat commander's suicide; in the final scene the commander thought, "The service pistol is a merciful thing."[4] Then a poem the commander liked: "Yes. Ah yes. Death, death and oblivion are God's greatest gifts."[5] Obviously the U-boat commander finds his present life intolerable and that death is a sweeter answer. The horrifying thought that Quentin, who projected what American Ace Eddie Rickenbacker said was "gay, hearty and absolutely square in everything he said or did"[6] was covering for a far darker world, where he saw death as his only out, puts into context his entire life. He was the son of a Rough Rider, a man who glorified courage, honor, and death. There was no room for a sensitive son who wrote short stories about U-boat commanders contemplating suicide or who had a fascination with the darker side of the world. One can only imagine the agony of daily existence in a wartime camp, learning how to fly to destroy other men. Then in December, Quentin came down with pneumonia from high-altitude flying. In a letter home he explained that he had written letters but the boat transporting them across the ocean had sunk and now he was sick. On December 28, 1917, he wrote to Flora,

I am in the hospital, the result of a mild case of pneumonia. You see, I have been trailing around here through mud and cold, and draughty, unheated barracks for the last month with a tremendous cold and cough. About three weeks ago it got pretty bad, but as I had lots of work on hand and no one else that I wanted to do it, I kept on going. About a week and a half ago it really began to hit me, and I turned into bed one night with a fever of one hundred and four . . . as soon as I am well enough I am to be sent off on a two weeks leave to recuperate.[7]

The flying had continued, and Quentin related more hair-raising reports on learning to fly the French planes:

We have had pretty good luck so far on this and tho we have had a good many pretty nasty smashes, no one has been killed yet . . . the French monitors make us do all the wild flying stunts that were considered tom fool tricks back home . . . formation flying is the prettiest, tho . . . it looks fairly easy too, but when you get up in the air trying to keep a hundred and twenty horse power kite in its position in a V formation with planes on either side of you, you begin to hold different ideas as to its easiness.[8]

Quentin went to the South of France in January to recuperate and posted a letter to Flora on the seventh speculating "that within six weeks or so things are going to be just about as hot up on the front as they have been since the Marne or Verdun."[9] Quentin then returns to his camp after recovering, but finds he is now behind in his training and unsure of himself. In describing one maneuver, he admits to almost losing control:

I had a rather hard time with my flying last week, thanks to having been sick, for I had to do my acrobatics, which is rather scary even when you are feeling thoroughly fit . . . they have one they call a glissade . . . you bank your machine up perpendicularly and then with your motor turning up at about three quarters speed, so as to keep the nose of the machine up, you slip perpendicular down toward the ground. . . . I got into it and after coming down three hundred meters, in it, got over onto my back, and, as I was all mixed up as to my whereabouts, didn't have the slightest idea of where I was or anything. I got down to within about a hundred meters of the earth before I finally did get over onto my right side again.[10]

The fact is, Quentin is not a natural flyer and with his bad back and poor eyesight he should have been kept out of the service. Another letter paints an even more alarming picture of a fragile young man just barely hanging on: "I have just finished up my acrobacy, doing it all in one day. It was rather strenuous, and I don't mind saying that I hope I don't get many more days like that. To begin with, the day before I had taken an altitude test, going up to four thousand meters and staying there for fifteen minutes. I did it all right, but thanks to having just gotten over being sick, it got to my lungs rather, and I picked up a bad cough and had a hard time breathing."[11]

Clearly even by January 27 Quentin is still suffering the effects of pneumonia and is still under the care of a doctor if not in the hospital. He finishes up sounding more like a young boy than an experienced flyer: "The doctor just happened along and as I am not supposed to stay up after 9:30 at the moment, has packed me off to bed."[12] The multitude of ailments has echoes of a young Teddy Roosevelt who overcame them with sheer will. The son would follow the father—even if it killed him.

CHAPTER FORTY

Of Hoary Age

1918

WILLIAM HOWARD TAFT WAS HAVING A BIG MEAL. HE ALWAYS HAD A big meal and he was discussing the article in the newspaper with his dinner companion. President Wilson had just unveiled his Fourteen Points for ending the war and one of the biggest points was the League of Nations. Wilson had told Edith that he could not face the mothers of all the boys who had lost their sons in the war and say it was over a land squabble. No. He must end war for all time and to this end the league, with its tripwire that ensured an attack on one was an attack on all, would keep the peace.

Taft shook his head. "I am sorry from the bottom of my heart for Colonel Roosevelt," Taft said to his dinner companion. "Here he is, the one man in the country most capable of doing things, of handling the big things in Washington, denied the opportunity . . . my heart goes out to him."[1] His dinner companion nodded. He didn't feel sorry for Teddy Roosevelt, but he loathed Woodrow Wilson. "I never expected to hate anyone in politics with the hatred I feel toward Woodrow Wilson,"[2] Henry Cabot Lodge would say later.

Lodge, the Republican leader, and President Wilson were constitutionally incapable of being in the same room. They saw the very traits in each other they despised most. Lodge was the Republican leader in the Senate, a Brahmin from Boston who graduated from Harvard and believed he was the smartest man in the room. He saw Woodrow Wilson as an arrogant Southern baboon and his new wife as a common climber;

he commented once after a presidential dinner that Edith Wilson had dirty fingernails. But more than that he hated Woodrow Wilson for what he had done to his good friend Teddy Roosevelt. He had beat him in the 1912 election and then he had taken revenge on him by denying him the right to go to the front and lead a final charge of the Rough Riders and die or triumph in a way befitting of his life. It was pure politics. Wilson did not want TR to eclipse him and Lodge, who was the apotheosis of a political animal, would take his revenge when the time was right.

But William Howard Taft need not feel sorry for Teddy Roosevelt. Not yet anyway. He had returned to Washington with his waistline still trimmed from Jack Cooper's Reducycle after having written his quota of articles for the *Metropolitan* magazine and delivered ten speeches in nine days in New York. The old action credo had kicked back in, and he met with Republican strategists in Washington in late January. Even Secretary Baker had to admit Roosevelt seemed to be back. "Roosevelt remains a virile and significant figure in American life," he wrote later.[3]

But the trip to Washington was bittersweet. They stayed with Alice and while Roosevelt enjoyed the social events, Edith could not help notice how much Washington had changed since 1909, when she had last been there: "M Street was noisy and dirty now with automobile traffic. There were uniforms everywhere and ugly wooden army buildings."[4] Many of their old friends had died off and when she stared at the White House it was a hard recognition that a different Edith reigned there now. "Mother found much sadness," Roosevelt reported to Kermit. "Our old friends are for the most part dead or else of hoary age."[5]

The cold hung on into February, when Roosevelt motored into Manhattan to work in an office set up for him in the Metropolitan Building. The temperature had plunged to seven degrees below zero and this exacerbated an abscess in his rectum that had become severely infected. The Brazilian pathogen had struck again with fever, and this had led to the abscess. A doctor had lanced the abscess the day before at Sagamore Hill, but the infection had not abated and Roosevelt was in severe pain as he lunched at the Harvard Club and dictated to his secretary, Mrs. Josephine Stricker, that afternoon. TR felt his pants filling with blood from the lanced abscess and went to the Langdon Hotel, where he kept a room.

Mrs. Stricker went with him and while she wrote down his words, she noticed Roosevelt's face had turned chalk white. She gave him some whiskey, which seemed to make him feel better, but then he stumbled over to a couch, leaving a trail of blood. Roosevelt passed out and when Dr. Walton Martin arrived he found his famous patient in a puddle of blood with a 103° temperature. He ordered him to bed with three nurses caring for him. When Edith reached the hotel, he sat up and shook his head, "What a jack I am. . . . Did you ever see such a performance?"[6]

But the infection took hold during the night with a throbbing in both ears. He was taken to Roosevelt Hospital at West Fifty-Ninth street for surgery and observation. The hospital had been named for his great-uncle and was rated one of the best hospitals in the country. Roosevelt was suffering from a long list of maladies. Malaria. Yellow fever. Infection from his leg. High blood pressure. Heart problems. Hardening of the arteries. Arthritis. A life of action was coming for its due. When he was wheeled into the operating room, Ethel Derby wrote her husband, "Father looks terribly white and seems so sick . . . I can't bear to have him suffering so."[7]

He was put under at 4:10 p.m., and it was found that Roosevelt's body was full of infection. The rectal abscess was removed but a "contributory fistula was found and had to be removed. Two more, potentially lethal abscesses were discovered in his left and right aural canals."[8] Both ears were punctured while the doctors worked quickly to avoid heavy bleeding. An hour and half later they were finished. Dr Martin told Edith and Ethel that the ex-president should have no more trouble. But the trouble began immediately.

The following morning a death watch was posted by newspapermen for Theodore Roosevelt. *The Philadelphia Inquirer* posted a front-page headline: "ROOSEVELT SERIOUS BUT SURGEONS HOPE AS HE RESTS BETTER."[9] "Spread of Inflammation in left ear to Internal passages Causes Hurried Call for Three Doctors—Mrs. Roosevelt Stays at Hospital Close By."[10] His fever took off and he vomited repeatedly as intense disorientation set in from the operation on his ears. He was permanently dizzy, and his eyes moved from side to side. He was given morphine for the pain from the three incisions and on the morning of February 8 a statement went out that TR was in serious condition after the infection had spread into both ears. "A sudden development of inflammation in the inner left ear was responsible for the hurried calling of a consultation of specialists during the day. This resulted in the issuing of a statement which in effect characterized the colonel's condition as 'serious but not critical.'"[11] By 9:00 a.m. a rumor swept the country that he had died.

The Washington Star posted a front-page headline: "ROOSEVELT'S DEATH RUMORED."[12] The paper reported that hundreds of telephone inquiries had been received after rumors of TR's death circulated through New York. The rumors "had it that Col Roosevelt had died in a New York hospital from the effects of operations to which he submitted earlier this week."[13] The rumors became so strong that the *Brooklyn Times Union* led with a front-page headline, "TR BETTER; NO DEAD MAN SAYS HOSPITAL." Roosevelt Hospital then released a statement: "Every report coming from Colonel Roosevelt's room, and they are coming every few minutes, say that he is improving. However if another abscess should form it might be a different story. At present, Colonel Roosevelt is very far from being a dead man."[14] The hospital refuted the rumor, but his surgeons were on standby as the infection spread from his ears to the base of the brain.

On February 9, the *St. Louis Star* led with the headline, "ROOSEVELT NOW FACING DANGER OF MENINGITIS."[15] "Infection in Roosevelt's left ear is reported spreading and threatening to develop into mastoiditis or meningitis. His condition would be serious, physicians said, if the case should take a turn for the worst. Twenty-four hours, they believe, will tell the tale."[16] Teddy was so covered with bandages Edith could not see his face. She and Alice spent the night at the hospital in adjoining rooms. Three special nurses were brought in to be with Roosevelt through the night. Woodrow Wilson sent Edith Roosevelt a telegram of sympathy: "May I express my warmest sympathy to you and the sincerest hope that Mr. Roosevelt's condition is improving."[17]

The infection and his temperature peaked and then both began to subside; by the end of the day Roosevelt asked for food. The hospital reported that "he has had a very satisfactory night, having slept about six hours. He will be able to take nourishment at regular intervals during the day. His temperature and pulse are normal."[18] But TR had almost died and would remain in the hospital for a month. The sepsis left but the vertigo plagued him until the middle of the month. If Roosevelt moved his head he felt nauseous and he was told that he was permanently deaf in his left ear. Edith read him the letters that came to his room in large sacks. William Howard Taft told him he suffered from the same rectal abscess and had a similar operation. Cables from King George V and Clemenceau were received as well, but none of these meant more to TR than the letter that came from Quentin. Unaware that his father was in the hospital, he complained about not being allowed to get to the front and being "called down" for insisting to be transferred forward. Roosevelt wrote back that he should remember he had been one of the first to enlist. "You stand as no other men of your generation can stand. You have won the great prize."[19] The next letter from Quentin told them a different story. It was the real reason for his lack of writing—pneumonia from high-altitude flying. Father and son were both recovering from life-threatening illnesses—but in very different circumstances.

CHAPTER FORTY-ONE

Blooding

MARCH 1918

A MONTH LATER ROOSEVELT WAS BACK AT SAGAMORE HILL. THE ICE
had cracked by the time Roosevelt returned, and with the springlike
weather Cove Neck "exuded its ancient reek of salt marsh, clam flats,
tangled rigging and seawater." Roosevelt would not be up and around for
some time. "The destruction of my left inner ear," he later wrote Quentin, "has made me lose my equilibrium . . . but in two or three months I
should be all right." Then he added, "I wish you could get darling Flora
to cross the ocean and marry you! I would escort her over."[1]

On March 13, Edith came down the stairs and found TR hanging
up from a phone call. It was the United Press. "Archibald Roosevelt of
Company B Twenty Sixth infantry had reportedly won France's Croix
de Guerre under dramatic circumstances."[2] Then a telegram arrived from
the war department stating that Archie had been "slightly wounded."[3]
Ted then cabled and said Archie had been wounded in the leg and
arm by shrapnel. He would stay in Paris until he was well enough to be
transferred; his wounding was doubly poignant as Grace had given birth
to Archibald Roosevelt Jr. But for now it was time to celebrate at Sagamore Hill for the first blooding of the Roosevelt brood. TR later wrote
Archibald of the toast: "At lunch mother ordered in some madeira, all
four of us filled the glasses, and drank them to you; then Mother, her eyes
shining, her cheeks flushed, as pretty as a picture, and as spirited as any
heroine of romance, dashed her glass on the floor, shivering it in pieces,
saying, 'That glass shall never be drunk out of again,' and the rest of us
followed suit and broke our glasses too."[4]

TR then read in the newspapers that an AEF official had made the prediction that "Quentin was a young officer worth watching . . . as game as they make them in aviation."[5] Roosevelt blared this news to reporters, adding his son Ted had almost been killed in the same battle as Archie and that Kermit had "acquitted himself bravely in Mesopotamia."[6] Roosevelt was now fully recovered and so was his appetite; the Reducycle and Jack Cooper's Health Farm became a distant gastrointestinal memory. Ethel wrote Dick Derby of one lunch: "Father had 2 plates . . . of tomatoes, 2 plates of applesauce, 1 plate of potato, grouped around . . . spare ribs of pork. I counted 18 he ate, & then he refused to let me count further!"[7] Meanwhile, the Germans had launched another offensive and the allies pleaded with Wilson to send over troops. Critics of Wilson began to see the wisdom of the Rough Riders brigade and many suggested he look to Oyster Bay for guidance. "Wilson always follows TR eventually," a guest sneered at a dinner party, attended by Secretary of the Treasury William McAdoo. "I suppose soon we will hear that he is deaf in one ear." "Many think he is already deaf in both," McAdoo replied.[8]

A medical report came through that Archie's wounds were more serious. His left arm been severely fractured with the main nerve severed, and his left kneecap was smashed by the shrapnel that was still in the bone. Amputation had been narrowly headed off by Ted's pleadings with the doctors. Edith had thrown her glass to the floor at the first blooding of the Roosevelt brood, declaring no one should drink from that glass again. She would need more glasses before the blooding was over. Many more. Quentin wrote Flora that he had just received news that a pilot he had trained with had been shot down. He mused on his death, philosophically pointing out to his fiancé, "Still—there's no better way if one has got to die. It solves things so easily, for you've nothing to worry about it, and even the people who you leave have the great comfort of knowing how you died. It's really very fine, the way he went, fighting hopelessly, against enormous odds—and then thirty seconds of horror and it's all over—for they say that on the average it's all over in that length of time, after a plane's been hit."[9]

It was a young man's way of facing the high prospect of his own death, but it was small comfort for the woman to whom he was engaged to be married. In fact, it was terrifying.

CHAPTER FORTY-TWO

The Lone Eagle

MARCH 1918

QUENTIN WAS IN A WHITE ROBE DRINKING COFFEE WHEN HE RECEIVED the letter from his brother Archie and endorsed by Ted, accusing him of slacking behind the lines. At that moment in the warm sunshine with the deep blue of the Mediterranean in front of him, a case might be made, but he had been ordered there for machine gun training. His view of the French planes had changed. The problem was that the French planes were "the most awful crocks. They have been in service for ages and have old motors and fuselages that are all warped and bent out of shape. Consequently, the French warn you when you go up, to be very careful to do no sort of acrobacy at all and even try steep dives."[1]

The training consisted of chasing parachutes and firing at them. One of the plane's wings folded up and "a Cornell boy, named Hagedorn" died. The life was not unpleasant. "I've actually got a room and a bath at a hotel, I dine with four or five officers every night and have a most delightful time."[2] There was sibling rivalry, though, and the Roosevelt code that roughly translated to putting yourself in danger as much as possible. Edith would have none of it and promptly cabled Quentin, the child most like her. She saw Ted and Archie closer to TR, cut from a coarser cloth, but Quentin had her sensitivity and "the elegance and subtle snobbery of French culture."

"AM SHOCKED BY ATTITUDE OF TED AND ARCHIE. IF YOU HAVE ERRED AT ALL IT IS IN TRYING TOO HARD

IN GETTING TO THE FRONT. YOU MUST TAKE CARE OF
YOUR HEALTH. WE ARE EXCEEDINGLY PROUD OF YOU."[3]

Quentin returned to Issodun and immediately began flying again. In
March 1918 he had a serious accident, although he downplayed it in a
letter to his parents: "I smashed it up beautifully. It was really a very neat
job, for I landed with a drift, touched one wing, and then, as there was
a high wind, did three complete summersaults ending up on my back. I
crawled out with nothing more than a couple of scratches."[4]

His father was right about American preparedness. There were
two thousand American pilots at the base who had to take turns flying
because there simply were not enough planes. "They are not going to send
any more pilots over here from the states for the present," Quentin wrote
in April 1918, "which is about the first sensible decision that they have
made as regards the Air Service. As it is they must have two thousand
pilots over here and Heaven knows it will be ages before we have enough
machines for even half that number."[5]

The upshot of this was that there was even less training time for
American pilots. Quentin described another harrowing flight to Flora
when he and another pilot went up after a storm:

> It was funny flying weather. We went through the first set of clouds
> at about three hundred meters. Then there was clear air for about a
> thousand meters with only occasional banks. . . . I had a most unpleas-
> ant time of it just at the end, for I was really scared, and it's the only
> time I have been, in the air. We were just about five miles from here,
> and I was getting ready to nose her down and come thru the clouds to
> land when for some unknown reason I began to feel faint and dizzy.
> I'm free to confess that I was scared, good and scared . . . so I nosed her
> down and went for the landing . . . I was mighty glad, tho, when on
> to good solid ground again.[6]

Even with the machine gun training and acrobatics, most pilots
would be thrown into battle and would have to learn on the job or perish.
On May 4, 1918, Quentin crashed again. He was on his way back when
"my motor blew up on me and I had to come down for a forced landing.

As luck would have it some fool people got in my way, just as I was coming in to land, and as between hitting them or crashing, I took the latter and hung myself up nicely in some trees." He was "rather battered" and broke his wrist, all part of a "general uncomfortableness."[7]

In June he was assigned to the Ninety-Fifth Aero Squadron and "took a half hour ride yesterday to get used to my plane and somewhat to the sector."[8] Quentin then went on patrol just behind the lines and was shot at "by the Archies [antiaircraft fire]. It is really exciting at first when you see the stuff bursting in great black puffs around you, but you get used to it after fifteen minutes." In July he flew through antiaircraft fire and wrote, "The best I can show for myself is a hole through my wing."[9]

Quentin then had his "crowded moment" on July 11, 1918, when he veered off from a fifteen-plane squadron and found himself trailing three enemy planes by accident. "A couple of kilometers inside the line we spotted six of them about a thousand meters below us. We circled and came back between them and dove on them. . . . I had my man just where I wanted. And after getting good and close, set my sight on him and pulled the trigger." The gun eventually jammed, and Quentin was reduced to firing one bullet at a time, but he could declare, "I've had my first real fight. I was doubtful before—for I thought I might get cold feet, or something, but you don't. You get so excited that you forget everything except getting the other fellow, and trying to dodge the tracers."[10]

Quentin decided to fly to Paris to see Archie in the hospital and almost ended up there himself. In low cloud cover he snapped a connecting rod and crashed in a pine grove. He broke his left arm and hurt his tenuous back. He wrote to Flora of a deep depression after the accident where "everything looked black." A new German offensive cut off communications between Roosevelt and his sons and his father wrote him, "I simply have no idea what you are doing . . . whether you are fighting or raging because you can't get into the fighting line."[11] Roosevelt didn't know Ted was in Flanders either, fighting against the German offensive at Saint Michel.

Quentin was busy. He was swimming in the Sauldre where Edith Normant took photos of Quentin and his friend Ham in front of their freshly painted Nieuports. They were ready to take off for the front, but their orders took them to a ferry-pilot field east of Paris in Orly. The German offensive was pushing back the allies all the way to the Marne, and it was not unreasonable to think the front might reach them. Quentin had been in Paris several times with shells falling and he felt it was a matter of time before the Germans would be marching in the streets of Paris if the Americans didn't get over there soon. In this way, his father was right.

He stopped in to see Eleanor Roosevelt, his brother's wife, in her house on the Avenue du Bois de Boulogne. German guns could be seen as pink flashes against the horizon from the east. But the worst pink flashes were his brother Ted's eyes. "I have never seen anyone look so ghastly," recalled Eleanor. "His face was scorched and inflamed and the whites of his eyes an angry red. He was thickly covered with dust and shaken by a racking cough."[12] It was reported that two hundred of his fellow soldiers had been killed around him but he refused to give up command of his battalion and received letters of commendation for his valor. Then it was reported that Kermit had been awarded the British Military Cross for bravery in Mesopotamia. Archie had taken shrapnel, Ted had been gassed, Kermit was collecting medals . . . no wonder Quentin felt he was next to prove himself worthy of the Roosevelt name. After seeing Archie, Quentin had taken a motorcycle and ridden to the front. The parting had been emotional, with a one-armed embrace. "He evidently felt that he was saying a last fond farewell to me,"[13] Archie later wrote.

Depression came flooding back with the news that there was no way Flora could get a passport to France. Her parents and his had consented to their marriage should she get over to France, but this was not to be. "It seems to me now, as though nothing could ever fill that void that the last year has left in my heart."[14] The war was going badly and French soldiers retreating were shouting at Americans going the other way, "*La guerre est finie.*" General Pershing didn't believe the war was over with a million men in France and more on the way, but to Quentin and others, the situation looked grim—if not for the war, for him personally.

Pilots had had a severe mortality rate with 80 percent dying in combat. Once a pilot reached the front in "their flaming coffins," they could only be expected to survive eleven days. Still, Quentin was a Roosevelt and Roosevelts could be expected to beat the odds. On a patrol, he started tailing what he thought were Allied planes "when the leader did a turn and I saw to my horror that they had white tails with black crosses on them." Quentin was high and behind and so he "put my sights on the end man and let go. I saw my tracers going all around him, but for some reason he never even turned, until all of a sudden his tail came up and he went down in a vrille."[15]

Quentin then turned and ran with the other planes trailing him. "I had a long chase of it for they followed me all the way back to our side of the lines."[16] Eddie Rickenbacker, his commanding officer, later recalled what happened: "Quentin fired one long burst . . . the aeroplane immediately preceding him dropped at once and within a second or two burst into flames. Quentin put down his nose and streaked it for home before the astonished Huns had time to notice what had happened. He was not even pursued."[17]

The downed German plane was confirmed, and Quentin had his first victory. It would be his last.

CHAPTER FORTY-THREE

Homefront

1918

ON THE FRONT PORCH OF SAGAMORE HILL, ROOSEVELT'S DAUGHTER Ethel is staring at TR. She would later write her husband Dick, "Just across from me is Father, rocking violently to and fro and ever so busy talking to himself. Poor lamb—he is having a horrid time, for he has much to do, and it frets him terribly, this looking ahead and feeling driven."[1] On June 7 he was beset with an attack of erysipelas, a streptococcal infection of his leg that had plagued him ever since the trolley car accident in 1902. Now he was in Chicago, headed for Omaha as a spokesman for the National Security League.

"Jack, I'm pretty sick,"[2] he confided to John Leary. He had a temperature of 104°, but Edith was with him, along with a nurse and a doctor. Still, Roosevelt kept up his schedule, giving every speech and distracting himself by reading hundreds of "ten-cent magazines." When he finally got home, there was a cable from Quentin that he and Ham had been ordered to the Front. "My joy for you and pride in you drown my anxiety," Roosevelt wrote. "Of course I don't know whether you are to go in pursuit planes—or battle planes or whatever you call them."[3] Then Roosevelt received news that Ted was to receive the Silver Star and the Croix de Guerre. The blooding was almost complete. As the infection ebbed, Roosevelt spent the rest of June on the porch at Sagamore Hill with a pile of books and listening to the birds he loved so much. "I have finished my last tour of speechmaking," he wrote Quentin, something he had said before. "From now on I shall speak . . . only just enough to put whatever power I have back of the war and to insist that we carry it through until we win such a peace as will ensure against danger from Germany for at least a generation to come."[4]

Roosevelt dined with Franny Parsons on Independence Day in Manhattan. She had a son in the army and they both talked about how the war would be won by America's might. The headwaiter brought a newspaper to the table reporting that Quentin had just made his first flight over enemy lines: "QUENTIN ROOSEVELT NOW AN AVIATOR. Nine German planes are unofficially reported to have been destroyed by American pursuit squadrons in the air fighting over the smoking battle zone of Vaux. Among the fighters engaged during the day was Quentin Roosevelt, youngest son of Colonel Theodore Roosevelt. He is flying a Newport machine."[5] TR read it quickly then set it aside, but Fanny noticed his face had darkened as if a cloud has just passed through a sunny day.

Roosevelt retreated to the deep summer of Sagamore Hill. The crickets lulled him to sleep, and the cicadas wound down the slow July tide. He rested with the slow steady breezes from Sagamore Bay reaching the front porch, where he often fell asleep with a book open on his stomach. It was the summer of 1918 in America. His last son was about to have his final crowded hour.

CHAPTER FORTY-FOUR

Angel of Death

1918

SHE WAS OUT THERE IN THE AIR OVER FRANCE. THIS ANGEL OF DEATH. And she was busy. Eleven days. That was the average life expectancy of a chase pilot in World War I. The planes were shot down. Their engines quit. They collided with other planes. Bad takeoffs. Bad landings. The Wright Brothers had flown just fifteen years before and flying any aircraft was dangerous. Being shot at in one was almost certain death. So the angel of death rode on the wings, in the cockpit, on top of the engine, sitting between the machine guns patiently waiting for these young pilots who had just touched twenty. When the inexperienced American pilots took off in their old, outdated planes, she was always sure to hitch a ride because up there in the skies over France in the twilight of the hour, there was death.

A letter to his mother in July sounded the Roosevelt gong of honor and glory: "The real thing is that I'm on the front—cheers oh cheers—and I'm very happy."[1] Already Quentin was making a name for himself. "He was so reckless," Rickenbacker later commented, "that his commanding officers had to caution him repeatedly about the senselessness of his lack of caution. His bravery was so notorious that we all knew that he would either achieve some great spectacular success or be killed in the attempt. Even the pilots in his own flight would beg him to conserve himself and wait for a fair opportunity for victory. But Quentin would merely laugh away all serious advice."[2]

A real chip off the old block. Danger was to be disdained. Full speed ahead. Charge into the maw of destruction and do what you are afraid of. These were the maxims of Teddy Roosevelt's life but not Quentin's. He was trying on a suit he had seen his whole life. But it was fitted perfectly for the man who faced down grizzly bears, Indians, Spanish Mauser bullets and came out without a scratch. Like all custom-made suits, it really only fit one person and everyone else has to make do. But Quentin was determined to wear that suit now that he was in the lion's den. What other protection did he have?

On July 10, he tasted battle in command of a squadron of Nieuports and was the lead man when he was blown off course at 5,200 meters. He flew down with the sun behind him and below appeared three Pfalz monoplanes. "Great excitement," he wrote Flora. "They had white tails with black crosses. . . . I was scared perfectly green but then I thought to myself that I was so near I might as well take a crack at one of them."[3] He let go with a blast from his machine gun and then turned for home, seeing one of the planes tumbling down.

On July 11, he was stationed in a French village not far from Reims in a white plaster house with a garden in full bloom behind. It was the type of setting one might see in a war movie, with no sign of war but the happy pilots setting off on their knight's errand. Quentin was writing Flora when he suddenly had to stop. "Oh ruin! There goes an alert and I must run or rather fly so I'll just finish this off. Goodbye dear sweetheart and a kiss from your QR."[4]

On July 14 he took off with his squadron headed for Chateau Thierry. His father had heard of his shooting down a German plane and had written Ethel: "Whatever now befalls Quentin, he has had his crowded hour, and his day of honor and triumph."[5] Quentin Roosevelt didn't think about that. He was more concerned with keeping his goggles clear from the engine oil blowing back with the exhaust. Those long, jaunty scarves were very necessary to continually wipe the motor oil off googles and keeping your hands from becoming slicked. Quentin held the stick and pulled back as his plane climbed and he felt the pressure in the seat of his pants. Flying by the seat of your pants. This had real meaning to a biplane pilot in 1918. If you ascended, then you felt the pressure in your rear. If you descended, you lifted up from the seat. It was critical in cloud cover to understand whether you were climbing or going down. One could become disorientated in seconds.

But Lieutenant Quentin Roosevelt felt the plane had its own voice and let him know what she needed. A little rough air then a touch on the elevator to climb up to smooth air. A little turbulence on the wing then a touch of the ailerons or the rudder. Born to fly. That was how he felt even though he had crash-landed multiple times and had been sent back to the hospital from high-altitude flying in winter, which gave him pneumonia.

No matter. He was looking for his "crowded hour." He had a taste when he came upon some Boche planes, let go a rip of his .50 caliber machine gun, and saw a German plane go down trailing smoke. But now he wanted the dogfight. The aerial combat that christened a pilot. He had heard lots of stories and now he wanted his own. He scanned the French countryside below. His brothers had all been christened in battle and it was his time for his blooding in battle. The Lion would approve. Then he would have his "crowded hour," return to his fiancé Flora, and marry.

Quentin stared out and saw the black crosses on the tails of no less than six German biplanes. He didn't wait for his group but broke off, soaring down from the clouds. He felt his stomach tighten as he floated up off his seat and pulled back the triggers on his machine guns. It would be just like before, a blast from his guns and the planes would fall. But now they were swarming. Quentin squeezed the triggers and now the angel of death was out there whirling in the clouds with him. It was a trap and three other Fokker triplanes descended on him.

Quentin broke off and the Germans saw his inexperience. He had given up his position quickly and now he was alone among the swarming yellowjackets swooping around him. The Americans had been thrown hastily into battle with little training. The German aviators had been fighting for years and their training was meticulous, but experience in a dogfight was the only way to really learn how to fight in the skies. The Americans were brash, brave, and foolish. They attacked boldly and were shot down just as boldly. The German flyers shook their heads at the foolish antics that allowed them to get behind and then it was a few bursts from their machine guns and the Americans fell.

But this one was not giving up. He had broken away and could have flown back toward France, but he dove further in over the German defenses over the Marne. The German officer saw him and got behind the American plane. The German officer pulled back and let go two bursts dead center on the American. The plane veered, then turned and headed straight down, tail spinning. The angel of death rode down on Quentin's wings with her hair flowing back and followed him down—down—down through the clouds, all the way down to the French countryside. But she knew the crash didn't matter now. That was just a period to the sentence. Death had come with the two bullets in Quentin Roosevelt's brain and the blood splattered back all over the fuselage as the g-force threw Quentin from the plane at impact. The angel of death floated slowly down. She had enjoyed this screaming torpedo of death unleashed.

The German officer turned his plane toward Germany with his squadron. He shook his head at the American pilot's brazen attack. He seemed possessed in his frontal attack; like a man charging up a hill in a hail of bullets on a horse. The officer looked at his .50 caliber twin machine guns. He could have turned and flown for home. He would have had a chance then, but he turned and charged. That sort of bravery might have worked in a different war, but in this one it was just death.

Chapter Forty-Five

The Boy in Him Had Died

July 16, 1918

THE SMELL OF COFFEE AND BACON. THE BREEZE SLIGHTLY REDOLENT OF marshy swamplands, juniper. The clunk of an oar on the bay. Teddy Roosevelt is dictating to his secretary, forty-year-old Mrs. Josephine Stricker, in his study with the windows open. It is midsummer. July 16. The world is taking a breather and the war overseas seems very far away. A strange rapping sounds at the front door.

Roosevelt opens the door and sees Philip Thompson, an Associated Press correspondent. He shows Roosevelt a cable from France: "WATCH SAGAMORE HILL FOR ___."[1] The message is censored, but it is ominous. TR stands in the doorway with the brilliant sunshine just beyond the porch. It is not Ted or Archie. They are both wounded. It is not Kermit, for he is not at the front. The math is brutal. The acrobat of death is the high-flyer, Quentin. The unlikely soldier who had put himself in the most hazardous job of all, a biplane pilot in World War I.

"Something has happened to one of the boys," he said in a low voice.[2]

Roosevelt stared at the suddenly incongruous summer day. Death always came this way. The very vitality of the day was now grotesque. He says nothing to Edith. Quentin might have been wounded. Missing. It was hard to know at this point. He writes a letter to Kermit, saying nothing of the AP cable, but there is a dawn, a glimmer of realization of what he had done. "It seems dreadful that I, sitting at home in ease and safety, should try to get the men I love dearest into the zone of fearful danger and hardship. . . . Mother, who has the heroic spirit if ever a woman had,

253

would not for anything in the world have you four behave otherwise than you have done, although her heartstrings are torn with terrible anxiety."[3]

Roosevelt passed the day waiting for more news, a hammering of guilt peppering his consciousness. Edith flows in the background and it must have begun to register. What he had asked of her. What he had done by taking the heroic ideal and using it as a battering ram to get his sons to the Western Front. When it was out there in the spangled patriotic sunshine it made perfect sense, but in this land of coffee, bedrooms, flower gardens, it smacked of unspeakable tragedy. A cable arrived from General Pershing: "REGRET VERY MUCH THAT YOUR SON LT QUENTIN ROOSEVELT REPORTED AS MISSING. ON JULY 14 WITH A PATROL OF TWELVE PLANES HE LEFT ON A MISSION OF PROTECTING PHOTOGRAPHIC SECTION. SEVEN ENEMY PLANES WERE SIGHTED AND ATTACKED, AFTER WHICH ENEMY PLANES RETURNED AND OUR PLANES BROKE OFF COMBAT RETURNING TO THEIR BASE. LT ROOSEVELT DID NOT RETURN. A MEMBER OF THE SQUADRON REPORTS SEEING ONE OF OUR PLANES FALL OF THE COMBAT AND INTO THE CLOUDS AND THE FRENCH REPORT AN AMERICAN PLANE WAS SEEN DESCENDING. I HOPE HE MAY HAVE LANDED SAFELY. WILL ADVISE YOU IMMEDIATELY ON RECEIPT OF FURTHER INFORMATION."[4]

Still like a little boy who does not want to tell his mother bad news, he waits. He bathes for dinner and changes into a knickerbocker suit. All niceties are observed as the long, white Victorian curtains swirl in the deep shadows of evening. It is just Edith and Roosevelt, and the house is even more quiet than usual. Edith goes to bed early while Roosevelt reads and prowls the house restlessly. He wants more information before he tells his wife that she might have lost her youngest child forever. Edith leaves her diary page blank for the sixteenth.

The next morning blooms with brilliant sunshine again. Roosevelt has slept little and sees the AP correspondent walking up the drive. They talk on the porch and Thompson tells him he has read dispatches from Europe that reported Quentin had been killed in combat. They would be in the morning papers, and though unconfirmed would tell the world Teddy Roosevelt's son had probably died in the war. TR paced up and down the porch, glancing into the shadows of the house. "But . . . Mrs. Roosevelt. How am I going to break it to her?"[5]

Roosevelt went into the house while Thompson waited outside, feeling the sea breeze from the bay. Teddy went upstairs like a man climbing Mount Olympus, his heavy tread reverberating through the house. How do you tell a mother her son is dead? He had no idea, but he had to do it. A few hours later he and Edith came downstairs. Thompson later recalled, "Her eyes were bright and her voice steady."[6] But he could see the pain and it was obvious now that she knew that her son had probably died in the skies over France. When TR walked away, Edith told Thompson that she and everyone in the household must do everything to help him. Quentin was their youngest, their closest child to their parenthood, and the searing pain of guilt and grief was nothing Roosevelt had ever felt before.

At 1:00 p.m. he issued a very Roosevelt statement: "Quentin's mother and I are very glad that he got to the front and had a chance to render some service to his country and to show the stuff there was in him before his fate befell him."[7]

But there was still a chance. There had been no official confirmation. His best friend and flying companion, "Ham," wrote a letter to Edith on July 16 describing the final patrol he and Quentin went on:

> On the morning of the fourteenth a report came in to Quentin's squadron, which was the one on duty at that time, that Boches were crossing the lines in the north eastern part of our sector. Accordingly a group of nine men, Q among them, set off to find the Huns. Just over the lines they encountered a Boche patrol of seven. The wind was blowing into their territory and the air was hazy even above the "ceiling." . . . The Boches at once started retreating and a running fight began. This soon developed into a series of individual combats . . . the combats finally ceased and the men all made their way home individually . . . no one remembers having seen Quentin after the shooting began. . . . I have talked to the men . . . and almost all seem to think that he is a prisoner and was not shot down.[8]

Roosevelt spent the rest of the day dictating and then left for Saratoga Springs to address the New York State Republican Convention. When asked if he wanted to cancel, Roosevelt refused, saying, "I must go, it is my duty."[9] He wanted to set the party on a course to humiliate Woodrow Wilson in the fall congressional elections. "Black care rarely sits close to the rider who rides fast enough."[10] This was Roosevelt's motto; this would be a tough one, but TR was not going to let this awful devastation catch him. He had cried while dictating to Mrs. Stricker, continually taking off his glasses, but he continued, and boarded a train for New York.

Herman Hagedorn, a young writer working on a biography of Roosevelt, picked him up for lunch. When he reached the Harvard Club, Albert Shaw, editor of the *American Review of Books* said to him, "Now, Colonel, you know it may not be true. . . . I would not make up my mind until I hear from General Pershing direct."

Roosevelt would have none of it.

"No, it is true. Quentin is dead."[11]

And then Roosevelt talked of other things. The elections. The Republican Party. Events from 1912. But Hagedorn could see the old burning light had dimmed behind his glasses. "The old side of him is gone," he wrote later. "The old exuberance . . . the boy in him has died."[12]

After his speech, he brushed off calls for him to be drafted as governor and later told his sister, "I have only one fight left in me . . . and I think I should reserve my strength in case I am needed in 1920."

Corinne looked at him. "Theodore, you don't really feel ill, do you?"

"No, but I am not who I was."[13]

When Roosevelt reached Sagamore Hill, hope flickered anew. A cable from his friend Ham lit the candle: "QUENTIN'S PLANE WAS SEEN TO DIVE 800 METERS, NOT IN FLAMES, SEEN TO STRIKE GROUND, COULD HAVE BEEN UNDER CONTROL AS DID NOT SPIN. CHANCE EXISTS HE IS A PRISONER."[14] A life raft for the drowning. Flora received a cable as well from Ted's wife, Eleanor, and she clung to the flotsam among the wreckage as newspapers seized on the story. Could the Roosevelt armor hold once again? Death was to be cheated one more time in a Rooseveltian haze.

The newspapers blared the news on July 17, 1918:

QUENTIN ROOSEVELT KILLED

Youngest son of Former President is Killed by Hun.

Lieutenant Roosevelt was last seen in combat on Sunday morning with two enemy airplanes about ten miles inside the German line in the Chateau Theirry sector. He started out a patrol of thirteen planes. They encountered seven Germans and were chasing them back when two of them turned on Lieutenant Roosevelt . . . then one of the machines was seen tumbling through the clouds.[15]

Still, there was hope. Maybe he had survived somehow. Then on Saturday, July 20, a lone German biplane flew over the French and American lines and dropped a package. A doughboy picked up the package and took it to his superiors. When it was opened, an identification bracelet was found inside and a long note confirming Quentin Roosevelt's death. This seesaw of rumor and reality continued until a cable arrived. The man who had stopped Theodore Roosevelt from going to France to fight and die and to put himself out there and protect his sons in the process, handed him the grim finality of death. President Woodrow Wilson sent Roosevelt a telegram that stated Quentin's death had been certified by German military authorities and broadcast by the Wolfe Press agency in Berlin. A handwritten version was passed to the Roosevelts:

On Saturday July 14th an American squadron comprising of 12 planes tried to break the German defense over the Marne. In a violent combat one American aviator stubbornly made attacks. This culminated in a duel between him and a German non Commissioned officer who after a short fight succeed at getting good aim at his brave but inexperienced opponent whose machine fell after a few shots near the village of Chamery 10 kilometers north of the Marne. His pocket case showed him to be Lieut. Quentin Roosevelt of the Aviation Section of the USA. The personal belongings of the fallen airman are being carefully kept with a view of sending them later to his relatives.[16]

Theodore Roosevelt now knew for certain that his youngest boy was dead. A casualty of the war he was denied. German soldiers had come upon the plane ten minutes after it crashed near the village Chamery in enemy territory. The plane was mangled and Quentin lay next to the plane as if laid out by some other hand. One of the soldiers checked the pilot's ID bracelet and personal effects in his pockets and was astounded. It was the son of an American president, Theodore Roosevelt. The Germans, who would have probably ransacked the corpse, stood in awe. One of the soldiers had a camera and took a picture that became world famous and would eventually be turned into a German postcard. In the picture Quentin is laid out by his plane.

TR wrote his son Kermit on Sunday, confirming the tragic news.

On Tuesday the first rumors of Quentin's death came; the final and definite announcement that he was killed and not captured came yesterday, Saturday, afternoon. Ethel and Alice had come on; and poor, darling heartbroken Flora had been spending the night here. There is not much to say. No man could have died in finer or more gallant fashion; and our pride equals our sorrow—each is limited only by the other. It is dreadful that the young should die; I hardly say to you, who know so intimately how I feel, that in hospital last winter my one constant thought was how I wished that by dying it were possible for me to save any of your from death; but after all how infinitely better death is than life purchased on unworthy terms; and you four, and Dick, being what you are—and neither your mother nor I would for anything in the world have you other than you are—it was unthinkable that you should do anything, any of you, except exactly what you have done.[17]

Some prisoners trudging by the wrecked plane the next day saw the twisted wreckage and Captain James E. McGee of the 110th infantry later wrote Roosevelt's son Ted:

In a hollow square about the open grave were assembled approximately one thousand German soldiers, standing stiffly in regular lines.

They were dressed in field gray uniforms, wore steel helmets, and carried rifles. Officers stood at attention before the ranks. Near the grave was the smashed plane and beside it was a small group of officers, one of whom was speaking to the men. I did not pass close enough to hear what he was saying. . . . At the time I did not know who was being buried, but the guards informed me later. The funeral certainly was elaborate. . . . They paid Lieutenant Roosevelt such honor not only because he was a gallant aviator, who died bravely fighting against odds, but because he was the son of Colonel Roosevelt, whom they esteemed as one of the greatest Americans.[18]

Then there was the quiet of the dead in Sagamore Hill. The wind blew though the high trees and whistled down the cold creosote-lined chimneys. Roosevelt and Edith took to rowing out in the bay on the glassy water. TR wrote to Archie that "it is hard for the women who weep—and hardest for those who weep a little."[19] They often took a swim and "as we swam she spoke of the velvet touch of the water and turning to me smiled and said, 'there is left the wind on the heath, brother!'"[20]

After the people had all left the house for the small funeral, TR walked down to the stables where the twenty-year-old pony, Algonquin, that was Archie's and Quentin's stood motionless in his stall. The rheumatic eyes, dulled by age, noticed the man approaching. In a prank years before in the White House, Quentin had taken him up the White House elevator in 1903 to cheer his ailing brother, Archie. Now there was the smell of hay. Dung. The enviable obliviousness of an animal that did not know one of his masters was now dead.

The pony was now one of the old toys that parents in later years would come across in the basement after children had grown and left. This fat rheumatic pony that Roosevelt could not bring himself to put down because it would be the finality of time past. It was the old rusted swing set in the yard still there while children have left for college. But now in the glittering sunshine and the fecund scent of hay and dung inside the stable, the world was away. Roosevelt stood patting the pony's mane, smoothing it down, his eyes blurring. It was coming now. The knee-buckling grief. The world was away, and he realized then that his son Quentin Roosevelt was dead and would never be coming back. He would never hear his footsteps on the stairs, see him walk in from the sunshine with Flora. All youth and vigor and freshness—gone—simple vanished from this world.

And the old ex-president buried his head in the mane of the pony and his knees buckled. "The iron of a Spartan father's soul gave way." Theodore Roosevelt sobbed. "Poor Quentin . . . poor Quentin."[21]

Chapter Forty-Six

Armistice

1918

LESS THAN FOUR MONTHS AFTER QUENTIN ROOSEVELT WAS KILLED over France, an armistice was signed on November 11, 1918. Edith Wilson, a woman less than four years before tooling around in her electric car and traveling the world, might have been the first person to receive the news in America that World War I had ended with the cessation of hostilities. She often deciphered top-secret cables for Wilson, and she might have been the one to reduce the cipher to letters, mouthing the words, "Armistice Signed." She had been trying to help Woodrow Wilson any way she could; he was not a well man.

The hypertension had become chronic, and the war had steadily worn down his iron constitution. Now they had to win the peace, and that meant the Fourteen Points and the League of Nations. Wilson would go to France himself on December 13 to negotiate the terms, and he would take Edith with him. Roosevelt read this out in Sagamore Hill after a bout of pain in his left leg and feet that left him unable to walk and under the care of Dr. Fuller. Rheumatism had racked his sister Bamie with pain almost her whole life, and TR dreaded the thought he might be afflicted with the same disease. The pain had come on after a tour for Liberty Loans out West, where he spent the night in Billings, Montana, talking with George Myers, an old cattleman, at his hotel. When Meyers stood to leave, Roosevelt looked up at him.

"Have you got a room, George?"

Meyers shook his head.

"Share mine with me and we'll talk about old times."[1]

Roosevelt divided the summer and fall between working on a book for Scribner's called *The Great Adventure* and giving speeches. He felt the enforced flaccidity of his situation acutely, writing Belle, "It's pretty poor business to be writing little books in these times of terrible action, but it's all I can do or at least all I am allowed to do by the people in power in Washington."[2] The speeches he gave on his Liberty Bond tour still attracted crowds, but there was nothing new now, just an echo of Teddy Roosevelt still blowing the same horn. When Quentin's personal effects had arrived at Sagamore Hill, he had to marvel at how little he knew of his youngest son. "It arrived, packed by Ham but also reflecting, in the orderliness of its contents (such as a sheaf of Flora's letters, neatly numbered and tied), Quentin's integrated personality. The mechanic in him had enjoyed fitting things together in sequences that made for power or taut structure. Even his poems were balanced, their meter meticulous, their rhyme schemes complex . . . but logical."[3]

Months later, Hamilton Coolidge would die in the skies over France. He left behind a letter reflecting on Quentin:

> *Death is certainly not a black unmentionable thing and I feel that dead people should be talked of just as though they were alive. At mess and sitting around in our quarters the boys that have been killed are spoken of all the time when any little thing reminds some one [sic] of them. To me Quentin is just away somewhere. I know we shall see each again and have a grand old "hoosh" talking over everything together. I miss him the way I miss mother or the family, for his personality or spirit are just as real and vivid as they ever were.*[4]

Archie Roosevelt had returned with a "bad case of nerves" that accounted for his skeletal frame; eating seemed to be a problem. He was to receive therapy for his left arm after two operations left his arm still paralyzed. But fall had come anyway to Sagamore Hill. "The dogwood berries are reddening, the maple leaves blush, the goldenrod and aster flaunt their beauty and log fires burn and crumble in the north room in the evenings,"[5] TR wrote to Kermit. On October 27 Roosevelt turned sixty with a small party attended by Archie and Ethel and their three children and Alice, who came in from Washington. Ethel noted later that Roosevelt became dizzy if he moved too fast and he complained about "queer feelings" in his head. While there was no ban on mentioning Quentin's name, he seemed to have passed into the Rooseveltian past along with other loved ones who had left his life.

"I can see how he constantly thinks of him," Edith wrote Kermit, "sad thoughts of what Quentin could have been counted for in the future."[6] Depressed and still grieving, Roosevelt had severe rheumatism, with a burning in his joints that was increasing to the point where he was losing all mobility. But he managed to get to Carnegie Hall to give a speech excoriating Woodrow Wilson once again for using the war as a weapon of partisan appeal.

The president had asked Edith Wilson if he should ask the people for a mandate in the upcoming congressional election so he could go to Europe knowing he had the full backing of the people to negotiate the peace. Edith, who had a sharper political nose than her husband many times, thought it was a bad idea and he would risk alienating people with what might be construed as a power grab. She was right, but Wilson went ahead anyway with his statement: "My fellow countrymen the congressional elections are at hand . . . if you have approved of my leadership and wish me to continue to be your unembarrassed spokesman in affairs at home and abroad, I earnestly beg that you express yourselves unmistakably to that effect by returning a Democratic majority to both the Senate and the House of Representatives."[7]

Wilson went on to say that a loss by his party would "certainly be interpreted on the other side of the water as repudiation of my leadership."[8] Woodrow had his eye on passage of the League of Nations. He knew that if Senator Henry Cabot Lodge were elected to the Senate Foreign Relations Committee, it would be a fight. He was a critic of the league and Wilson's hatred for him went back to Mexico where Lodge accused him of being "womanish." So Roosevelt went for the jugular in his speech, sticking it to Wilson one more time: "If the President of the United States is right in the appeal he has just made to voters, then you and I, my hearers, have no right to vote in this election or to discuss public questions while the war lasts."[9] Wilson's appeal backfired, and the Democrats lost the Senate and the House.

Roosevelt felt everything was lining up nicely for 1920, but after a speech on the day the Armistice was signed, he found he could barely walk for the pain in his legs. The next morning his shoe wouldn't fit. The doctors diagnosed "rheumatism, lumbago, sciatica, or gout." He hobbled into the blacksmith's shop on Oyster Bay, the polling station, and cast his vote in the midterms on November 5. On November 10 he read in his bed that Kaiser Wilhelm II had resigned after mass desertions and mutinies.

"If I had been the Kaiser," Roosevelt snorted, "when my generals told me that the war was lost, I would have surrounded myself with my six healthy and unharmed sons, and would have charged up the strongest part of the Allied lines in the hope that God in his infinite goodness and mercy would give me a speedy and painless death."[10]

The Rough Rider in him was still there, ready to ride at a moment's notice. Roosevelt remained bedridden, feeling steadily worse except for the news on November 5 that the Republicans had gained control of the Senate and the House of Representatives. Then he heard that Teddy Roosevelt Junior had gone AWOL from military convalescence and reassumed command of the Twenty-Sixth Infantry regiment and Kermit had reached the front as well for Pershing's final offensive.

On the day the Armistice was signed, Roosevelt was driven into Manhattan and was back in the Roosevelt Hospital. The day had been pandemonium unleashed with the news of the armistice. Roosevelt could hear the celebrations in the streets as "fire crackers, cap pistols, brass bands, air raid sirens, and even cow bells added to the cacophony. Impromptu parades joined together and marched up Fifth Avenue . . . airplanes roared overhead at dangerously low altitudes."[11]

TR lay in his bed listening to the pandemonium that seemed to make Quentin's death strangely pointless. His son should have been there participating in the revelry, not lying in the cold, dark earth of France. It should have been him, he had thought not once but a hundred times. If only he had died, then his son might have survived. There was no logic there, but fate was not logical.

Dr. John H. Richards announced Roosevelt was in the hospital for sciatica and declared, "The Colonel's general condition is excellent, his blood pressure and heart being that of a man of forty years. The Colonel was brought to Roosevelt Hospital so that he might be enabled more speedily to return to work."[12] Other bulletins were upbeat, but Edith had moved into an adjoining room and there was no date for his discharge. Hamlin Garland came to see him, an old literary friend. "He looked heavier than was natural to him and his mustache was almost white. There was something ominous in the immobility of his body,"[13] he later wrote in his diary.

Garland brought up Quentin and proposed that he and some friends buy the field he was buried in and turn it into a memorial park. Roosevelt thanked him for the thought. When Edith came in, Garland rose, but Teddy ordered him to stay. For the next three hours they talked about books and poetry and then Roosevelt veered. "I wanted to see this war put through and I wanted to beat Wilson. Wilson is beaten and the war is ended."[14] When Garland returned, he thought Roosevelt stronger, but when he shook hands detected he was much sicker than the hospital was letting on.

Roosevelt shot down the park idea, declaring that other men should be honored like Quentin, without special treatment. Then a who's who of political heavyweights came to see Roosevelt. William Howard Taft, Henry Cabot Lodge, Elihu Root, and Henry White, all wanting to discuss Wilson's League of Nations proposal. Lodge was dead set against the league and Roosevelt, while not endorsing the league, thought maybe a scaled-down version would be better. November passed to December and Roosevelt was walking, but only for short distances.

From his hospital bed he navigated entreaties by party loyalists to be the 1920 nominee for president. Roosevelt played coy, saying, "I am indifferent to the subject . . . since Quentin's death the world seems to have shut down on me." But then William Allen White told Roosevelt that Leonard Wood might be running. TR said, "Well, probably I shall have to get in this thing in June." Hiram Johnson wrote a journalist on December 14, "I tell you no secret when I say the cards are arranged for the nomination of TR . . . he has gained immeasurably in public esteem I think."[15]

But the public esteem of the world now belonged to Woodrow Wilson. He had arrived in Paris to a hysteria never seen before and was much greater than the welcome Roosevelt found there in 1910. Two million people greeted the president "as the savior of Western civilization," showering him with roses as he rode up the Champs-Élysées to the Arc de Triomphe. Woodrow Wilson was far from being beaten, as proclaimed by the man in the hospital bed. He was in Paris with his new wife Edith Wilson, and he was riding high.

The next morning Roosevelt's wrist had to be splinted against intense pain but more ominous was that he was showing signs of a pulmonary embolism that the doctors did not tell the press about. His temperature reached 104° and then fell back. Dr. Richards had wanted to send him home, but now he required round-the-clock observation. Edith stayed by his bedside, reading him Shakespeare, later lamenting privately that Roosevelt might not be able to fulfill his own plans for the first time. "Poor dear, I wish I could take the pain . . . there are so many things which he wants to do but cannot."[16]

After seven weeks, it was looking like TR might be stuck in the hospital for Christmas and could not play Santa Claus at the Cove School in Oyster Bay, a thirty-year tradition. "I am pretty low," he admitted to old friend Margaret Chandler, "but I shall get better. I cannot go without having done something to that old gray skunk in the White House."[17] Finally Roosevelt improved enough to go home for Christmas. They thought it was best to leave early on Christmas morning when few reporters would be around. His sister Corinne came to visit him on Christmas Eve, when TR told her the Republicans wanted him to run in 1920 for president but his health might prevent that.

"Well anyway, no matter what comes, I have kept the promise that I made to myself when I was twenty-one."

"What promise, Teddy?"

"I promised myself that I would work up to the hilt until I was sixty and I have done it."[18]

On Christmas morning vertigo in the elevator made him unsteady and Dr. Richards reached out to help him. Teddy flinched. "Don't do that doctor, I am not sick and it will give the wrong impression,"[19] he said, bracing himself as the door opened, and then walking in a straight line to a waiting car. He then was driven home to Sagamore Hill, where he spent Christmas with Alice, Ethel, Archie, and Grace. Roosevelt was pale and moved unsteadily but he was glad to be back home among his books, trophies, animal heads, and the old smell of burned wood that permeated the home. On the table was a great turkey, and mince pie and plum pudding and ice cream. Teddy enjoyed the hilarity of the grandchildren opening gifts and the general pandemonium of Christmas morning in the North Room with the giant Christmas tree and the torn-open wrappings of children's joy.

CHAPTER FORTY-SEVEN

Warmed Our Hands by the Fire

JANUARY 5, 1919

ROOSEVELT LAY IN THE WARMEST ROOM IN THE HOUSE, A SMALL ADJA-cent chamber to their bedroom that Ethel had been in before she married and before that had been a nursery. A coal fire glowed in the hearth. It had windows east and south, with high sunny exposure. There were no bearskin rugs or buffalo heads, but there were some carved masks on the wall along with some carved heads. A blue plush armchair, chest of drawers, and a lift-top desk with a walnut nightstand surrounded the fireplace. Edith wanted Teddy to be warm, but also she wanted to have direct access to his room.

Theodore Roosevelt lay in his bed watching the fire in his bedroom but in the morning he did get up and dress; shaving was impossible so a barber came every morning. Then a limping gait down the stairs to his study where a fire burned and he could recline on a chaise longue. He was anemic, and pain shot through his body from his toes to his fingers. His temperature rose to 103°.

One New Year's Day he could not leave his bedroom—the pain was too much. So he worked from the sofa, dictating letters and a *Kanas City Star* editorial. His editorial was on the League of Nations, which was before the Paris Peace Conference, due to open in the middle of the month. "We all of us desire such a league, only we wish to be sure that it will help and not hinder the cause of world peace and justice."[1] Then Roosevelt shut down Wilson's league with one sentence, saying that America "did not wish to send any more of their sons to die in wars provoked by obscure foreign quarrels."[2] He also put himself on record with the *Metropolitan* in coming out for a constitutional amendment awarding suffrage to women. Roosevelt went on to say it was "a misfortune" that Henry Cabot Lodge and others were "so very bitter about woman suffrage."[3]

TR was exhausted and told Edith he felt even worse than when he was in the hospital. Edith hired a full-time nurse Saturday morning, and his longtime valet, James Amos, from his White House years to assist Roosevelt for the last two days. Amos was shocked when he arrived to see how weak Roosevelt looked. He bathed the former president and then got him into some pajamas. "By George," Roosevelt said gratefully, "you never hurt me a bit."[4] Roosevelt had been in so much pain all day Saturday that Edith called the doctor. On Sunday morning when Dr. Fuller arrived, he seemed better. He stayed in his room and dictated to Edith some letters and corrected the *Metropolitan* article. "As it got dusk," she later wrote Ted, "he watched the dancing flames and spoke of the happiness of being home and made little plans for me. I think he had made up his mind he would have to suffer for some time and with his high courage has adjusted himself to bear it."[5]

At around ten o'clock Roosevelt asked her to help him sit up, saying he felt as if heart or lungs might fail. "I know it is not going to happen but it is a strange feeling." Edith gave him "a sniff of sal volatile"[6] and sent for Dr. Fuller, who came again and found his pulse steady and his breathing clear. Edith went down with the doctor and said Roosevelt was an insomniac and asked permission on Sunday night for the nurse to give the president morphine. Dr. Fuller nodded his assent and left. Edith watched the nurse administer two shots of morphine and she and the nurse turned in for the night, leaving James Amos to watch over Roosevelt. The president lay on the sofa in his bedroom watching the flames lick the sputtering oak logs. Now he was tired, and the morphine was lulling him away. He looked at his old valet. "James . . . don't you think I might go to bed now?"[7]

His valet half lifted him onto the mattress and helped him turn to his side, where he could still see the fire. There was a small yellow desk lamp that circled the room with a dim glow. Teddy Roosevelt lay staring at the licking flames. The big house was still, the moon bright and cold on Oyster Bay. Only the crackling of the fire now. Roosevelt watched the fire for a while, then looked at James sitting quietly by the bed in a chair. "James, will you please put out the light?"[8]

The small lamp was electric and threw a sepia halo into the room. The old valet switched it off. Now there was only the coal-red logs and the flickering firelight. The moon poured in the windows. James Amos sat back down with his long hands on his knees. He could dimly see Roosevelt and, more importantly, he could hear him. Teddy stared at the flames, his eyes curiously naked without the ever-present pince-nez. James watched his eyes slowly close.

Then the Rough Rider's breathing became heavy and regular. James Amos sat for the next hour listening to the creak of the wind and watching his old boss. At 12:30 Edith came in and checked on her husband. She did not kiss him for fear she might wake him and left. James moved over by the dying fire and continued to watch over Theodore Roosevelt. The room became cooler. The fire just embers, red coals from a once mighty blaze. The house creaked. Groaned. Time slowed down as Theodore Roosevelt's breathing became more rhythmic. Then he began to dream.

The Germans were facing him in the far trench. He could see the points on their helmets. Teddy turned on his white charger with the Rough Riders behind him in the French lines. Morning mist rose from the ground. He was in his old uniform with his hat brim pinned up. TR turned the horse around several times as his men all came up behind him. They were the cream of the crop. The best America had to give him, and Teddy eyed the Germans low in their trenches with the early morning fog blowing off. It was time. It was time to avenge his son and win this war. His big white horse turned around again, and Teddy faced his men. *"Goddamn them, men. Let's charge them and win this war!"*

Roosevelt turned then, lifted his saber, and shouted as his men all shouted with him. And now he galloped as fast as his horse would carry him, pounding between the shell holes of No Man's Land toward the Germans, who are in shock to see a man with a saber charging them on a large white horse. The men are behind Colonel Roosevelt; they are shouting and this is unnerving to the Germans too, as it was some sort of primordial scream that made them want to run. And now the bullets were flying from the machine guns and the Rough Riders were dropping all around Roosevelt, but he was not stopping. He could see the Huns, the Germans who had killed his son, and he would have vengeance now. He shouted again. "Come on men! Goddamn them anyway!" Teddy had his saber high and was standing up in his saddle when the .50 caliber bullets ripped through his chest and he fell back from his horse to the ground below, with his heart silent and his eyes still. He stared up at the sky as the willowy angel of death came for him and then mercifully lifted him away.

It was the last charge of the Rough Rider.

Theodore Roosevelt died at 4:00 a.m. on January 6, 1919.

CHAPTER FORTY-EIGHT

The Old Lion Is Dead

1919

THE CABLE WENT OUT FROM ARCHIE ROOSEVELT TO TED AND KERMIT in Europe on January 6, 1919. It was five simple words that summed up Theodore Roosevelt's death: "THE OLD LION IS DEAD."[1] Biplanes droned over Sagamore Hill with the wind from the propellors shaking the trees. The Air Corps was maintaining an around-the-clock vigil over the dead president's home. Papers thumped onto sidewalks and porches and were left in diners and hotels—all proclaiming the same incredible news: "ROOSEVELT DEAD."[2] It simply wasn't believable. Edith Roosevelt handled it all, the logistics, the telegrams letting the family and the world know that Theodore Roosevelt had left the earth. Edith then had the more immediate concerns, from James Amos crying in the library with his long brown hands over his face, sobbing, "gone . . . gone,"[3] to Charlie Lee, the coachman, and others who had walked from the railroad stations, like George Syran, a New York porter who sent coffee to Roosevelt's room in the hospital every morning.

Edith faced them and told George, "He's gone now, so you must take good care of me."[4] In a later letter describing the visit, the old porter wrote, "She had a crying smile on her, I'm sorry I haven't the power to describe that divine face . . . her heart was torn out by the roots."[5] The country was in shock. Most people did not know Theodore Roosevelt was ill; if they did they were assured that the Rough Rider who charged up San Juan Hill was fine. The doctors and TR's family were well practiced at the art of deception. So when people woke on Monday morning on

January 6, 1919, and opened their papers, they were stunned to see that this most vigorous of men had succumbed to disease and the ravages of old age like any other mortal. But he never did seem like a mortal, and so the press stepped up. The *Winnipeg Evening Tribune* in Canada summed up the shock most people felt. In bold 30-point type across the top of the page over the masthead, the paper announced the news:

COL ROOSEVELT DIES SUDDENLY AT OYSTER BAY
Found Dead in his Bed.[6]

The paper, like so many others, stated, "The colonel suffered a severe attack of rheumatism and sciatica on New Year's Day, but none believed his illness would be fatal."[7] Of course it wouldn't be fatal. The *Morning Star* on January 7 led with the headline, "COL. THEODORE ROOSEVELT DIES AT HIS HOME AT OYSTER BAY; FUNERAL TOMORROW AFTERNOON. Put Out the Light Please His Last Words."[8] The paper speculated that "the death of Colonel Roosevelt is believed by the physicians to have been hastened by grief over Quentin's death."

Roosevelt's silver-handled coffin was placed in front of the fireplace in the North Room. His daughter Ethel looked upon her father one last time. "He looked as if he were asleep—and weary."[9] The coffin was set upon one of his lion skins and then blanketed with the Stars and Stripes and a pair of Rough Rider flags crossed on the foot. Theodore Roosevelt was buried on top of a hill in Young's Cemetery, which required his pallbearers to climb up the hill in slippery snow with the coffin held high at a forty-five-degree angle. Everyone, including William Howard Taft, was huffing and puffing all the way up the hill and had to rest at the summit. Theodore Roosevelt would have had it no other way.

From the top of the hill was a view of the bay, half-covered with snow. Woodsmoke whiffed in the hard sunshine that came through the bare trees. Red cheeks and watery eyes with hands crossed against the cold. "Taps" was blown with the sibilant notes lingering in the cold air, then fading to just the wind in the trees. The flag was folded from the coffin and then the coffin lowered into the ground with the rectangle of silver:

THEODORE ROOSEVELT
OCTOBER 27 1858–JANUARY 6 1919

Everyone left except for William Howard Taft, who remained, staring at the grave, weeping for his old friend.

President Wilson was in Paris negotiating the Treaty of Versailles to end World War I. He put out an official statement, but Vice President Marshall summed up the essence of Roosevelt's life: "Death had to take him when he was sleeping, for if Roosevelt had been awake, there would have been a fight."[10] Newspapers tried and failed to sum up Theodore Roosevelt's life. The *New York Evening Post* tried anyway: "Something like a superman in the political sphere has passed away. He saw the nation steadily and he saw it as a whole . . . he boldly thrust out his hand and captured the hearts and sufferings of a whole race."[11] It took writers to sum up the life another writer. "He was the most encouraging person that ever breathed," Edna Ferber declared.[12] Will H. Hay told a reporter, "The strongest character in the world has died. . . . I have never known a person so vital."[13]

When Woodrow Wilson returned with his League of Nations in hand, he met Henry Cabot Lodge, who had given a moving speech to a joint memorial session of Congress, ending with, "So he passed over and all the trumpets sounded for him on the other side."[14] Lodge fell back, sobbing for the loss of his good friend. But he was not done with Woodrow Wilson, whom he never forgave for beating Roosevelt in the 1912 election and then denying him his chance to go to France and end his life in triumph or glorious defeat.

Henry Cabot Lodge made it his mission to destroy the League of Nations, and this sent Wilson on a whistlestop tour to take the issue to the people, which ended when he had a stroke outside Pueblo, Colorado, in October 1919. A final, more serious stroke occurred two days later and in something that TR could never have imagined in a hundred years, Edith Wilson took over as president.

The League of Nations came up for a vote twice in the Senate, and both times Henry Cabot Lodge defeated it, essentially handing Wilson the biggest defeat of his presidency. Wilson would die in 1924 unsure of his legacy, which he had pinned to an organization that would bring world peace. In the back-and-forth that encapsulated the relationship of Teddy Roosevelt and Woodrow Wilson, one could make the case that Wilson thought he had beaten Teddy Roosevelt forever by denying him his final moment of glory in France, but victory belongs to he who laughs last.

Henry Cabot Lodge's slaying of Wilson's dream of a League of Nations was the final arrow in Wilson's back. Destroyed by a devastating stroke, defeated by his nemesis, Wilson died a broken man. In a sense, Woodrow Wilson stopped Teddy Roosevelt from going to France, but not the last charge of the Rough Rider. And yet, to sum up any life is difficult, but Theodore Roosevelt's life never more so, with his twists and turns and complete transformations. Maybe a summary of the last days of Teddy Roosevelt—or all his days—is best put by a schoolchild, Thomas Maher, a boy given the assignment at Cove School in Oyster Bay to write a tribute about the late president on June 16, 1922. In one sentence he nailed the life of Theodore Roosevelt for all time.

"He was a fulfiller of good intentions."[15]

CHAPTER FORTY-NINE

The Last Charge of the Rough Rider

IN THE END, TEDDY ROOSEVELT WAS THE LAST ROUGH RIDER. HE WAS the last of a certain type of American born in the nineteenth century when Indians still prowled the West but ending in the twentieth century after industrialization, mechanized war, and national markets had changed America forever. Some would say it is impossible that a man should propose that cavalry would charge Germans with tanks, machine guns, and mustard gas at their disposal. But Teddy Roosevelt said he was going to do it and, amazingly, he came very close to pulling it off. His proposal to lead a division of Rough Riders against the Germans had passed the Senate and the House and had landed on President Woodrow Wilson's desk. With a stroke of the pen Wilson could have sent TR into battle for one last heroic charge that would have been immediately cut down by Germans with machine guns and high-explosive shells. It would have been a bloodbath, but of course everything on the Western Front was a bloodbath.

By 1917, Teddy Roosevelt had lived ten lives and he knew those lives were coming for their due. Roosevelt was not a man who cared to grow old and fall apart gracefully. It was not in his DNA. He would go out the way he came in and lived his life, charging straight ahead. And what better way to go out than facing down the Germans. Roosevelt was the last man of action where action could change destiny. The picture of Roosevelt with his men on San Juan Hill said it all. Here was a group of cowboys who had turned the tide of a war. This would never happen again. The world had spiraled too much beyond that world of personal initiative changing the tides of large battles. There was still plenty of heroism to go around, but overcoming the Germans with American bravery on such a small scale had become a quaint idea.

Why Woodrow Wilson did not let Roosevelt have his last "crowded hour" is a complicated question. He could have very easily authorized the volunteer units and let Roosevelt go over to France with his men. The Allies were all for it. But Woodrow Wilson saw the battlefield as no place for volunteer militias. It was a war of mass killing on a scale not known before and to have an ailing old man go over on a horse and get shot down, an ex-president no less, made no sense to Woodrow Wilson. And there was that political animal that did not want to give the man who had charged up an unknown hill in Cuba and parlayed it into the presidency another chance to do the same if somehow he should survive. Roosevelt might be the man who could survive such a charge, although it is doubtful. Still one cannot discount the political animal and the human being that was Woodrow Wilson. Theodore Roosevelt had been attacking Wilson for years and Wilson did not want to give his nemesis a final shot at glory for all time.

F. Scott Fitzgerald once said there could never be a good biography of a writer because he is too many people. This could be said of Teddy Roosevelt. Explorer. Author. Politician. Naturalist. President. Speaker. We are talking about a man who read Tolstoy in the Badlands in the dead of winter while going down the Little Missouri River in a boat after some outlaws that he was determined to bring to justice. That kind of fire burns very brightly. And Roosevelt was a Roman candle of sorts and when that fire began to dim it was fitting that it should not just sputter and then go out but blaze up one more time before going out altogether. After the death of his son Quentin, TR was but a shadow of himself. His son had taken all glory away from death. There was none. He had simply lost his youngest son and that pain was unbearable.

Still, action cures all. And Teddy was aiming for the 1920 election and a run for president with his party behind him, but even he knew that he would never make it that far. The irony, of course, is that six months after Woodrow Wilson turned him down to lead a division of Rough Riders, he was at death's door. Of course he was ailing. Of course he didn't have much time. This is exactly why he wanted to go to France and fight the Germans and die in battle. He saw what his life would be. His official cause of death would be listed as "embolism of the lung, with multiple arthritis as a contributing factor."[1] They also said a blood clot might have gone to the brain. They didn't know that Roosevelt might have had had rheumatic heart disease as a child that can recur in winter. The Amazon, the bullet from John Shrank, the trolley accident, multiple broken bones, severe grief, chronic asthma, a diet to stunt a bull. A more modern review of his medical history would have been "the cause of death was a myocardial infarction, secondary to chronic atherosclerosis with possible acute coronary occlusion."[2]

Or put this way, Theodore Roosevelt died in his sleep. James Amos had noticed his breathing was irregular, then it became intermittent, and then James had to lean very close to hear any breathing at all. At 4:00 a.m. Edith woke and saw the nurse standing over her bed. By the time she reached Teddy, he was gone. And one can hope that in his last dream he finally got what he wanted—to lead the Rough Riders one last time in a charge that would make the world right again. It was what Woodrow Wilson probably should have given him. And that would be his final moment.

So now Teddy Roosevelt is standing in the morning sun at the head of his men. The cavalry is lined up behind him. He turns around on his great white horse, twice inspecting the men staring toward the German lines. He faces forward, then looking back at the men who would follow him anywhere one more time, he lifts his arm, points the way with his gleaming saber extended, and shouts, "Goddamn 'em men . . . *let's charge them!*"

Endnotes

Foreword

1. Edwin C. Hargrove Jr., "The Tragic Hero in Politics: Theodore Roosevelt, David Lloyd George, and Fiorello La Guardia" (PhD diss., Yale University, 1963), 348.
2. Una Stannard, *A Few Kind Words About Hate* (Ashland, OR: Germain Books, 1968), 134.
3. Michael Canfield, *Theodore Roosevelt in the Field* (Chicago: University of Chicago Press, 2015), 463.
4. *New York Tribune*, April 15, 1917.
5. Ibid.
6. Ibid.

Prologue

1. American Heritage, Part 4 (Nashville: American Association for State and Local History, 1955), 25.

Chapter One

1. Roosevelt, *The Works of Theodore Roosevelt* (New York: PF Collier, 1899), 69.
2. Richard Davis, *The Cuban and Puerto Rican Campaigns* (New York: Charles Scribner's Sons, 1898), 108.
3. Edmund Morris, *The Rise of Theodore Roosevelt* (New York: Random House, 2010), 665.
4. Ibid., 667.
5. Clay Risen, *The Crowded Hour: Theodore Roosevelt, the Rough Riders, and the Dawn of the American Century* (New York: Scribner, 2020), 149.
6. Nathan Miller, *Theodore Roosevelt: A Life* (New York, Quill, 1992), 292.
7. *Brooklyn Times Union*, May 6, 1898.
8. *Kansas City Star*, 1917.
9. Ibid.
10. Ibid.
11. Morris, *Rise of Theodore Roosevelt*, 641.
12. Ibid., 669.
13. H. W. Crocker III, *Don't Tread on Me: A 400-Year History of America at War, from Indian Fighting to Terrorist Hunting* (New York: Crown, 2006), 240.
14. Richard E. Killblane, *They Were the Rough Riders: Inside Theodore Roosevelt's Famed Cavalry Regiment* (Jefferson, NC: McFarland, 2022), 126.

15. Morris, *Rise of Theodore Roosevelt*, 674.
16. Ibid.
17. Ibid., 661.
18. Ibid., 675.
19. Ibid., 676.
20. US Congress, "Awarding of the Medal of Honor to Theodore Roosevelt," 1998, 79.

Chapter Two

1. Roger L. Di Silvestro, *Theodore Roosevelt in the Badlands: A Young Politician's Quest for Recovery in the American West* (New York: Bloomsbury, 2012), 16.
2. Edward P. Kohn, *A Most Glorious Ride: The Diaries of Theodore Roosevelt, 1877–1886* (Albany: State University of New York Press, 2015), 86.
3. Edmund Morris, *The Rise of Theodore Roosevelt* (New York: Random House, 2010), 100.
4. Michael Schuman, *Theodore Roosevelt* (New York: Enslow, 1997), 26.
5. Morris, *Rise of Theodore Roosevelt*, 102.
6. Ibid., 107.
7. Ibid.
8. Kohn, *Most Glorious Ride*, 145.
9. Morris, *Rise of Theodore Roosevelt*, 109.
10. Ibid.
11. Paul Rego, *American Ideal: Theodore Roosevelt's Search for American Individualism* (Lanham, MD: Lexington Books, 2008), 54.
12. Albert Vollweiler, *Roosevelt's Ranch Life in North Dakota* (Grand Forks: University of North Dakota, 1918), 41.
13. Edmund Morris, *Colonel Roosevelt* (New York: Random House, 2011), 352.
14. Ibid.
15. *Wilmington Morning News*, "TR Visits Wilson at White House," May 27, 1914.
16. Ibid.

Chapter Three

1. Greg King and Penny Wilson, *Lusitania: Triumph, Tragedy, and the End of the Edwardian Age* (New York: St. Martins, 2015), 169.
2. Lowell Thomas, *Raiders of the Deep* (New York: Doubleday, 1928), 96.
3. Erik Larson, *Dead Wake: The Last Crossing of the Lusitania* (New York: Crown, 2015), 229.
4. Ibid.
5. Thomas, *Raiders of the Deep*, 97.

Chapter Four

1. David Pietrusza, *TR's Last War: Theodore Roosevelt, the Great War, and a Journey of Triumph and Tragedy* (Guilford, CT: Lyons Press, 2018), 7.
2. Ibid., 8.

3. Kathleen Dalton, *Theodore Roosevelt: A Strenuous Life* (New York: Vintage, 2007), 410.

4. Pietrusza, *TR's Last War*, 8.

5. Edmund Morris, *Colonel Roosevelt* (New York: Random House, 2011), 366.

6. William Atherton Du Puy and John Wilber Jenkins, *The World War and Historic Deeds of Valor* (Berkeley: University of California Press, 1919), 69.

7. *The News*, May 12, 1915.

8. Ibid.

9. Ibid.

10. Morris, *Colonel Roosevelt*, 411.

11. Ibid., 413.

12. Francis Trevelyan Miller, ed., *True Stories of the Great War* (New York Review of Books, 1918), 330.

13. *Derby Daily Telegraph*, "Oh for a Day of Roosevelt," May 5, 1915.

14. Morris, *Colonel Roosevelt*, 419.

15. Petruscza, *TR's Last War*, 14.

16. Theodore Roosevelt, *The Roosevelt Policy* (New York: The Current Literature Publishing Co., 1908), 848.

17. *The News*, "One Hundred and Fifty Innocent Babies," May 12, 1915.

18. John Milton Cooper, *Woodrow Wilson: A Biography* (New York: Vintage, 2011), 287.

19. A. Scott Berg, *Wilson* (New York: Penguin, 2013), 364.

20. Morris, *Colonel Roosevelt*, 425.

21. Ibid., 421.

22. H. W. Crocker III, *Don't Tread on Me: A 400-Year History of America at War, from Indian Fighting to Terrorist Hunting* (New York: Crown, 2006), 255.

23. Pietruscza, *TR's Last War*, 41.

CHAPTER FIVE

1. Godfrey Hodgson, *Woodrow Wilson's Right Hand: The Life of Colonel Edward M. House* (New Haven, CT: Yale University Press, 2006), 110.

2. A. Scott Berg, *Wilson* (New York: Penguin, 2013), 370.

3. Woodrow Wilson, *The Papers of Woodrow Wilson* (Princeton, NJ: Princeton University Press, 1980), 87.

4. Erik Larson, *Dead Wake: The Last Crossing of the Lusitania* (New York: Crown, 2015), 109.

5. Ibid.

6. Ibid., 110.

7. Kristie Miller, *Ellen and Edith: Woodrow Wilson's First Ladies* (Lawrence: University Press of Kansas, 2010), 109.

8. John Milton Cooper, *Woodrow Wilson: A Biography* (New York: Vintage, 2011), 283.

9. Ibid.

10. Wilson, *Papers of Woodrow Wilson*, 109.

11. Ibid.

12. John Whitcomb, *Real Life at the White House: 200 Years of Daily Life at America's Most Famous Residence* (New York: Routledge, 2002), 253.

13. Miller, *Ellen and Edith*, 112.

14. Wilson, *Papers of Woodrow Wilson*, 311.

15. Henry Cabot Lodge, *The Senate and the League of Nations* (New York: Scribner's, 1925), 32.

16. Phyllis Lee Levin, *Edith and Woodrow: The Wilson White House* (New York: Scribner's, 2002), 78.

17. Wilson, *Papers of Woodrow Wilson*, 135.

18. Edward House, *The Intimate Papers of Colonel House* (New York: Houghton Mifflin, 1926), 434.

19. Ibid.

20. Cooper, *Woodrow Wilson*, 4.

21. Wilson, *Papers of Woodrow Wilson*, 136.

22. Ibid., 147.

23. Woodrow Wilson, *President Wilson's State Papers* (New York: George H. Doran, 1918), 117.

24. Lodge, *Senate and the League of Nations*, 33.

25. Wilson, *Papers of Woodrow Wilson*, 162.

26. Jennings C. Wise, *Woodrow Wilson: Disciple of Revolution* (New York: Paisley Press, 1938), 308.

CHAPTER SIX

1. Kristie Miller, *Ellen and Edith: Woodrow Wilson's First Ladies* (Lawrence: University Press of Kansas, 2010), 114.

2. Richard F. Welch, *Long Island's Gold Coast Elite & the Great War* (Charleston, SC: History Press, 2021), 39.

3. Ray Stannard Baker, *Woodrow Wilson, Life and Letters: Neutrality, 1914–1915* (Westport, CT: Greenwood, 1940), 408.

4. Edward House, *The Intimate Papers of Colonel House* (New York: Houghton Mifflin, 1926), 6.

5. Edith Bolling Wilson, *My Memoir* (Indianapolis: Bobbs-Merrill, 1939), 63.

6. Ibid.

7. Edmund Morris, *Colonel Roosevelt* (New York: Random House, 2011), 428.

8. Ibid.

9. Ibid.

10. *Enid Morning News,* June 10, 1915.

11. Morris, *Colonel Roosevelt*, 430.

12. Ibid., 431.

13. William Nester, *Theodore Roosevelt and the Art of American Power* (Lanham, MD: Lexington Books, 2019), 271.

14. David Siefkin, *The City at the End of the Rainbow: San Francisco and its Grand Hotels* (New York: Putnam, 1976), 72.

CHAPTER SEVEN

1. Ralph Perry, *The Plattsburg Movement: A Chapter of America's Participation in the World War* (New York: Dutton, 1921), 121.
2. Edmund Morris, *Colonel Roosevelt* (New York: Random House, 2011), 433.
3. Ibid.
4. Ibid., 434.
5. Ibid.
6. Ibid., 435.
7. Ibid., 436.
8. Ibid.
9. Ibid.
10. Kristie Miller, *Ellen and Edith: Woodrow Wilson's First Ladies* (Lawrence: University Press of Kansas, 2010), 113.
11. John Milton Cooper, *Woodrow Wilson: A Biography* (New York: Vintage, 2011), 290.
12. Miller, *Ellen and Edith*, 113.
13. Woodrow Wilson, *The Papers of Woodrow Wilson* (Princeton, NJ: Princeton University Press, 1980), 301.
14. Ibid., 334.
15. A. Scott Berg, *Wilson* (New York: Penguin, 2013), 372.
16. Phyllis Lee Levin, *Edith and Woodrow: The Wilson White House* (New York: Scribner's, 2002), 379.
17. Arthur S. Link, *Wilson: Confusion and Crises: 1915–1916* (Princeton, NJ: Princeton University Press, 1947), 3.
18. John Whitcomb, *Real Life at the White House: 200 Years of Daily Life at America's Most Famous Residence* (New York: Routledge, 2002), 254.

CHAPTER EIGHT

1. Edmund Morris, *The Rise of Theodore Roosevelt* (New York: Random House, 2010), 190.
2. Rick Marschall, *Bully! The Life and Times of Theodore Roosevelt* (Washington, DC: Regnery, 2011), 67.
3. Morris, *Rise of Theodore Roosevelt*, 198.
4. Ibid., 274.
5. Ibid., 279.
6. Theodore Roosevelt, *Hunting Adventures in the West* (New York: Putnam, 1913), 221.
7. David McCullough, *Mornings on Horseback* (New York: Simon and Schuster, 2001), 324.
8. Theodore Roosevelt, *An Autobiography of Theodore Roosevelt* (Createspace, 2011), 116.
9. Ibid.
10. Ibid.
11. Morris, *Rise of Theodore Roosevelt*, 277.

12. Ibid.

13. Ibid., 280.

14. William Nester, *Theodore Roosevelt and the Art of American Power* (Lanham, MD: Lexington Books, 2019), 48.

15. Morris, *Rise of Theodore Roosevelt*, 306.

16. Ibid.

17. Ibid.

18. Michael Blake, *The Cowboy President: The American West and the Making of Theodore Roosevelt* (Guilford, CT: Twodot, 2018), 108.

19. H. Paul Jeffers, *Roosevelt the Explorer: Teddy Roosevelt's Amazing Adventures as a Naturalist, Conservationist, and Explorer* (Lanham, MD: Taylor Trade Publishing, 2002), 64.

20. Morris, *Rise of Theodore Roosevelt*, 322.

21. Ibid., 325.

22. Ibid., 296.

23. Ibid., 297.

24. Ibid.

25. Ibid.

26. Ibid., 308.

27. Theodore Roosevelt, *The Works of Theodore Roosevelt* (New York: P. F. Collier, 1899), 15.

CHAPTER NINE

1. *Anaconda Standard*, "Attempt to Reorganize," June 26, 1916.

2. Edmund Morris, *Colonel Roosevelt* (New York: Random House, 2011), 451.

3. Theodore Roosevelt, *Letters Selected and Edited* (Cambridge, MA: Harvard University Press, 1954), 1024.

4. Morris, *Colonel Roosevelt*, 452.

5. Ibid., 456.

6. "Citing Mrs. Wilson," *The Commoner* 15, no. 16 (1915): 21.

7. Morris, *Colonel Roosevelt*, 455.

8. Ibid., 462.

9. John Thompson, *Woodrow Wilson: Profiles in Power* (New York: Longman, 2015), 86.

10. Roosevelt, *Letters Selected and Edited*, 1014.

11. David Pietrusza, *TR's Last War: Theodore Roosevelt, the Great War, and a Journey of Triumph and Tragedy* (Guilford, CT: Lyons Press, 2018), 165.

12. Theodore Roosevelt, *The Works of Theodore Roosevelt*, vol. 24 (New York: Scribner's, 1925), 366.

13. Theodore Roosevelt, *Letters and Speeches* (New York: Library of America, 2004), 707.

CHAPTER TEN

1. Michael Bie, *Wisconsin Myths and Legends* (Lanham, MD: Rowman and Littlefield, 2022), 102.

2. *San Francisco Call*, "Colonel Does Not Feel Bullet Strike Him," October 15, 1912.

3. Ibid.

4. Joseph Bishop, *Theodore Roosevelt and His Time* (New York: Scribner's, 1920), 343.

5. Theodore Roosevelt, *The Works of Theodore Roosevelt* (New York: Scribner's, 1926), 395.

6. *San Francisco Call*, "Colonel Does Not Feel Bullet."

7. Ibid.

8. Bishop, *Theodore Roosevelt and His Time*, 337.

9. Theodore Roosevelt, *The Works of Theodore Roosevelt* (New York: Scribner's, 1925) 441.

10. Edmund Morris, *Colonel Roosevelt* (New York: Random House, 2011), 246.

11. James Strock, *Theodore Roosevelt on Leadership* (New York: Crown, 2009), 50.

12. David Healy, *US Expansionism* (Madison: University of Wisconsin Press, 2011), 125.

13. Morris, *Colonel Roosevelt*, 250.

14. Ibid.

15. Kathleen Dalton, *Theodore Roosevelt: A Strenuous Life* (New York: Vintage, 2007), 409.

CHAPTER ELEVEN

1. Edmund Morris, *Colonel Roosevelt* (New York: Random House, 2011), 519.

2. Ibid., 465.

3. Ibid., 466.

CHAPTER TWELVE

1. Edmund Morris, *Colonel Roosevelt* (New York: Random House, 2011), 468.

2. Ibid.

3. Ibid.

4. Ibid., 469

5. Ibid.

6. Ibid., 309

7. Ibid., 471.

8. Theodore Roosevelt, *The Works of Theodore Roosevelt*, vol. 20 (New York: Scribner's, 1925), 526.

9. Morris, *Colonel Roosevelt*, 472.

CHAPTER THIRTEEN

1. Edmund Morris, *Colonel Roosevelt* (New York: Random House, 2011), 472.

2. William Hazelgrove, *Madam President* (Washington, DC: Regnery, 2016).

3. A. Scott Berg, *Wilson* (New York: Penguin, 2013), 389.

4. Michael Beschloss, *Presidents of War: The Epic Story, from 1807 to Modern Times* (New York: Crown, 2019), 307.

5. Berg, *Wilson*, 415.

6. Patricia O'Toole, *The Moralist: Woodrow Wilson and the World He Made* (New York: Simon and Schuster, 2019), 226.

7. Ibid.

8. Edmund Morris, *Theodore Rex* (New York: Random House, 2010), 142.

9. Ibid.

10. Ibid.

11. Ibid.

12. Ibid.

13. Morris, *Colonel Roosevelt*, 472.

CHAPTER FOURTEEN

1. Jacob Riis, *The Making of an American* (New York: Harper and Row, 2011), 214.

2. Daniel Henderson, *Great Heart: The Life Story of Theodore Roosevelt* (New York: Knopf, 1919), 74.

3. H. Paul Jeffers, *Commissioner Roosevelt* (New York: Wiley, 1994), 67.

4. *Theodore Roosevelt* (New York: Random House, 2010), 503.

5. Ibid., 504.

6. Ibid., 507.

7. Ibid.

8. Ibid.

9. Ibid., 512.

10. Thomas Bailey, *Theodore Roosevelt, A Literary Life* (Lebanon, NH: University Press of New England, 2018), 91.

11. Morris, *Rise of Theodore Roosevelt*, 512.

12. Ibid., 509.

13. Ibid., 511.

14. Ibid., 512.

15. Ibid., 513.

16. Ibid., 517.

17. Ibid., 522.

18. Richard Zacks, *Island of Vice: Theodore Roosevelt's Quest to Clean Up Sin-Loving New York* (New York: Anchor Books, 2012), 119.

19. James Lardner, *NYPD* (New York: Holt, 2001), 120.

CHAPTER FIFTEEN

1. *The Fortnightly* 109 (1918): 294.

2. United States Naval Institute *Proceedings* (1917): 414.

3. Woodrow Wilson, *The Papers of Woodrow Wilson* (Princeton, NJ: Princeton University Press, 1980), 228.

4. Edmund Morris, *Colonel Roosevelt* (New York: Random House, 2011), 474.

5. Thomas Knock, *To End All Wars: Woodrow Wilson and the Quest for a New World Order* (Princeton, NJ: Princeton University Press, 2019), 115.

6. H. W. Brands, *T. R.: The Last Romantic* (New York: Basic Books, 2019).

7. Morris, *Colonel Roosevelt*, 475.

8. Ibid., 476.

9. Theodore Roosevelt, *The Days of Armageddon, 1900–1914* (Bloomington: Indiana University Press), 1156.

10. J. Lee Thompson, *Never Call Retreat: Theodore Roosevelt and the Great War* (New York: Palgrave Macmillan, 2014), 168.

11. Theodore Roosevelt, *The Foes of Our Own Household* (New York: Scribner's, 1925), 187.

12. Thompson, *Never Call Retreat*, 165.

13. Morris, *Colonel Roosevelt*, 477.

14. Theodore Roosevelt, *Letters and Speeches* (New York: Library of America, 2004), 717.

15. David Pietrusza, *TR's Last War: Theodore Roosevelt, the Great War, and a Journey of Triumph and Tragedy* (Guilford, CT: Lyons Press, 2018), 187.

16. Theodore Roosevelt, *The Works of Theodore Roosevelt*, vol. 21 (New York: Scribner's, 1923) 199.

17. Woodrow Wilson, *Second Inauguration of Woodrow Wilson* (Washington, DC: Government Printing Office, 1918), 46.

18. Ibid.

19. A. Scott Berg, *Wilson* (New York: Penguin, 2013), 426.

CHAPTER SIXTEEN

1. *Des Moines Register*, April 5, 1917.

2. Ibid.

3. J. Lee Thompson, *Never Call Retreat: Theodore Roosevelt and the Great War* (New York: Palgrave Macmillan, 2014), 29.

4. Peter Collier, *The Roosevelts: An American Saga* (New York: Simon and Schuster, 1995), 181.

5. Edith Bolling Wilson, *My Memoir* (Indianapolis: Bobbs-Merrill, 1939), 116.

6. John Milton Cooper, *Woodrow Wilson: A Biography* (New York: Vintage, 2011), 383.

7. US Government, *Army Navy Air Force Register*, 1917, 191.

8. Theodore Roosevelt, *The Foes of Our Own Household* (New York: Scribner's, 1925), 191.

9. Ibid.

10. Michael Canfield, *Theodore Roosevelt in the Field* (Chicago: University of Chicago Press, 2015), 366.

11. Edmund Morris, *Colonel Roosevelt* (New York: Random House, 2011), 481.

12. Ibid.

13. Ibid.

14. Ibid.

15. Patricia O'Toole, *The Moralist: Woodrow Wilson and the World He Made* (New York: Simon and Schuster, 2019), 257.

16. Theodore Roosevelt, *Literary Digest* 54 (1917): 881.

17. Theodore Roosevelt, *Selections from the Correspondence of Theodore Roosevelt* (New York: Scribner's, 1925), 512.

CHAPTER SEVENTEEN

1. Richard David, *Notes of a War Correspondent* (New York: Scribner's, 1910), 89.
2. Clay Risen, *The Crowded Hour: Theodore Roosevelt, the Rough Riders, and the Dawn of the American Century* (New York: Scribner, 2020), 205.
3. Robert C. V. Meyers, *Theodore Roosevelt, Patriot: The True Story of an Ideal American* (Philadelphia: Ziegler, 1902), 287.
4. Risen, *Crowded Hour*, 205.
5. Ibid.
6. Ibid.
7. Theodore Roosevelt, The Rough Riders (Mineola, NY: Dover, 2006), 76.
8. Ibid.,128.
9. Ibid.
10. Theodore Roosevelt, *An Autobiography* (New York: Scribner's, 1913), 266.
11. Edward Marshall, *The Story of the Rough Riders, 1st U.S. Volunteer Cavalry: The Regiment in Camp and on The Battle Field* (New York: Literary Licensing, 1899), 118.
12. Ibid.
13. Theodore Roosevelt, *Selections from the Correspondence of Theodore Roosevelt and Henry Cabot Lodge 1884–1918* (New York: Scribner's, 1925), 328.

CHAPTER EIGHTEEN

1. William White, *Woodrow Wilson: The Man, His Times, and His Task* (Boston: Houghton Mifflin, 1924), 354.
2. Christopher McKnight Nichols, *Promise and Peril: America at the Dawn of a Global Age* (Cambridge, MA: Harvard University Press, 2011), 206.
3. Ibid.
4. Ibid.
5. J. W. Schulte Nordholt, *Woodrow Wilson: A Life for World Peace* (Berkeley: University of California Press, 1991), 229.
6. Ibid.
7. *New York Times*, "War Call Sounded by Col. Roosevelt," March 20, 1917.
8. David Pietrusza, *TR's Last War: Theodore Roosevelt, the Great War, and a Journey of Triumph and Tragedy* (Guilford, CT: Lyons Press, 2018), 187.

CHAPTER NINETEEN

1. Theodore Roosevelt, *Selections from the Correspondence of Theodore Roosevelt and Henry Cabot Lodge 1884–1918* (New York: Scribner's, 1925), 499.
2. Ibid.
3. Paul Grondahl, *I Rose Like a Rocket: The Political Education of Theodore Roosevelt* (New York: Free Press, 2007), 370.
4. Ibid., 376.

5. John S. D. Eisenhower, *Teddy Roosevelt and Leonard Wood: Partners in Command* (Columbia: University of Missouri Press, 2014), 85.

CHAPTER TWENTY

1. Paul Grondahl, *I Rose Like a Rocket: The Political Education of Theodore Roosevelt* (New York: Free Press, 2007), 360.
2. David Pietrusza, *TR's Last War: Theodore Roosevelt, the Great War, and a Journey of Triumph and Tragedy* (Guilford, CT: Lyons Press, 2018), 190.
3. Theodore Roosevelt, *The Works of Theodore Roosevelt* (New York: Scribner's, 1926), 496.
4. Pietruscza, *TR's Last War*, 190.
5. Resa Willis, *FDR and Lucy: Lovers and Friends* (New York: Routledge, 2012), 29.
6. Edmund Morris, *Colonel Roosevelt* (New York: Random House, 2011), 485.
7. *Star Gazette*, "TR Change of Heart," April 4, 1917.
8. Ibid.

CHAPTER TWENTY-ONE

1. Nathan Miller, *Theodore Roosevelt: A Life* (New York: Quill, 1992), 43.
2. David McCullough, *Mornings on Horseback* (New York: Simon and Schuster, 2001), 94.
3. Henry Hyde Salter, *On Asthma: Its Pathology and Treatment* (New York: William Wood, 1882), 82.
4. Kathleen Dalton, *Theodore Roosevelt: A Strenuous Life* (New York: Vintage, 2007), 50.
5. Carleton Putnam, *Theodore Roosevelt: The Formative Years* (New York: Scribner's, 1958), 75.

CHAPTER TWENTY-TWO

1. Samuel Lyman Atwood Marshall, *World War I* (Boston: Houghton Mifflin, 2001), 281.
2. Joseph Tumulty, *Woodrow Wilson as I Know Him* (New York: Doubleday, 1921), 258.
3. J. W. Schulte Nordholt, *Woodrow Wilson: A Life for World Peace* (Berkeley: University of California Press, 1991), 229.
4. Michael Beschloss, *Presidents of War: The Epic Story, from 1807 to Modern Times* (New York: Crown, 2019), 320.
5. *Flying Magazine*, January 1942, 216.
6. John Macgavock Grider, *War Birds: Diary of an Unknown Aviator* (Sydney: Cornstalk Publishing, 1926), 75.
7. Roger A. Bruns, *Preacher: Billy Sunday and Big-Time American Evangelism* (Champaign: University of Illinois Press, 2002), 210.
8. *Des Moines Register*, "Ready for Call," April 15, 1917.
9. Ibid.
10. Ibid.

11. David Pietrusza, *TR's Last War: Theodore Roosevelt, the Great War, and a Journey of Triumph and Tragedy* (Guilford, CT: Lyons Press, 2018), 184.

12. Ibid.

CHAPTER TWENTY-THREE

1. Edmund Morris, *Colonel Roosevelt* (New York: Random House, 2011), 486.

2. John Leary, *Talks with TR* (Boston: Houghton Mifflin, 1920), 94.

3. Richard Striner, *Woodrow Wilson and World War I: A Burden Too Great to Bear* (Lanham, MD: Rowman & Littlefield, 2014), 109.

4. John Milton Cooper, *Woodrow Wilson: A Biography* (New York: Vintage, 2011), 395.

5. Striner, *Woodrow Wilson and World War I*, 109.

6. Leary, *Talks with TR*, 97.

7. Ibid.

8. *McClure's Magazine* 51, 1920.

9. Patrick Tumulty, *Woodrow Wilson* (New York: Doubleday, 1921), 286.

10. Ibid., 288.

11. Morris, *Colonel Roosevelt*, 486.

12. Ibid., 487.

13. Ibid.

14. Ibid.

15. Editorial reports, *The New York Times*, 1939 v 2 p 294.

16. "Editorial on Roosevelt," *Dispatch Republican*, April 16, 1917.

17. *Des Moines Register*, April 5, 1917.

18. *Scranton Times*, "Roosevelt Supports Wilson," June 12, 1915.

19. *Chattanooga News*, "Roosevelt Eager to Go to France," April 13, 1917.

20. Ibid.

CHAPTER TWENTY-FOUR

1. Edmund Morris, *Theodore Rex* (New York: Random House, 2010), 3.

2. Ibid., 4.

3. Ibid.

4. Ibid.

5. Ibid.

6. Ibid., 7.

7. Ibid., 10.

8. Ibid., 11.

9. Theodore Roosevelt, *In the Words of Theodore Roosevelt* (Ithaca, NY: Cornell University Press, 2012), 105.

10. Edward Wagenknecht, *Seven Worlds of Theodore Roosevelt* (Guilford, CT: Lyons Press, 2010), 222.

11. Edmund Morris, *Theodore Rex* (New York: Random House, 2010), 50.

12. Ibid., 52.

13. Ibid.
14. Ibid., 53.
15. Ibid., 54.
16. Ibid.
17. Lori Cox Han, ed., *Hatred of America's Presidents: Personal Attacks on the White House from Washington to Trump*, (Santa Barbara, CA: ABC-CLIO, 2018), 175.
18. Ibid., 55.
19. Ibid.
20. Ibid.
21. Ibid.
22. Aida D. Donald, *Lion in the White House: A Life of Theodore Roosevelt* (New York: Basic Books, 2008), 139.
23. *Yale Alumni Weekly* 28 (1918): 536.
24. Edmund Morris, *Theodore Rex* (New York: Random House, 2010), 56.
25. Kathleen Dalton, *Theodore Roosevelt: A Strenuous Life* (New York: Vintage, 2007), 216.
26. Morris, *Theodore Rex*, 57.
27. Ibid., 57.

CHAPTER TWENTY-FIVE

1. *Kansas City Times*, April 5, 1917.
2. Ibid.
3. Edmund Morris, *Colonel Roosevelt* (New York: Random House, 2011), 488.
4. Theodore Roosevelt, *The Works of Theodore Roosevelt*, vol. 21 (New York: Scribner's, 1925), 204.
5. Ibid.
6. Ibid.
7. David Pietrusza, *TR's Last War: Theodore Roosevelt, the Great War, and a Journey of Triumph and Tragedy* (Guilford, CT: Lyons Press, 2018), 195.

CHAPTER TWENTY-SIX

1. *Washington Post*, May 19, 1917.
2. Ibid.
3. Ibid.
4. Ibid.
5. Ibid.
6. Ibid.
7. William Hazelgrove, *Madam President* (Washington, DC: Regnery, 2016).

CHAPTER TWENTY-SEVEN

1. Theodore Roosevelt, *The Works of Theodore Roosevelt* (New York: Scribner's, 1925), 208.
2. Ibid.

3. Ibid., 225
4. Ibid.
5. *New York Times*, "New Rush Sets in to Join Roosevelt," May 8, 1917.
6. Ibid.
7. Ibid.
8. Ibid.
9. *St. Louis Dispatch*, "Nelson Loyal to TR," April 14, 1917.
10. Edmund Morris, *Colonel Roosevelt* (New York: Random House, 2011), 490.
11. Ibid.
12. Linda Robertson, *The Dream of Civilized Warfare* (Duluth: University of Minnesota Press, 2003), 80.
13. Morris, *Colonel Roosevelt*, 490.
14. Thomas Athridge, *American Presidents at War* (AOIS 21, 2017), 120.

CHAPTER TWENTY-EIGHT

1. Theodore Roosevelt, *The Works of Theodore Roosevelt* (New York: Scribner's, 1924), 114.
2. *Vignettes of Military History*, vol. 3 (Carlisle Barracks, PA: U.S. Army Military History Institute), 27.
3. Theodore Roosevelt, *The Works of Theodore Roosevelt* (New York: Scribner's, 1899), 312.
4. Ibid., 312.
5. Mark Lee Gardner, *Rough Riders: Theodore Roosevelt, His Cowboy Regiment, and the Immortal Charge Up San Juan Hill* (New York: HarperCollins, 2016), 168.
6. Ibid.
7. Ibid., 169.
8. *Buffalo Enquirer*, "Buffalo Soldier Writes of Charge," July 26, 1898.
9. Gardner, *Rough Riders*, 179.
10. Ibid.
11. Ibid.
12. Peggy Samuels and Harold Samuels, *Teddy Roosevelt at San Juan: The Making of a President* (College Station: Texas A&M University Press, 1997, 269.
13. Gardner, *Rough Riders*, 171.
14. Corinne Roosevelt Robinson, *My Brother Theodore Roosevelt* (New York: Scribner's, 1921), 174.

CHAPTER TWENTY-NINE

1. Edmund Morris, *Colonel Roosevelt* (New York: Random House, 2011), 495.
2. *Akron Beacon Journal*, November 28, 1902.
3. Ibid.
4. Ibid.
5. Morris, *Colonel Roosevelt*, 491.
6. Ibid.

7. Edmund Morris, *The Rise of Theodore Roosevelt* (New York: Random House, 2010), 690.

CHAPTER THIRTY

1. *The Oklahoman*, May 2, 1917.
2. Ibid.
3. Edmund Morris, *Colonel Roosevelt* (New York: Random House, 2011), 490.
4. Ibid.
5. *The Oklahoman*, May 2, 1917.
6. *New York Times*, May 8, 1917.
7. Ibid.
8. Ibid.
9. Ibid.
10. *York Dispatch*, "House Votes For TR," May 12, 1917.
11. Ibid.
12. Ibid.
13. *Washington Times*, May 13, 1917.

CHAPTER THIRTY-ONE

1. *Democrat Chronicle*, "House Votes for Roosevelt's Division," May 13, 1917.
2. Ibid.
3. William Maynard, *Woodrow Wilson* (New Haven, CT: Yale University Press, 2008), 199.
4. Edmund Morris, *Colonel Roosevelt* (New York: Random House, 2011), 492.
5. John Leary, *Talks with TR* (Boston: Houghton Mifflin, 1920), 223.
6. *Democrat Chronicle*, "House Votes."
7. Ibid.
8. Morris, *Colonel Roosevelt*, 493.
9. Theodore Roosevelt, *The Foes of Our Own Household* (New York: Scribner's, 1925), 215.
10. *The York*, "House for TR Going to France," May 12, 1917.

CHAPTER THIRTY-TWO

1. *Pittsburg Press*, "President's Son is Worse," February 10, 1902.
2. Ibid.
3. Ibid.
4. Ibid.
5. Ibid.
6. Ibid.
7. Ibid.
8. Ibid.
9. Ibid.
10. Ibid.

11. Ibid.

12. Ibid.

CHAPTER THIRTY-THREE

1. *Washington Post*, May 19, 1917.

2. Ibid.

3. Theodore Roosevelt, *Literary Digest* 54 (1917): 1580.

4. *A Compilation of Messages and Papers of the Presidents* (New York: Bureau of National Literature and Art, 1897), 8261.

5. Edmund Morris, *Colonel Roosevelt* (New York: Random House, 2011), 494.

6. James McMaster, *McMaster's Commercial Cases* (New York: McMaster Company, 1917), 119.

7. *A Compilation of Messages and Papers of the Presidents* (New York: Bureau of National Literature and Art, 1897), 8261.

8. Alfred Maurice Low, *Woodrow Wilson, an Interpretation* (Boston: Little, Brown, 1918), 265.

9. *Washington Post*, "Roosevelt Silent on Wilson's Stand," May 19, 1917.

10. J. Lee Thompson, *Never Call Retreat: Theodore Roosevelt and the Great War* (New York: Palgrave Macmillan, 2014), 185.

11. Morris, *Colonel Roosevelt*, 494.

12. H. W. Brands, *T. R.: The Last Romantic* (New York: Basic Books, 2019).

13. Ibid.

14. Ibid.

15. Morris, *Colonel Roosevelt*, 495.

16. Ibid.

17. Ibid., 496.

18. *El Paso Morning Times*, "Volunteers Await Teddy's Next Move," May 21, 1917.

19. Ibid.

20. Ibid.

21. Ibid.

22. John Leary, *Talks with TR* (Boston: Houghton Mifflin, 1920), 239.

CHAPTER THIRTY-FOUR

1. Edmund Morris, *Theodore Rex* (New York: Random House, 2010), 552.

2. Una Stannard, *A Few Kind Words About Hate* (Ashland, OR: Germain Books, 1968), 134.

3. Theodore Roosevelt, *An Autobiography of Theodore Roosevelt* (Createspace, 2011), 341.

4. Edmund Morris, *Colonel Roosevelt* (New York: Random House, 2011), 19.

5. Michael Canfield, *Theodore Roosevelt in the Field* (Chicago: University of Chicago Press, 2015), 372.

6. Morris, *Colonel Roosevelt*, 18.

7. Ibid.

8. Ibid.
9. Ibid., 19.

CHAPTER THIRTY-FIVE
1. Edmund Morris, *Colonel Roosevelt* (New York: Random House, 2011), 496.
2. *Fort Wayne News*, July 16, 1917.
3. Morris, *Colonel Roosevelt*, 498.

CHAPTER THIRTY-SIX
1. Edmund Morris, *Colonel Roosevelt* (New York: Random House, 2011), 502.
2. Ibid.
3. Ibid., 500.
4. Ibid., 501.
5. Ibid.
6. Ibid.
7. Ibid.
8. Ibid., 502.
9. Ibid., 503.
10. Ibid., 504.
11. Ibid., 507.
12. Ibid.
13. Ibid.
14. Ibid.
15. Ibid.

CHAPTER THIRTY-SEVEN
1. Edmund Morris, *Colonel Roosevelt* (New York: Random House, 2011), 504.
2. Quentin Roosevelt, *Quentin Roosevelt: A Sketch with Letters* (New York: Scribner's, 1921), 42.
3. Morris, *Colonel Roosevelt*, 505.
4. Quentin Roosevelt, *Quentin Roosevelt: A Sketch with Letters*, 47.
5. Ibid.
6. Morris, *Colonel Roosevelt*, 505.
7. Quentin Roosevelt, *Quentin Roosevelt: A Sketch with Letters*, 70.
8. Ibid., 78.
9. Ibid., 79.
10. Ibid., 80.
11. Morris, *Colonel Roosevelt*, 508.
12. Ibid.
13. Ibid.
14. Quentin Roosevelt, *Quentin Roosevelt: A Sketch with Letters*, 80.

CHAPTER THIRTY-EIGHT

1. *Brooklyn Daily Eagle*, October 22, 1917.
2. Ibid.
3. Edmund Morris, *Colonel Roosevelt* (New York: Random House, 2011), 507.
4. Ibid.
5. Ibid., 508.
6. *Philadelphia Inquirer*, October 17, 1917.
7. *Brooklyn Daily Eagle*, October 22, 1917.
8. Ibid.
9. Ibid.
10. Morris, *Colonel Roosevelt*, 505.
11. Ibid., 510.
12. David Pietrusza, *TR's Last War: Theodore Roosevelt, the Great War, and a Journey of Triumph and Tragedy* (Guilford, CT: Lyons Press, 2018), 236.
13. *Kansas City Star*, 1921, 24.
14. Kathleen Dalton, *Theodore Roosevelt: A Strenuous Life* (New York: Vintage, 2007), 487.
15. Theodore Roosevelt, *The Days of Armageddon, 1900–1914* (Bloomington: Indiana University Press), 1216.
16. Roosevelt, *Days of Armageddon*, 1216.
17. Ibid., 1217.
18. William White, *Autobiography* (New York: Macmillan, 1946), 545.

CHAPTER THIRTY-NINE

1. Quentin Roosevelt, *Quentin Roosevelt: A Sketch with Letters* (New York: Scribner's, 1921), 251.
2. Ibid., 27.
3. Edward J. Renehan Jr., *The Lion's Pride: Theodore Roosevelt and His Family in Peace and War* (New York: Oxford University Press, 1999).
4. David Pietrusza, *TR's Last War: Theodore Roosevelt, the Great War, and a Journey of Triumph and Tragedy* (Guilford, CT: Lyons Press, 2018), 288.
5. Ibid.
6. Eddie Rickenbacker, *Fighting the Flying Circus* (New York: Stokes, 1919), 193.
7. Quentin Roosevelt, *Quentin Roosevelt: A Sketch with Letters*, 87.
8. Ibid., 89.
9. Ibid., 91.
10. Ibid., 99.
11. Ibid., 104.
12. Ibid., 105.

CHAPTER FORTY

1. Edmund Morris, *Colonel Roosevelt* (New York: Random House, 2011), 516.
2. Michael Farquhar, *Bad Days in History: A Gleefully Grim Chronicle of Misfortune, Mayhem, and Misery for Every Day of the Year* (Washington, DC: National Geographic Society, 2017) 414.

3. Morris, *Colonel Roosevelt*, 516.
4. Ibid.
5. Ibid.
6. Ibid., 517.
7. Ibid.
8. Ibid.
9. *Philadelphia Inquirer*, February 8, 1918.
10. Ibid.
11. Ibid.
12. Ibid.
13. *Evening Star*, February 8, 1918.
14. Ibid.
15. *Brooklyn Daily Eagle*, February 8, 1918.
16. Ibid.
17. *Brooklyn Daily Eagle*, February 8, 1918.
18. Ibid.
19. Morris, *Colonel Roosevelt*, 519.

CHAPTER FORTY-ONE
1. Edmund Morris, *Colonel Roosevelt* (New York: Random House, 2011), 520.
2. Ibid.
3. Ibid.
4. Ibid.
5. Ibid., 521.
6. Ibid.
7. Ibid.
8. Ibid., 522.
9. Mark De Wolfe, *Memoirs of the Harvard Dead* (Cambridge, MA: Harvard University Press, 1922), 361.

CHAPTER FORTY-TWO
1. Quentin Roosevelt, *Quentin Roosevelt: A Sketch with Letters* (New York: Scribner's, 1921), 125.
2. Ibid., 126.
3. Edward J. Renehan Jr., *The Lion's Pride: Theodore Roosevelt and His Family in Peace and War* (New York: Oxford University Press, 1999).
4. Quentin Roosevelt, *Quentin Roosevelt: A Sketch with Letters*, 133.
5. Ibid., 136.
6. Ibid., 134.
7. Ibid., 140.
8. Ibid., 151.
9. Ibid.
10. Ibid., 159.

11. Edmund Morris, *Colonel Roosevelt* (New York: Random House, 2011), 524.

12. Harry Jeffers, *Theodore Roosevelt Jr.: The Life of a War Hero* (Novato, CA: Presidio, 2002), 103.

13. Morris, *Colonel Roosevelt*, 526.

14. Ibid.

15. *Quentin Roosevelt: A Sketch with Letters*, 163.

16. Ibid., 164.

17. Eddie Rickenbacker, *Fighting the Flying Circus* (New York: Stokes, 1919), 194.

CHAPTER FORTY-THREE

1. Edmund Morris, *Colonel Roosevelt* (New York: Random House, 2011), 524.

2. Ibid., 526.

3. Ibid.

4. Ibid., 527.

5. *Sacramento Bee*, "Quentin Roosevelt Now An Aviator," July 4, 1918.

CHAPTER FORTY-FOUR

1. Edmund Morris, *Colonel Roosevelt* (New York: Random House, 2011), 527.

2. Eddie Rickenbacker, *Fighting the Flying Circus* (New York: Stokes, 1919), 193.

3. Quentin Roosevelt, *Quentin Roosevelt: A Sketch with Letters* (New York: Scribner's, 1921), 163.

4. Morris, *Colonel Roosevelt*, 528.

5. Ibid.

CHAPTER FORTY-FIVE

1. Bill Bleyer, *Sagamore Hill: Theodore Roosevelt's Summer White House* (Charleston, SC: History Press, 2016), 90.

2. Ibid.

3. Edmund Morris, *Colonel Roosevelt* (New York: Random House, 2011), 528.

4. Ibid., 529.

5. Bleyer, *Sagamore Hill*, 90.

6. David Pietrusza, *TR's Last War: Theodore Roosevelt, the Great War, and a Journey of Triumph and Tragedy* (Guilford, CT: Lyons Press, 2018), 240.

7. Bleyer, *Sagamore Hill*, 90.

8. Quentin Roosevelt, *Quentin Roosevelt: A Sketch with Letters* (New York: Scribner's, 1921), 166.

9. Joseph Bishop, *Theodore Roosevelt and His Time* (New York: Scribner's, 1920), 451.

10. Richard White, *Roosevelt the Reformer: Theodore Roosevelt as Civil Service Commissioner, 1889–1895* (Tuscaloosa: University of Alabama Press, 2003), 64.

11. Morris, *Colonel Roosevelt*, 530.

12. Ibid.

13. Ibid., 496.

14. Ibid., 531.

15. *Tampa Morning Tribune*, "Quentin Roosevelt Killed," July 18, 1918.

16. Morris, *Colonel Roosevelt*, 532.

17. H. W. Brands, *T. R.: The Last Romantic* (New York: Basic Books, 2019).

18. Quentin Roosevelt, *Quentin Roosevelt: A Sketch with Letters* (New York: Scribner's, 1921), 175.

19. J. Lee Thompson, *Never Call Retreat: Theodore Roosevelt and the Great War* (New York: Palgrave Macmillan, 2014), 254.

20. Brands, *T. R.*

21. Pietruscza, *TR's Last War*, 240.

CHAPTER FORTY-SIX

1. Edmund Morris, *Colonel Roosevelt* (New York: Random House, 2011), 541.

2. Ibid.

3. Ibid.

4. Quentin Roosevelt, *Quentin Roosevelt: A Sketch with Letters* (New York: Scribner's, 1921), 169.

5. Morris, *Colonel Roosevelt*, 540.

6. Ibid., 543.

7. Ernest Young, The Wilson Administration and the Great War (Westport, CT: Gorham Press, 1922), 355.

8. Robert Saunders, *In Search of Woodrow Wilson: Beliefs and Behavior* (Westport, CT: Greenwood Press, 1998), 122.

9. Morris, *Colonel Roosevelt*, 544.

10. Ibid., 545.

11. Ibid.

12. Ibid.

13. Ibid., 546.

14. Ibid.

15. Ibid., 548.

16. Ibid.

17. Ibid.

18. Ibid., 549.

19. Edward J. Renehan Jr., *The Lion's Pride: Theodore Roosevelt and His Family in Peace and War* (New York: Oxford University Press, 1999), 219.

CHAPTER FORTY-SEVEN

1. Edmund Morris, *Colonel Roosevelt* (New York: Random House, 2011), 550.

2. Ibid.

3. Ibid.

4. Ibid., 551.

5. Ibid.

6. Ibid.

7. Ibid.

8. Ibid.

CHAPTER FORTY-EIGHT

1. Bill Bleyer, *Sagamore Hill: Theodore Roosevelt's Summer White House* (Charleston, SC: History Press, 2016), 92.

2. *The York*, "Ex-President Dies," January 6, 1919.

3. Edmund Morris, *Colonel Roosevelt* (New York: Random House, 2011), 554.

4. Ibid., 555.

5. Ibid.

6. Ibid.

7. *Bellman* 26 (1919): 38.

8. *Morning Star*, "Colonel Theodore Roosevelt Dies," January 7, 1919.

9. Morris, *Colonel Roosevelt*, 556.

10. William Thayer, *Theodore Roosevelt: An Intimate Biography* (Boston: Houghton Mifflin 1919), 213.

11. Morris, *Colonel Roosevelt*, 559.

12. Ibid.

13. Ibid.

14. Ibid., 560.

15. Ibid., 570.

CHAPTER FORTY-NINE

1. Michael Medved, *God's Hand on America: Divine Providence in the Modern Era* (New York: Crown, 2019), 198.

2. Edmund Morris, *Colonel Roosevelt* (New York: Random House, 2011), 725.

Bibliography

American Heritage, Part 4. Nashville: American Association for State and Local History, 1955.

The Anaconda Standard Attempt to Reorganize. New York: Standard Publishing Company, 1983.

Athridge, Thomas. *American Presidents at War.* New York: AOIS 21, 2017.

Bailey, Thomas, and Katherine Joslin. *Theodore Roosevelt: A Literary Life.* Lebanon, NH: University Press of New England, 2018.

Baker, Ray Stannard. *Woodrow Wilson, Life and Letters: Neutrality, 1914–1915.* Boston: Greenwood Press, 1940.

Berg, A. Scott. *Wilson.* New York: Penguin, 2013.

Beschloss, Michael. *Presidents of War: The Epic Story, from 1807 to Modern Times.* New York: Crown, 2019.

Blake, Michael F. *The Cowboy President: The American West and the Making of Theodore Roosevelt.* Guilford, CT: TwoDot, 2018.

Brands, H. W. *T. R.: The Last Romantic.* New York: Basic Books, 2019.

Bruns, Roger. *Preacher: Billy Sunday and Big-Time American Evangelism.* Champaign: University of Illinois Press, 2002.

Canfield, Michael R. *Theodore Roosevelt in the Field.* Chicago: University of Chicago Press, 2015.

"Citing Mrs. Wilson." *The Commoner,* Volume 15, 1915.

Collier, Peter. *The Roosevelts: An American Saga.* New York: Simon and Schuster, 1995.

Cooper, John Milton Jr. *Woodrow Wilson: A Biography.* New York: Vintage, 2011.

Crocker, H. W. III. *Don't Tread on Me: A 400-Year History of America at War, from Indian Fighting to Terrorist Hunting.* New York: Crown, 2006.

Dalton, Kathleen. *Theodore Roosevelt: A Strenuous Life.* New York: Vintage, 2007.

Davis, Richard Harding. *The Cuban and the Puerto Rican Campaigns.* New York: Scribner and Sons, 1898.

Di Silvestro, Roger L. *Theodore Roosevelt in the Badlands: A Young Politician's Quest for Recovery in the American West.* New York: Bloomsbury, 2012.

Donald, Aida. *Lion in the White House: A Life of Theodore Roosevelt.* New York: Basic Books, 2008.

Du Puy, William Atherton, and John Wilber Jenkins. *The World War and Historic Deeds of Valor.* Berkeley: University of California Press, 1919.

"Editorial on Roosevelt." *Dispatch Republican,* April 16, 1917.

Eisenhower, John S. D. *Teddy Roosevelt and Leonard Wood: Partners in Command.* Vol. 1. Columbia: University of Missouri Press, 2014.

Farquhar, Michael. *Bad Days in History: A Gleefully Grim Chronicle of Misfortune, Mayhem, and Misery for Every Day of the Year.* Washington, DC: National Geographic Society, 2017.

Gardner, Mark Lee. *Rough Riders: Theodore Roosevelt, His Cowboy Regiment, and the Immortal Charge Up San Juan Hill.* New York: HarperCollins, 2016.

"Getting into the War with the Colonel." *New York Tribune*, April 15, 1917.

Grider, John Macgavock. *War Birds: Diary of an Unknown Aviator.* Sydney: Cornstalk Publishing, 1926.

Grondahl, Paul. *I Rose Like a Rocket: The Political Education of Theodore Roosevelt.* Lincoln: University of Nebraska Press, 2007.

Han, Lori Cox, ed. *Hatred of America's Presidents: Personal Attacks on the White House from Washington to Trump.* Santa Barbara, CA: ABC-CLIO, 2018.

Hargrove, Erwin C. Jr. "The Tragic Hero in Politics: Theodore Roosevelt, David Lloyd George, and Fiorello LaGuardia." PhD diss., Yale University, 1968.

Hazelgrove, William. *Madam President: The Secret Presidency of Edith Wilson.* Washington, DC: Regnery, 2016.

Healy, David. *US Expansionism: The Imperialist Urge in the 1890s.* Madison: University of Wisconsin Press, 2011.

Henderson, Daniel. *Great Heart: The Life Story of Theodore Roosevelt.* New York: Knopf, 1919.

Hodgson, Godfrey. *Woodrow Wilson's Right Hand: The Life of Colonel Edward M. House.* New Haven, CT: Yale University Press, 2006.

House, Edward Mandell. *The Intimate Papers of Colonel House.* New York: Houghton Mifflin, 1926.

"House Votes for Roosevelts Division." *Democrat Chronicle*, May 13, 1917.

"House Votes For TR." *York Dispatch*, May 12, 1917.

Killblane, Richard E. *They Were the Rough Riders: Inside Theodore Roosevelt's Famed Cavalry Regiment.* Jefferson, NC: McFarland, 2022.

King, Greg. *Lusitania: Triumph, Tragedy, and the End of the Edwardian Age.* New York: St. Martin's, 2015.

Knock, Thomas. *To End All Wars: Woodrow Wilson and the Quest for a New World Order.* Princeton, NJ: Princeton University Press, 2019.

Kohn, Edward P. *A Most Glorious Ride: The Diaries of Theodore Roosevelt, 1877–1886.* New York: State University of New York Press, 2015.

Larson, Erik. *Dead Wake: The Last Crossing of the Lusitania.* New York: Crown, 2015.

Leary, John J. *Talks with T. R.* Boston: Houghton Mifflin, 1920.

Levin, Phyllis Lee. *Edith and Woodrow: The Wilson White House.* New York: Scribner's, 2002.

Link, Arthur. *Wilson: Confusion and Crises, 1915–1916.* Princeton: Princeton University Press, 1947.

Literary Digest 54 (1917).

Lodge, Henry Cabot. *The Senate and the League of Nations.* New York: Scribner's, 1925.

Low, Alfred Maurice. *Woodrow Wilson: An Interpretation*. Boston: Little, Brown, 1918.

Marschall, Rick. *Bully! The Life and Times of Theodore Roosevelt*. Washington, DC: Regnery, 2011.

Marshall, Edward. *The Story of the Rough Riders, 1st U.S. Volunteer Cavalry: The Regiment in Camp and on The Battle Field*. New York: Literary Licensing, 1899.

Marshall, Samuel Lyman Atwood. *World War I*. New York: Houghton Mifflin, 2001.

McCullough, David. *Mornings on Horseback: The Story of an Extraordinary Family, a Vanished Way of Life and the Unique Child Who Became Theodore Roosevelt*. New York: Simon and Schuster, 2001.

McKnight Nichols, Christopher. *Promise and Peril: America at the Dawn of a Global Age*. Cambridge, MA: Harvard University Press, 2011.

Miller, Francis Trevelyan. *True Stories of the Great War*. New York: Review of Books, 1918.

Miller, Kristie. *Ellen and Edith: Woodrow Wilson's First Ladies*. Lawrence: University Press of Kansas, 2010.

Miller, Nathan. *Theodore Roosevelt: A Life*. New York: Quill, 1992.

Morison, Elting. *Letters Selected and Edited*. Cambridge, MA: Harvard University Press, 1954.

Morris, Edmund. *Colonel Roosevelt*. New York: Random House, 2011.

———. *The Rise of Theodore Roosevelt*. New York: Random House, 2010.

———. *Theodore Rex*. New York: Random House, 2010.

Nester, William R. *Theodore Roosevelt and the Art of American Power: An American for All Time*. Lanham, MD: Lexington Books, 2019.

"New Rush Sets in to Join Roosevelt." *New York Times*, May 8, 1917.

Nordholt, J. W. *Woodrow Wilson A Life for World Peace*. Berkeley: University of California Press, 1917.

O'Toole, Patricia. *The Moralist: Woodrow Wilson and the World He Made*. New York: Simon and Schuster, 2019.

"Oklahomans Want to Go with Teddy." *Kansas City Times*, April 5, 1917.

"Pershing to Lead US Forces." *Washington Post*, May 19, 1917.

Pietrusza, David. *TR's Last War: Theodore Roosevelt, the Great War, and a Journey of Triumph and Tragedy*. Guilford, CT: Lyons Press, 2002.

Putnam, Carleton. *Theodore Roosevelt: The Formative Years 1858–1886*. New York: Scribner's, 1935.

"A Real Boy." *Akron Beacon Journal*, November 28, 1902.

Rego, Paul. *American Ideal: Theodore Roosevelt's Search for American Individualism*. Lanham, MD: Lexington Books, 2008.

Richardson, James. *President of the United States: A Compilation of Messages and Papers*. Alexandria, VA: Library of Alexandria, 1911.

Rickenbacker, Eddie. *Fighting the Flying Circus*. New York: Stokes, 1919.

Riis, Jacob A. *The Making of An American*. New York: Harper and Row, 2011.

Risen, Clay. *The Crowded Hour: Theodore Roosevelt, the Rough Riders, and the Dawn of the American Century*. New York: Scribner's, 2020.

Robertson, Linda. *The Dream of Civilized Warfare*. Duluth: University of Minnesota Press, 2003.

Roosevelt, Kermit. *Quentin Roosevelt*. New York: Scribner's, 1921.

"Roosevelt Men Ready for Call." *Des Moines Register*, April 15, 1917.

"Roosevelt Now Facing Danger." *The Brooklyn Daily Eagle*, February 9, 1918.

Roosevelt, Theodore. *The Autobiography of Theodore Roosevelt*. New York: Scribner's, 1913.

———. *An Autobiography of Theodore Roosevelt*. New York: Scribner's, 1922.

———. *The Foes of Our Own Household*. New York: Scribner's, 1925.

———. *Hunting Adventures in the West*. New York: Putnam, 1913.

———. *The Letters of Theodore Roosevelt: The Days of Armageddon*. Vol. 7. Bloomington: Indiana University Press, 1914.

———. *The Roosevelt Policy*. New York: The Current Literature Publishing Co., 1908.

———. *The Rough Riders*. Mineola, NY: Dover, 2006.

———. *The Works of Theodore Roosevelt*. New York: P. F. Collier, 1899.

Salter, Henry Hyde. *On Asthma: Its Pathology and Treatment*. Lansing, MI: William Wood, 1882.

Samuels, Peggy, and Harold Samuels. *Teddy Roosevelt at San Juan: The Making of a President*. College Station: Texas A&M University Press, 1997.

Schuman, Michael. *Theodore Roosevelt*. New York: Enslow Publishers, 1997.

Siefkin, David. *The City at the End of the Rainbow: San Francisco and its Grand Hotels*. New York: Putnam, 1976.

Stannard, Una. *A Few Kind Words About Hate: The Dark Side of Family Life and the Bible*. Ashland, OR: Germain Books, 1968.

Striner, Richard. *Woodrow Wilson and World War I: A Burden Too Great to Bear*. Lanham, MD: Rowman & Littlefield, 2014.

Strock, James. *Theodore Roosevelt on Leadership: Executive Lessons from the Bully Pulpit*. New York: Crown, 2009.

Thomas, Lowell. *Raiders of the Deep*. New York: Doubleday, 1928.

Thompson, J. *Never Call Retreat: Theodore Roosevelt and the Great War*. New York: Palgrave Macmillan, 2014.

Thompson, John. *Woodrow Wilson*. New York: Longman, 1915.

"TR Better." *Brooklyn Times Union*, May 6, 1898.

"TR Change of Heart." *Star Gazette*, April 4, 1917.

"TR to March Under Old Rough Rider Flag." *Washington Times*, May 13, 1917.

"TR Visits Wilson at White House." *Wilmington Morning News*, May 27, 1914.

Tumulty, Joseph P. *Woodrow Wilson as I Know Him*. New York: Doubleday, 1921.

US Congress. "Awarding the Medal of Honor to Theodore Roosevelt." Washington, DC: US Government Printing Office, 1998.

Vollweiler, Albert Tangeman. *Roosevelt's Ranch Life in North Dakota*. Grand Forks: University of North Dakota Press, 1918.

"Volunteers Await Teddy's Next Move." *El Paso Morning News*, May 21, 1917.

Wagenknecht, Edward. *Seven Worlds of Theodore Roosevelt*. Guilford, CT: Lyons, 2010.

Welch, Richard F. *Long Island's Gold Coast Elite and the Great War*. Charleson, SC: The History Press, 2021.

Whitcomb, John, and Claire Whitcomb. *Real Life at the White House: 200 Years of Daily Life at America's Most Famous Residence*. New York: Routledge, 2002.

White, William Allen. *Woodrow Wilson: The Man, His Times, and His Task*. New York: Houghton Mifflin, 1924.

Willis, Resa. *FDR and Lucy: Lovers and Friends*. New York: Routledge, 2012.

Wilson, Edith Bolling. *My Memoir*. Indianapolis: Bobbs Merrill, 1939.

"Wilson May Approve Roosevelt War Move." *Oklahoman News*, May 2, 1917.

Wilson, Woodrow. *The Papers of Woodrow Wilson*. Princeton, NJ: Princeton University, 1980.

———. *President Wilson's State Papers*. New York: George H. Doran, 1918.

———. "Second Inauguration of Woodrow Wilson." Washington, DC: Government Printing Office, 1918.

Wise, Jennings C. *Woodrow Wilson: Disciple of Revolution*. New York: Paisley Press, 1938.

Young, Ernest William. *The Wilson Administration and the Great War*. Westport, CT: Gorham Press, 1922.

Zacks, Richard. *Island of Vice: Theodore Roosevelt's Quest to Clean Up Sin-Loving New York*. New York: Anchor Books, 2012.

INDEX

acute coronary occlusion, 279
Adams, Henry, 149
African safari, 9, 10, 38; number
    of kills, 203; after Presidency,
    202–3; with Roosevelt, K.,
    202–3
airplanes, 75, 182, 257, 264;
    biplanes, 205, 207, 273;
    Boche, 251; as crude, 136;
    Curtis, 217; Fokker triplanes,
    251; formation flying, 231;
    Newport machine, 248;
    Nieuports, 217, 243, 250;
    Pfalz monoplanes, 250;
    pursuit and battle, 247. *See
    also* fighter pilots
Air Service, 242
Akron Beacon Journal, 176
Amazon River expedition, 279;
    disaster on, 9–10; emergence
    from, 10, 16–17, 124; leg
    infection from, 209
American exceptionalism, xiii, xiv
American Expeditionary Force,
    157
American Review of Books, 256
American Revolution, 44

Amos, James, 196, 270–71, 279;
    grief of, 273
Anna Karenina (Tolstoy), 54
antiaircraft fire (archies), 243
Applegarth, William B., 171–72
Arabic sinking, 47, 61
archies. *See* antiaircraft fire
armed neutrality, 102
Armed Ships Bill, 102
Army, US, 163, 197, 248; Air
    Service, 242; Army League,
    158; bases, 45; Commander
    in Chief, 110, 198; Company
    B Twenty Sixth infantry,
    239; fighter pilots, 136,
    207; 1st United States
    Volunteer Cavalry, 110, 114;
    general staff, 183; infantry,
    65; innovative spirit in, 44;
    Ninety-Fifth Aero Squadron,
    207, 243; Ninth Cavalry,
    113–14; resources of, 143;
    signal reserve corps, 207;
    training and, 157; Twenty-
    Sixth Infantry, 264. *See also*
    military; volunteer army
arteriosclerosis, 85, 235

speeches, 278; of Bryan, 41;
Carnegie Hall, 263; in
Cooper Union, New York,
80; on courage, 109; Liberty
Bond tour, 262; National
Geographic Society speech,
10; National Security League
speech, 247; New York State
Republican Convention,
256; on pacifists, 41, 212; at
Panama Pacific Exposition
World's Fair, 41; speaking
engagements, 212–13; at
Union League, New York,
108, 138; whistlestop
speeches, 202, 275
Star Gazette, 127–28
state governments, 24; Rough
Riders proposal supported by,
155–56
Stickney, Victor, 55
Stillman, Fred, 136
St. Louis Dispatch, 165
St. Louis Star, 236
Stoker, Bram, 95
Stricker, Josephine, 234–35, 253,
256
suffrage. *See* women's suffrage
Sumner, Samuel, 110
Sussex sinking, 60–62, 85
swashbuckling glory, 177
swimming with sharks, 177–78
swords, xi, 7, 118, 155
Syran, George, 273

Taft, William Howard, 29, 63,
67, 128, 184, 222; at burial,
274–75; inauguration
of, 201; Lodge on, 203;
as major general, 211;
meeting with Wilson, W.,
233–44; sympathy from,
237; visiting hospital,
265
Tammany Hall, 13–14, 94
tanks, xiii, 124, 138, 158, 194,
277
Tarkington, Booth, 15
Thayer, William Roscoe, 56
Thompson, Philip, 253–55
Tolstoy, Leo, 278
tragedy: death of Roosevelt, Q.,
as, 254, 278; glory and, 41;
Wilson, W., on, 61
Treaty of Versailles, 275
trench warfare, 145, 164, 226
tributes, 276
trolley accident, Pittsfield,
Massachusetts, 86–87, 247,
279
Tuckerman, Emily, 211
Tumulty, Joseph, 17, 117,
135; greeting of, 142;
scheduling by,
159
Turner, Frederick Jackson, 88
Tuskegee Institute, 150
Twain, Mark, 152–53
Twenty-Sixth Infantry, 264

U-boats, 65; *Lusitania* sinking,
19–21, 34; in Newport,
Rhode Island, 77–79, 81,
98–99; Roosevelt, Q., short
story, 230
Uncle Sam, 172
Union League, New York, speech,
108, 138
Unrestricted Warfare plan, 98

Vanderbilt, Alfred G., 26
vice presidency, 177
victories: first, for Roosevelt,
Q., 245; peace without, 98;
Rickenbacker on Roosevelt,
Q., 245; of Rough Riders, 6,
16, 123
Vigilancia sinking, 119
Villa, Pancho, 59–60, 62, 71
volunteer army: Baker on, 193;
Congress and, 156; history
of, 43–44; Rough Riders
proposal for World War I,
141, 143–44, 165–67, 175,
179–80, 278; Wilson, W.,
direct statement on, 193–96

Wadsworth, Craig, 3
War College, 157
War Department, 163, 226;
deficiencies of, 166
warfare: American Revolution,
44; cavalry, xiii, 40, 164;
dogfights, 206; gallantry
lacking in, 219; against

Germany, 124–25; with
horses, 156; lack of honor
in, 219; mechanization
and megadeath in, 195;
mechanized war, 277;
military preparedness camps,
30, 43–48; Plain Wars,
197; Roosevelt, Q., on, 218;
trench warfare, 145, 164,
226; Unrestricted Warfare
plan, 98; War Resolution,
135; Wilson, W., address
to Congress, 100, 108–9,
117–19, 135; Wilson, W.,
school of, 195–96; worry over
preparedness, 166. *See also*
Civil War, US; Rough Riders,
proposal for World War I
action; San Juan Hill, Cuba;
Spanish American War;
World War I
Washington, Booker T., 165;
academic procession of,
152–53; letter from, 153;
meeting Roosevelt, E., 151;
press condemning, 151–52; at
White House, 150–53
Washington, DC: bureaucracy of,
167; departure from, 202;
National Geographic Society
speech, 10; Roosevelt, E.
C., on, 234; Roosevelt, Q.,
summoned to, 176; walking
streets of, 34; Wilson, E. B.
G., disliking, 85; Wilson, W.,

nose of, 263; sheep raising by, 136; taking over presidency, 275; Wilson, W., courting, 32–36; Wilson, W., first meeting, 31–32

Wilson, Ellen, 11, 14–16, 18, 34; on Peck letters, 184

Wilson, Margaret, 87

Wilson, Woodrow: affair with Peck, 183–84; appeal to country, 263–64; armed neutrality proposed by, 102; awards to, 152; Balfour plea for troop deployment, 156; blackballing by, 213; bomb threats against, 106; on break with Mexico, 62; as brooding, 142; broomstick preparedness accusation, 226; bullying of, 97, 103, 142–43, 278; confirming death of Roosevelt, Q., 257; Congressional address, 108–9, 117–19, 135; as co-president, 84–85; courting by, 32–36; cruise on Potomac River, 161–63; death of, 275–76; denying crowded hour, 278; direct statement on volunteer divisions, 193–96; as egghead, 182; election of, xii, 9, 29; engagement of, 47–48; failing health, 17–18, 84, 106–7, 159; first meeting Edith Galt, 31–32; flattery

and, 143; Fourteen Points of, 233, 261; golf playing, 117–18; honesty of, 194; ignoring *Lusitania* sinking, 28, 36, 79–80; inaction of, xv, 75, 79; inauguration of, 102–3, 106; League of Nations proposed by, 97–98, 188, 233, 261; letters from, 47–48; as "lily-livered skunk," 99; Lodge on, 233–44; love letters to Peck, 184–85, 210; luncheon with, 9–11, 14–18; marriage of, 62, 76; meeting with Taft, 233–44; *Metropolitan Magazine* blasting, 226–27; as nemesis, x, xvi; offer to, xiii; in Paris, 266; passionate side of, 16; paying Peck's mortgage, 188; as political animal, 125, 278; politics driving, 159; polling for war declaration, 107; press appeals to, 160–61; public esteem for, 266; re-election of, 87–88; riding through Washington, DC, 106; Roosevelt, A., on, 29; school of warfare, 195–96; selective service (draft) enacted, 141, 143; severing from Germany, 99–100; at Shadow Lawn, 75–76, 79–80, 83, 88; strokes suffered by, 275–76; support for, 39; sympathy from, 70,

236; on tragedy, 61; view of,
as war commander, 62–63;
War Resolution signed by,
133–34; worry over war
preparedness, 166
The Winning of the West (Roosevelt,
T.), 15
Winnipeg Evening Tribune, 274
Wister, Owen, 150
women's suffrage: address to, 144;
Lodge and, 270; support for,
270; at White House, 97, 144
Wood, John, 132
Wood, Leonard, 43–46, 62, 110,
113, 265
World War I: American
Expeditionary Force, 157;
armistice, 261–67; carnage
of, xiii, 40; dogfights, 206;
gasless Mondays in, 136;
heatless Mondays in, 136;
progress of, 24; *Over There,*

as US theme song, 205;
Treaty of Versailles ending,
275; trench warfare, 145;
US entry, 19–21, 135–36;
volunteers for, 205; as war
of mass killing, 278; War
Resolution signed, 133–34;
Wilson, W., Congressional
address, 100, 108–9, 117–19,
135. *See also* Army, US;
fighter pilots; France;
Germany; Rough Riders,
proposal for World War I
action; Wilson, Woodrow
World War II, 177
Wright Brothers, 149

Yale University, 45, 152
yellow fever, 141, 177, 235
Young, S. B. M., 110

Zimmerman, Arthur, 102